Authentic Project-based Learning in Translation and Interpreting Studies

This book delves into the dynamic world of authentic project-based learning (PjBL) in translation and interpreting (T&I) education.

With translation and interpreting programs on the rise, especially in China, the book merges academic rigor with market realities and provides valuable insights for the cultivation of school-based translation projects that prepare students for the global stage. Using a cross-analysis of eleven representative projects, Li's research identifies patterns, trends, and commonalities in PjBL and distinguishes traditional classroom exercises from innovative internship projects. The chapters offer an in-depth analysis of a unique internship project in collaboration with the United Nations at Shanghai International Studies University, from recruitment to leadership selection and from teamwork to task management, where students gain real-world skills, collaborate seamlessly, and tackle continuous challenges. By situating a unique case within this broader education context, this book provides holistic understanding, meaningful comparisons, and a detailed depiction of not only the productive side of an internship project but also the selection, training, assessment, knowledge-building, and maintenance that ensures the continuity of the team.

By combining a broad view of project-based learning with an in-depth investigation of a single case, this book serves as a valuable resource for researchers, students and educators in T&I programs, providing guidance, insights, and best practices for designing and implementing authentic translation projects.

Rui Li is a Lecturer at the School of Translation Studies, Xi'an International Studies University, China. She has a PhD in Translation Studies from Shanghai International Studies University.

Routledge Studies in East Asian Interpreting
Series edited by Riccardo Moratto and Irene A. Zhang

Routledge Studies in East Asian Interpreting aims to discuss practical and theoretical issues in East Asian interpreting. This series encompasses scholarly works on every possible interpreting activity and theory involving the use of Chinese (Mandarin, Cantonese, and other topolects), Japanese, Korean and other East Asian languages/dialects. At a time when Western interpreting studies has reached its maturity and scholars are looking for inspiration from elsewhere in the world, the field of East Asian interpreting offers the greatest potential for discovery of new frontiers and formulation of new theories The topics included in this series set out to include all the subfields of interpreting in the broader East Asian region, with Chinese, Japanese, and Korean being the main research languages. Topics can range from interpreter education, conference interpreting, medical or healthcare interpreting, educational interpreting, public service interpreting (also known as community interpreting), sign language interpreting, police interpreting, legal interpreting, interpreting for children, diplomatic interpreting, interpreting in war zones, social services interpreting, liaison or dialogue interpreting, business interpreting, remote interpreting, new models in consecutive and simultaneous interpreting, chuchotage or whispered interpreting, simconsec interpreting, telephone interpreting, shadowing, and respeaking. The series primarily consists of focus/shortform books, monographs, edited volumes, handbooks, and companions dedicated to discussing the above issues in East Asia.

Translating Chinese in Malaysia
The Rise of a New Cultural and Linguistic Enclave
Edited by Riccardo Moratto and Lay Hoon Ang

Authentic Project-based Learning in Translation and Interpreting Studies
Zooming Out and Zooming In
Rui Li

For more information about this series, please visit: www.routledge.com/Routledge-Studies-in-East-Asian-Interpreting/book-series/RSEAI

Authentic Project-based Learning in Translation and Interpreting Studies
Zooming Out and Zooming In

Rui Li

LONDON AND NEW YORK

First published 2025
by Routledge
4 Park Square, Milton Park, Abingdon, Oxon OX14 4RN

and by Routledge
605 Third Avenue, New York, NY 10158

Routledge is an imprint of the Taylor & Francis Group, an informa business

© 2025 Rui Li

The right of Rui Li to be identified as author of this work has been asserted in accordance with sections 77 and 78 of the Copyright, Designs and Patents Act 1988.

All rights reserved. No part of this book may be reprinted or reproduced or utilised in any form or by any electronic, mechanical, or other means, now known or hereafter invented, including photocopying and recording, or in any information storage or retrieval system, without permission in writing from the publishers.

Trademark notice: Product or corporate names may be trademarks or registered trademarks, and are used only for identification and explanation without intent to infringe.

British Library Cataloguing-in-Publication Data
A catalogue record for this book is available from the British Library

ISBN: 9781032893792 (hbk)
ISBN: 9781032893808 (pbk)
ISBN: 9781003542469 (ebk)

DOI: 10.4324/9781003542469

Typeset in Times New Roman
by Newgen Publishing UK

Contents

Acknowledgments vi

1 Introducing project-based learning in T&I studies 1

2 Theoretical basis for authentic project-based learning 9

3 Meta-analysis of authentic cases of project-based learning 37

4 Revisiting facets of authentic project-based learning 65

5 Zooming in on a new case 75

6 The DGC project under the microscope 91

7 Analysis, comparison and discussion of the DGC project 154

8 Conclusions and pedagogical implications 166

Index *176*

Acknowledgments

This book is based on my doctoral thesis. I chose to study project-based learning motivated by my personal experience as a teacher reviser in a news translation project at the School of Translation Studies, Xi'an International Studies University, and a raw sense of scientific curiosity, but the research process has turned out to be an extremely fulfilling experience. I have taken the time to read relevant literature, as well as to observe the DGC project firsthand, to fill many gaps in my knowledge. As this book is about to come to fruition, I must thank a few important people who have made all of this happen.

First and foremost, I'm filled with gratitude for my chief doctoral supervisor, Professor Hannelore Lee-Jahnke. She always gives me the utmost luxury of time to discuss the research design and list all the references helpful to my research. I'm also thankful for Professor Irene Ailing Zhang, my co-supervisor, who has brought me on board several translation and research projects at the Graduate Institute of Interpreting and Translation, Shanghai International Studies University, which have opened my eyes to many best practices in curriculum design, training, and research.

My observation of the DGC project would not have been possible without Professor Xie'an Huang's support. I'm impressed by his quality, consistency and efficiency in translation and the commitment he has given to the project over the past decade. My special thanks go to the participants of the 2018 class by allowing me to be a witness of their growth story. I'm indebted to Professor Gary Massey for giving me initial inspiration on using collaborative protocol analysis as a research tool and to Professor Donald Kiraly for sparking and sustaining my interest in project-based learning through his publications.

I'd also like to warmly thank Professor Riccardo Moratto for giving me this chance to publish the book under his East Asian Interpreting Studies Series at Routledge. Although the research is mainly about translation projects, as many scholars can attest, interpreting and translation are not exclusive to each other, and the overarching aim of T&I education is to enhance the career prospects of students, making them versatile and adaptable in the language service industry. It is in this sense that I hope the book may be relevant to interpreting students and trainers as well.

During the preparation of the manuscript, Ms. Katie Peace and Ms. Khin Thazin from Routledge led my hands in navigating different stages with their professional acumen and generous guidance. Any errors or omissions are thus solely my responsibility, and I welcome feedback from readers for further refinement.

1 Introducing project-based learning in T&I studies

1.1 Definition of subject

Modern Translation and Interpreting (T&I) education often employs a diverse array of methodologies to facilitate effective learning. To enhance student employability, many T&I programs in higher education are aligning their training methods closely with industry standards and practices at the advanced stages of training (e.g., FIT 2003; Mu 2012; Chai 2017; Schnell and Rodríguez 2017; Cui 2017). One method is to involve them in authentic translation projects (Lee-Jahnke 2005; Hurtado Albir 2015). This approach falls under the umbrella of project-based learning (PjBL) (Morgan 1983) and draws inspiration from principles of situated learning (González-Davies and Enríquez-Raído 2016). It emerged in T&I education during the 1990s, with pioneers such as Gouadec (1991), Vienne (1994), and Mackenzie and Nieminen (1997) leading the way. Vienne (1994, 51–52) defines "projects" as the translation of texts "in their real communicative situation" as opposed to "in a void." He also posits that as students coordinate with, monitor, and critique each other to produce a joint product, this activity can activate a wide range of skills.

Based on their degree of authenticity, translation projects can be categorized into simulated and authentic ones (Mackenzie 2004). Simulated projects involve texts that have either been translated in real context before or have been created with the purpose of requiring translation. Trainers may assume the roles of clients, expert consultants, or language revisers, while students take on the roles of terminologists, translators, revisers, or project managers. In contrast, authentic projects entail entirely new texts for actual communication needs. In terms of progression, authentic projects are preceded by simulated ones (Kelly 2005). In some instances, they may even be followed by work placements[1], where students work as interns with external language service providers (LSPs) (Chai 2015; Astley and Hostench 2017). It is noteworthy that Vienne (1994, 52) vehemently opposes the simulation of professional tasks, contending that "it is difficult, indeed sometimes impossible, to carry out a realistic analysis of the situation and to answer the questions that might arise." Building on Vienne's proposal, Kiraly advances authentic experiential PjBL and defines a project as "a comprehensive undertaking by a team of students in the service of a real-world client or user" (2012a, 84). He

DOI: 10.4324/9781003542469-1

also provides a multi-vortex co-emergent model illustrating participants' competency growth during training (2000, 2005, 2012a, 2012b, 2013, 2015, 2016).

1.2 Context of subject

While authentic translation projects have gained popularity in T&I education, there has been a lack of efforts to map out the practices in various contexts. We believe that this oversight poses at least two risks.

To begin with, the landscape of translation projects and translation tools is evolving. In the industry, a project is defined as "a temporary endeavor undertaken to create a unique product" (Project Management Institute 2013, 3). Here, "temporary" does not necessarily imply a short duration but rather denotes the engagement and lifecycle of the project. A successful project requires the completion of various tasks, each with its own timeline, resources, and dependencies (Rico 2002; Walker 2023). Yet, in the era of continuous delivery, TAUS (Massardo and van der Meer 2017) indicate that clients might increasingly demand shorter translations as opposed to lengthy ones. This means that traditional project timelines could become less defined, requiring new methods for incorporating such projects into educational contexts.

At the same time, different learning environments also come with their own conventions, priorities, expectations, and resource limitations. When applying PjBL, adjustments are necessary to accommodate these unique realities, inevitably leading to changes in the types of processes and tools undertaken. There are few rigid universal best practices. A process that works well in one context may not necessarily work in another (Sfard 1998; Kiraly, Massey and Hofmann 2018). Unfortunately, current descriptions of PjBL predominantly consist of isolated case studies, lacking the effort to analyze and juxtapose them.

Following Hammersley's process of analytic induction (1989), there is a clear imperative to compile a collection of representative studies for a broad view. This will empower us to build a more intricate comprehension of PjBL and unveil patterns and trends.

Indeed, upon our review, we've identified a new trend in T&I education in China. In contrast to the traditional approach, where teachers introduce one-off projects as part of the syllabus, this emerging model involves collaborative efforts between external industry partners and translation programs. These projects operate outside the regular curriculum and take the form of internships, with student participation being voluntary. Depending on the partner's requirements, these teams may undertake a single or multiple tasks, and in some cases, they engage in ongoing work, which introduces a cyclical dynamic to such projects. The challenges associated with organizing and sustaining long-term projects are notably different from those of a single-class project. However, existing studies have not adequately addressed this distinction.

We propose using the concept of "Community of Practice" (CoP), as introduced by anthropologists Lave and Wenger (1991), to describe this new type of project. A CoP consists of individuals who share a common interest or passion for a particular field and engage in regular interactions to improve their expertise. It is characterized by members' mutual engagement, shared knowledge, and a common purpose. Historically, CoPs have been used to describe how professionals continue learning after entering the workforce, contrasting with how students learn in school, where terms like "learning community," "knowledge community," or "community of inquiry" are more relevant (Bielaczyc and Collins 1999).

Many scholars have seen the goal of professional-oriented T&I education as preparing students for full membership in a CoP (Kiraly 2003; Lee-Jahnke 2011; Berthaud and Mason 2018). However, in recent years, the concept has also been applied to PjBL research. Some educators have compared one-off class projects they run to CoPs (e.g., Kiraly 2013; Marco 2016; Colina and Venuti 2017; González Davies 2017). We find this analogy confusing because none of these projects involve selecting student translators or maintaining a consistent team structure. In a one-off project, the team dissolves after delivering a single comprehensive work, whereas a CoP must consistently produce high-quality work to maintain the trust of clients and secure future tasks. While both learning contexts are guided by similar principles of situated learning, a CoP is additionally characterized by members who share a common identity, a shared heritage, and a reproduction cycle in which experienced members are succeeded by new recruits (Barab and Duffy 2000). The newcomers gradually progress from peripheral roles, working alongside more experienced members, to central roles, where they take ownership and mentor new members (Lave and Wenger 1991). It is these features that lead us to believe that comparing an ongoing internship project to a CoP is more appropriate. In essence, our research indicates that current research tends to focus on the workflow of a single significant task and its impact on students' individual translation competence while overlooking the routine practices and social learning that truly define a CoP.

1.3 Initial questions and problematics

If a translation project could run as a CoP, it would be valuable to put its practices under the microscope. The case we choose to investigate is known as the DGC project. It is an internship the Department of Global Communications (DGC) of the United Nations (UN) has been running with the Graduate Institute of Interpretation and Translation (GIIT), Shanghai International Studies University (SISU) since 2014. It is designed to give the selected students a hands-on opportunity to translate DGC content that will be published across the DGC's media platforms. Each November, some 20 first-year students are recruited into the project. They are trained and supervised jointly by the second-year members and a teacher reviser until they are competent to translate the DGC materials and take charge of the project themselves. With this experience, some even successfully applied to do in-site internships at the United Nations headquarters and its offices. The cycle repeats itself in this way, and to date, over 100 students from five years of classes have participated in the project.

The project immediately captured our interest, partly because of the "halo effect" of the United Nations and its rigorous language service requirement (Shaaban

2012), partly because the team seems to have built up a set of practices governing its recruitment, training, leadership, resource management, workflow, and quality control procedures. Intrigued, we sought the approval of the gatekeepers to see how the participants learn from the day they are recruited to the time they exit. We joined the team's online chat group and its cloud-based translation platform to track all the dialogues and artifacts they make. We conducted field trips to their meetings as participant observers. We interviewed key informants on an ongoing basis and distributed questionnaires to the participants at different points in their learning journey. In the sequential order, some initial questions include:

- If the internship project is carried out at the program level, what is the mechanism to recruit student participants?
- How are the new recruits trained by the senior, more competent students?
- What is the content and volume of work? how often are the tasks sent and how short is their turnaround time?
- How, in a routine task, the participants collaborate with each other as a distributed team?
- To what extent are the translation technologies integrated in the workflow? How do the new members shorten their learning curve of the technologies if the project is carried outside the formal curriculum?
- To what extent does the workflow meet the criteria of industry best practice?
- What kind of scaffoldings are offered to students? How does the feedback process work?
- How are the participants evaluated in the program?
- For a long-running project like this, what changes have taken place over the years?
- What do the students feel they have learned from the project?

To our knowledge, there are few studies that have provided an ethnographic account of the practices adopted by an internship project and the learning accrued by its participants. As T&I programs across the world embrace various forms of PjBL in their curriculum, we hope our description of the case could yield relevant insights and contribute to the broader conversation about these new developments.

1.4 General outline of adopted methodology

We choose to employ the case study approach for our research strategy, as it incorporates an "emergent design" (Gillham 2000) and allows for the exploration of a naturally occurring phenomenon over time and in depth (Meyer 2015). Considering the extended duration of the DGC project, we are also keen on adopting an ethnographic perspective.

The time frame of our observation lasts from late October in 2018 to early April in 2020. This covers the length of time starting from the recruitment of the participants of the 2018 class to the time they exited the project. We adopt a combination of qualitative and quantitative methods, including documentation analysis, verbal analysis, observation records, physical artifacts, interviews, and questionnaires, to raise the validity of the findings.

Saldanha and O'Brien (2014) emphasize that a single case, by itself, may not yield findings that can be broadly generalized. However, when considered within the context of its own development and in comparison to existing studies, it may contribute to a particularly comprehensive view of the subject. Ultimately, we believe that the knowledge obtained through cross-case analysis and the examination of the DGC project would provide us with a deeper knowledge of the field and offer insights into new approaches of PjBL in T&I education.

1.5 Objective and structure

This study serves a twofold purpose: Firstly, our aim is to construct a comprehensive understanding of how authentic translation projects are put into practice in different contexts and how academic research examines these events, enabling us to draw meaningful comparisons. Secondly, by focusing on a new case study, we aim to discern the conceptual distinctions between single classroom projects and continuous internship projects and understand how the latter is implemented across different stages.

Chapter 1 is the introductory chapter. It lays the ground by introducing the objective, plan, contributions, and structure of the book.

Chapter 2 delves into the theoretical underpinnings of these projects. Section 2.1 contextualizes the necessity of authentic PjBL in the rise of the process-oriented competence-based T&I education. Section 2.2 describes the evolution of standards and workflow of a translation project informed by industry perspectives. In section 2.3, we use findings from the learning sciences, cognitive science, and expertise studies to examine the origins, conditions, and benefits of PjBL and its common research tools.

The theoretical review is complemented in Chapter 3 by a cross-case analysis of 11 sample studies. We start by explaining the framework used to make the comparison, followed by a detailed description of their respective research and practice features before we synthesize their convergence, heterogeneity, and gaps.

In Chapter 4, we will home in on "authenticity" and "collaboration" as two critical features of PjBL. We will clarify the differences between class projects and internship projects and explain why the latter correlates with the social learning concept represented by CoP.

Chapter 5 gives a detailed description of the research design of a new case. We first provide the background of the project and justify the necessity of combining the case study and ethnographic study as our main research methodology. Then, we describe the research questions, the data collection instruments, the analysis procedures and the ethical measures taken to raise the credibility of the findings.

As the main body of this new study, Chapter 6 tracks how the research participants were taken in and trained and how they have grown competent to take on the project. The description, hopefully, replete with details, will yield a layered picture of how the DGC project was run in different stages in one cycle from late 2018 to early 2020.

Building on the descriptions in Chapter 6, Chapter 7 summarizes the changes identified in the observed cycle. We will compare the research design of the DGC project against the existing studies on PjBL. We will also take a reflective stance to put in context the strengths and weaknesses that are revealed in the cycle compared with those of the previously reviewed studies.

The last chapter concludes the whole research by answering the original question: how the DGC project runs as a CoP and what benefits the student participants have taken away. We will take stock of the deficiencies in the research design and the difficulties experienced, as well as point out the paths of further investigations. This whole research ends on a positive note by bringing about the significance of the issues exposed and drawing implications for T&I pedagogy.

Note

1 For instance, China National Committee for Graduate Education of Translation and Interpreting (GETI) has made work placement a mandatory credit-based component in translation curriculum guidelines.

References

Astley, H., and O. T. Hostench. 2017. "The European Graduate Placement Scheme: An Integrated Approach to Preparing Master's in Translation Graduates for Employment." *The Interpreter and Translator Trainer* 11 (2–3): 204–222. doi:10.1080/1750399X.2017.1344813.

Barab, S. A., and T. Duffy. 2000. "From Practice Fields to Communities of Practice." In *Theoretical Foundations of Learning Environments*, edited by D. H. Jonassen and S. M. Land, 25–56. Mahwah: Lawrence Erlbaum & Associates.

Berthaud, S., and S. Mason. 2018. "Embedding Reflection Throughout the Postgraduate Translation Curriculum: Using Communities of Practice to Enhance Training." *The Interpreter and Translator Trainer* 12 (4): 388–405. doi:10.1080/1750399X.2018.1538847.

Bielaczyc, K., and A. Collins. 1999. "Learning Communities in Classrooms: A Reconceptualization of Educational Practice." In *Instructional Design Theories and Models*, Vol. II, edited by C. M. Reigeluth, 1–16. Mahwah: Lawrence Erlbaum & Associates.

Chai, M. 2015. "The Internship Mechanism of the MTI Program in GIIT, SISU." In *CIUTI-Forum 2014. Pooling Academic Excellence with Entrepreneurship for New Partnerships*, edited by M. Forstner, H. Lee-Jahnke, and M. Chai, 277–291. Frankfurt am Main: Peter Lang.

Chai, M. 2017. "Understanding the Current Situation, Enhancing Quality, and Pioneering Progress: The Future Development of Translation Studies [认识现状 提升质量 开拓前行——翻译专业的未来发展.]." *East Journal of Translation* 6: 4–8.

Colina, S., and L. Venuti. 2017. "A Survey of Translation Pedagogies." In *Teaching Translation: Programs, Courses, Pedagogies*, edited by L. Venuti, 203–215. London and New York: Routledge.

Cui, Q. 2017. *China's MTI Education and Employment Survey Report [全国MTI教育与就业调查报告.]*. Beijing: University of International Business and Economics Press.

FIT. 2003. "Translator Training & the Real World: Concrete Suggestions for Bridging the Gap." *Translation Journal* 7(1). https://translationjournal.net/journal/23roundtablea.htm.

Gillham, B. 2000. *Case Study Research Methods*. London: Continuum.

González Davies, M. 2017. "A Collaborative Pedagogy for Translation." In *Teaching Translation: Programs, Courses, Pedagogies*, edited by L. Venuti, 118–131. London and New York: Routledge.

González Davies, M., and V. Enríquez Raído. 2016. "Situated Learning in Translator and Interpreter Training: Bridging Research and Good Practice." *The Interpreter and Translator Trainer* 10 (1): 1–11. doi: 10.1080/1750399X.2016.1154339.

Gouadec, D. 1991. "Autrement Dire Pour une Redéfinition des Stratégies de Formation des Traducteurs." *Meta* 36 (4): 543–557.

Hammersley, M. 1989. *The Dilemma of Qualitative Method*. London: Routledge.

Hurtado Albir, A. 2015. "The Acquisition of Translation Competence. Competences, Tasks, and Assessment in Translator Training." *Meta* 60 (2): 256–280. doi: 10.7202/1032857ar.

Kelly, D. 2005. *A Handbook for Translator Trainers*. Manchester: St. Jerome Publishing.

Kiraly, D. 2000. *A Social Constructivist Approach to Translator Education. Empowerment from Theory to Practice*. Manchester: St. Jerome Publishing.

Kiraly, D. 2003. "From Instruction to Collaborative Construction: A Passing Fad or the Promise of a Paradigm Shift in Translator Education?" In *Beyond the Ivory Tower*, edited by B. J. Baer and G. S. Koby, 3–27. Amsterdam and Philadelphia: John Benjamins.

Kiraly, D. 2005. "Project-Based Learning: A Case for Situated Translation." *Meta* 50 (4): 1098–1111. doi: 10.7202/1012742ar.

Kiraly, D. 2012a. "Growing a Project-Based Translation Pedagogy: A Fractal Perspective." *Meta* 57 (1): 82–95. doi: 10.7202/1012742ar.

Kiraly, D. 2012b. "Skopos Theory Goes to Paris: Purposeful Translation and Emergent Translation Projects." *mTm. Minor Translating Major—Major Translating Minor—Minor Translating Minor, Special issue: In memoriam Hans J. Vermeer*, 4: 119–144.

Kiraly, D. 2013. "Towards a View of Translator Competence as an Emergent Phenomenon: Thinking Outside the Box(es) in Translator Education." In *New Prospects and Perspectives for Educating Language Mediators*, edited by D. Kiraly, S. Hansen-Schirra, and K. Maksymski, 197–224. Tubingen: Narr Francke Attempo.

Kiraly, D. 2015. "Occasioning Translator Competence: Moving Beyond Social Constructivism Towards a Postmodern Alternative to Instructionism." *Translation and Interpreting Studies* 10 (1): 8–32. doi: c10.1075/tis.10.1.02kir.

Kiraly, D. 2016. "Beyond the Static Competence Impasse in Translator Education." In *Translation and Meaning. New Series*, edited by B. Lewandowska-Tomaszczyk et al., Vol. 1, 129–142. Frankfurt am Main: Peter Lang.

Kiraly, D., G. Massey, and S. Hofmann. 2018. "Beyond Teaching Towards Co-Emergent Praxis in Translator Education." In *Translation-Didaktik-Kompetenz*, edited by B. Ahrens 11–64. Berlin: Frank Timme.

Lave, J., and E. Wenger. 1991. *Situated Learning: Legitimate Peripheral Participation*. Cambridge: Cambridge University Press.

Lee-Jahnke, H. 2005. "New Cognitive Approaches in Process-Oriented Translation Training." *Meta* 50 (2): 377. doi: 10.7202/010942ar.

Lee-Jahnke, H. 2011. "Trendsetters and Milestones in Interdisciplinary Process-Oriented Translation: Cognition, Emotion, Motivation." In *CIUTI-Forum 2010. Global Governance and Intercultural Dialogue: Translation and Interpreting in a New Geopolitical Setting*, edited by M. Forstner and H. Lee-Jahnke, 109–153. Frankfurt am Main: Peter Lang.

Mackenzie, R. 2004. "The Competencies Required by the Translator's Roles as a Professional." In *Translation in Undergraduate Degree Programmes*, edited by K. Malmkjær, 31–38. Amsterdam and Philadelphia: John Benjamins.

Mackenzie, R., and E. Nieminen. 1997. "Motivating Students to Achieve Quality in Translation." In *Transferre Necesse Est*, edited by K. Klaudy and J. Kohn, 339–344. Budapest: Scholastica.

Marco, J. 2016. "On the Margins of the Profession: The Work Placement as a Site for the Literary Translator Trainee's Legitimate Peripheral Participation." *The Interpreter and Translator Trainer* 10 (1): 29–43. doi: 10.1080/1750399X.2016.1154341.

Massardo, I., and J. van der Meer. 2017. *The Translation Industry in 2022. A Report from the TAUS Industry Summit*. TAUS. www.taus.net/insights/reports/the-translation-industry-in-2022.

Meyer, B. 2015. "Case Studies." In *Researching Interpreting and Translation*, edited by C. V. Angelelli and B. James Baer, 177–184. London and New York: Routledge.

Morgan, A. 1983. "Theoretical Aspects of Project-Based Learning in Higher Education." *British Journal of Educational Technology* 14 (1): 66–78.

Mu, L. 2012. "Professionalization of Translation and Professional Translation Education [翻译的职业化与职业翻译教育.]." *Chinese Translators Journal* 4: 13–14.

Project Management Institute. 2013. *A Guide to the Project Management Body of Knowledge (PMBOK® Guide)*, 5th ed. Newtown Square: Project Management Institute.

Rico, P. C. 2002. "Translation and Project Management." *Translation Journal*, 6 (4). https://translationjournal.net/journal/22project.htm.

Saldanha, G., and S. O'Brien. 2014. *Research Methodologies in Translation Studies*. London and New York: Routledge.

Schnell, B., and N. Rodríguez. 2017. "Ivory Tower Vs. Workplace Reality." *The Interpreter and Translator Trainer* 11 (2/3): 160–186. doi: 10.1080/1750399X.2017.1344920.

Sfard, A. 1998. "On Two Metaphors for Learning and the Dangers of Choosing Just One." *Educational Researcher* 27 (2): 4–13. doi: 10.2307/1176193.

Shaaban, S. M. 2012. "Global Strategic Partnership Policy and Its Effect on the Translation and Interpreting Industry and Professional Organizations—The United Nations Model." In *CIUTI-Forum Beijing 2011. A Global Vision: Development of Translation and Interpreting Training*, edited by H. Lee-Jahnke et al., 1–6. Beijing: Foreign Language Teaching and Research Press.

Vienne, J. 1994. "Towards a Pedagogy of 'Translation in Situation'." *Perspectives* 2 (1): 41–50. doi: 10.1080/0907676X.1994.9961222.

Walker, C. 2023. *Translation Project Management*. London and New York: Routledge.

2 Theoretical basis for authentic project-based learning

2.1 Intra-disciplinary foundations of PjBL

This section sketches out these key concepts in T&I pedagogy and explains why and when authentic translation projects as a training approach fit into competence-based T& I education.

2.1.1 Evolution in perceptions of translation

The definition and practice of translation have always been shaped by the evolution and shifts in translation theories.

The first major impact on translation emerged from the linguistic theories of the 1950s and 1960s. During this period, translation centered on the source text as the exclusive benchmark to which target language elements needed to be equivalent. Consequently, translation was mainly taught as part of second language education, involving prescriptive "transcoding" exercises, and students were assessed solely on the final product through error analysis (González Davies and Kiraly 2006).

As Holmes (1972) proposed to make "translation studies" an autonomous discipline away from linguistics, the field of translation studies became more descriptive. The "cultural turn" of that period highlighted the importance and role of the target text within the target culture (Snell-Hornby 2006). The translation was recognized as a rewriting process influenced by the ideology, patronage, and poetics of the target audience (Lefevere 1992).

Accompanying the cultural turn, functional theory became a major pushing force in translation pedagogy. Holz-Mänttäri (1984) contended that translation should be viewed as an activity that brings the initiator, the commissioner, the source text producer, the target text producer, and the target text user together. Translators are empowered to make changes to the source text based on textual types (Newmark 1988; Reiss 2000) and by the "*skopos*" (Vermeer 2000). Consequently, students should be taught to be mindful of the purpose and readers of the target text (Nord 1997, 2005; Kautz 2002).

Starting in the 1990s, inspired by the neighboring disciplines such as second-language acquisition, psycholinguistics and cognitive sciences, researchers shifted their interest to the process that led to a product, using tools such as retrospective protocols and think-aloud protocols (Alves 2003; Hurtado Albir and Alves 2009). They availed the construct of translation competence to explain the knowledge and skills required of a successful student translator. Findings were then plowed back into the instructional design to help students acquire such competence (e.g. Gile 1995; Kußmaul 1995; Tirkkonen-Condit and Jääskeläinen 2000).

Entering the new century, the traditional view of translation as an individual activity dominated by literary translation has increasingly been transformed by the rise of language service provision as an industry. With methodological innovations in collecting empirical data (Jakobsen 2017), researchers and educators have increasingly recognized the "social turn" and "technological turn" in translation. Translation is not solely a cognitive process confined to translators' minds but a practice situated in real-world contexts (Risku 2002). Translators collaborate not only with other people but also with various resources and tools (O'Brien 2012). The quality of a product is influenced not only by translation competence but also by multiple parameters (Drugan 2013).

These shifts have paved the way for the emergence of the competence-based translation (CBT) training approach, which has become firmly established over the past two decades (Hurtado Albir 2007). This approach emphasizes social needs and employability within the curriculum (Li 2000a, 2000b). Internally, the translation curriculum connects each learning objective or outcome to a specific competence or component that students are expected to develop. Externally, the curriculum aims to align with professional practices and market assessments (Lee-Jahnke 2009).

2.1.2 Key concepts in T&I education

The key concept behind the CBT is competence. Nevertheless, competence as a general concept is already contentious (Weinert 2001). When it is applied in T&I, a plethora of models have emerged. It is important we start by distinguishing several interrelated concepts.

Specific competence vs. generic competence

The first distinction is to be made between specific competence and generic competence. Generic competence encompasses a versatile and transferable set of knowledge, skills, and attitudes that are essential for personal growth, inclusion, and gainful employment (González and Wagenaar 2003). It serves as the foundation for students to acquire subject-specific knowledge and skills, and it directly contributes to the interpersonal dimension of translation competence.

Specific competence, on the other hand, is discipline related. Hurtado Albir (2007, 166) believes "translation competence is a complex know *how to act* resulting from integration, mobilization and organization of a combination of capabilities and skills (which can be cognitive, affective, psycho-motor or social) and knowledge (declarative knowledge) used efficiently in situation with common characteristics." González Davies and Enrique Raído (2016) provides a more succinct synthesis of the three strands of translation competence, including (1) to know; (2) to know how to do; (3) to know how to be. In terms of the relationship between the three, while the first two elements—knowledge and skills—may give people qualifications, it is only when people act in accordance with the rules, values, and norms of the profession that they can transform competence into performance that is outwardly visible to others (Lee-Jahnke 2009). This is also the reason why some scholars use "translatorial competence" (Kautz 2002) and "translator competence" (Kiraly 2003) rather than "translation competence" as more apt goals of CBT.

Competence vs. expertise vs. professionalism

Ambiguity also exists between translation competence and translation expertise. Expertise is defined as the consistently superior performance on representative tasks for a domain (Ericsson 2010). In Dreyfus and Dreyfus' (1980) five-stage model of skill acquisition, expertise denotes the second highest level of skill and knowledge one could possess in a field, whereas competence is merely the effective performance. Expertise is often used as a cognitive construct (Shreve, Angelone, and Lacruz 2018). Since expertise constantly develops throughout the career of a translator (Muñoz Martín 2009), research on translation expertise mainly "grapples with what happens *after* graduation from translation school" (Shreve 2002: 154). By comparison, the didactic approach to competence is mainly concerned with what and how the content should be taught while students are in training. It is, therefore, unrealistic to expect students to achieve expertise in school (Angelone and Marín García 2017).

Likewise, there is a distinction between professionalism and expertise. Professionalism is understood as "acting in a manner befitting a member of a profession" (Liu 2021, 2). Today's language service professionals encompass not only translators or interpreters but also terminologists, post-editors, trans-creators, language consultants, product localizers, project managers, etc. Empirical studies have already shown that not all professional translators qualify as experts (Jääskeläinen 2010). Generally, it takes at least ten years for a professional to become an expert in his/her area of specialization (Ericsson 2010). The key factor contributing to such transformation is "deliberate practice," which is underpinned by a) a well-defined task, b) the task is of appropriate difficulty, c) there is informative feedback, d) opportunities for repetition and the correction of errors, and e) motivation and support (Shreve 2006, 2020).

T&I education is a pathway for students to accumulate practical experience and understand the fundamental norms of their chosen profession. It prepares them to enter the field with a reasonable level of competence, but still, they need to embrace lifelong learning to be experts in their chosen field. In this sense, senior T&I students are often referred to as "semi-professionals" (Jääskeläinen, 2010) or "pre-professionals (Kiraly 2016)."

2.1.3 Translation competence models

As the central concept governing CBT, models of translation competence are divided by their epistemological origins, the methodological approaches, and the specific content. We will capitalize on the existing reviews to bring some quick clarity to the discussion.

Pym (2003) categorizes early competence models into competence viewed as a natural extension of linguistic competence, competence seen as non-existent, competence as a multi-componential concept, and lastly, competence portrayed as a minimalist two-fold functional competence.

Lesznyák (2007) maps ten translation models to Pym's (2003) and Weinert's (2001) classifications. She finds Pym's typology in need of two modifications. First, the category of "competence as no such thing" should be eliminated because it is unnecessary to include a category that denies the existence of translation competence. Second, the multi-componential category should be further divided into procedural models, which list the steps for a translation activity, and prerequisite models that identify the qualities one must possess to translate.

It is this latter type of multi-componential model that is most relevant to T&I education. Early models in this category are invariably heuristic (e.g. Neubert 2000; Kiraly 2003, Kelly 2005). In other words, they are founded on the educator's practical teaching or translation experiences. To address this weakness, empirical models began to surface. Among them, the one introduced by the PACTE Group stands out as the most extensively documented. It encompasses five sub-competencies, accompanied by a set of psycho-physiological mechanisms. In the center of the model is the strategic sub-competence, an essential procedural sub-competence that affects all the other sub-competences in a translation activity. PACTE has been working to validate this model through experiments over the past two decades (2017). Another model comes from Göpferich (2009, 2013), which is modeled after PACTE and is used as a basis to investigate the acquisition of translation competence of students compared with professionals.

Hague, Melby, and Wang (2011) pick three widely quoted models for comparison. They first note Neubert's use of the terms 'equivalence' and 'transfer competence' recalled the linguistic approaches to translation (ibid., 248)." Secondly, Neubert gave little consideration to the technological influence on translation[1]. In contrast, PACTE and Kelly, despite their different epistemological origins, have moved beyond the linguistic models to highlight a translator's strategic abilities and instrumental competence explicitly.

In China, although professional T&I education started relatively late (Tao 2016; Dawrant, Wang, and Jiang 2022), scholars (Wen 2004; Mu 2008; Li R. L. 2011; Liu 2011) have been advocating competence-based education. Several heuristic models have been put forth (e.g. Miao 2007; Wang and Wang 2008; Fang 2011; Qian 2012; Fu 2015; Zhang and Wang 2020). While these models may appear visually distinct, their underlying content aligns with well-established Western multi-componential models that emerged in the early 21st century.

In the second decade of the 21st century, significant advancements were made in the understanding of translation competence. Recognizing the profound impact of machine translation, Pym (2013) identified ten crucial skills that had previously been overlooked in existing models. He then organized them into three categories: the "ability to learn" incorporates elements of generic competence, "data management skills" have elevated instrumental competence, and the "ability to revise machine-generated translations" intersects with revision competence and post-editing competence[2].

Another impetus comes from Kiraly (2016). Inspired by the cognitive and learning sciences, he argues that the empirical attempts to validate translation competence are incapable of capturing the full complexity of a translation event. The weakness he finds with most componential models is that they are all static representations of an idealized translator, but they don't show the relationship or sequence of acquisition of the different elements. For each learner, the makeup of translation competence is divergent. As they acquire more experience, the links between these components will grow far more diffusive, complex, and intuitive, making it even harder to specify.

In addition to the models put forward by individual researchers/trainers, several academic associations have also put forward their interpretations[3]. The European Master's in Translation's (EMT) wheel of competence (EMT Expert Group 2009) first uses the concept of service provision, which includes interpersonal attributes and professional ethics, as a central element in linking the rest of the components together. The subsequent adoption of the model across the EMT network has promoted a change in the aim of a translation program from training translators to translation service providers in all stages of translation (Biel 2011; Schäffner 2012).

The revised EMT Competence Framework (EMT Board 2017) separates language and culture, interpersonal competence, technological competence, and service competence, all of which used to belong to translation competence, and puts them on equal footing with the latter. Each component contains specific requirements that add up to a total of 35 desired skills. The changes in the status of different types of competencies symbolize the divergent skillsets required of a language service professional. It also reflects EMT's continuous efforts to re-orient the goal of translation programs to prepare students for a wide range of career possibilities (Massey 2017).

To sum up, except for very few early models, there is wide consensus that translation competence requires additional components beyond linguistic components. This is the very reason that justifies the existence of translation as a separate discipline and translator education as an independent area of specialization away from language education. The evolution of multi-componential models also epitomizes changes in the understanding of the very practice of translation itself. Early models invariably see translation as a text-based activity that requires little technological assistance or collaboration. Later, with the changing method of production in the market, it has been extended to include not only elements required of translators but also of those who work in other capacities in a joint endeavor. As a result, their content is expanding; the status of different components is in the flux; and the boundary between generic competence and translation competence is shifting (Massey 2021).

Nevertheless, some scholars have pointed out drawbacks of these models: they are often presented from top-down perspectives, laden with assumption, and prone to becoming overly complex (e.g. Li 2022; Schäffner and Adab 2000; Shreve,

Angelone, and Lacruz 2018; Piotrowska 2016). However, we believe that these constructs still hold utility. Unlike cognitive models, pedagogical translation competence models are developed based on professional profiles to guide curriculum and syllabus design. With unstoppable technological advances, it is only natural for the method, medium, and modality of translation to change. A proper conceptualization of translation competence must incorporate these changes to better prepare students for the market. In a way, the pedagogical concept of translation competence features some built-in flexibility. This will push translator education providers to stay in tune with industry trends. It will also sustain interest from educators, practitioners and industry stakeholders and open new pathways in T&I education.

2.1.4 Interpreting competence models

Kalina (2002) is among the first scholars to emphasize the importance of utilizing interpreting competences as both a foundation and an objective in teaching. Similar to Kiraly's distinction between translation competence and translator competence, Pöchhacker (2007) argues in favor of framing interpreting training as a means to develop student interpreter competence, which entails physiological aptitude, professional ethics, and familiarity with the market rather than interpreting only as a skill. With insights from professional interpreters, Albl-Mikasa (2013) takes a process- and experience-based model of interpreter competence and argues competence development requires targeted practice and feedback to integrate the various elements and turn them into routine practice. Wang, Xu and Mu (2018) come up with an elaborated rubric to assess competence that comprises interpreting skills, strategies, specialist knowledge, service provision awareness and quality parameters. Wang and Li (2021) conduct the most extensive review of interpreting competence models in the existing literature. They identify a comprehensive array of nine types of interpreting competence, including physiological competence, psychological competence, interpersonal skills, cross-cultural competence, language proficiency, knowledge expertise, transfer capabilities, strategic acumen, and instrumental competence.

Interpreting and translation engage overlapping yet distinct cognitive skills and practices, thereby necessitating distinct pedagogical approaches (Kelly 2005; Setton and Dawrant 2016). However, it is also crucial to recognize that interpreting and translation are not exclusive to each other and are rarely the sole activity undertaken in today's market (Albl-Mikasa 2020; Schäffner 2020). There appears to be a lack of research pinpointing the convergence of skills between translation and interpreting. However, Kalina (2002) does encourage research on the extent to which translation can contribute to interpreting competence. It is also worth noting that Wang and Li (2021) reveal striking similarities, at least in name, between many interpreting sub-competencies and those found in prominent translation competence models. Tentatively, we suggest the existence of shared skills between translation and interpreting, such as a deep understanding of source and target languages and cultures, technological literacy, research, and preparation proficiency, as well as ethical and professional awareness.

Translation activities often expose students to a wide array of textual genres and contexts, enriching their cultural awareness. This heightened awareness can significantly benefit interpreters, particularly in their preparations for assignments or when dealing with written materials. Furthermore, translation often necessitates the use of various tools and technologies, including Computer-Assisted Translation (CAT) tools, which can be equally valuable for interpreters in terms of glossary management and preparation. Training in translation can reinforce these concepts related to quality, accountability, and professional ethics. It also enhances students' understanding of the demands and expectations in translation settings, sharpening their awareness of client needs and professional standards in interpreting.

From a career development perspective, some professional contexts may require practitioners to perform both interpreting and translation tasks. Proficiency in both fields can open a broader range of professional opportunities, rendering graduates more versatile and marketable. Whether in training or in the marketplace, interpreting is often a group effort, so training on a translation project can teach soft skills related to providing interpreting services. Furthermore, as we discuss later, given the diverse needs of students and the limited availability of internships directly related to translation and interpretation, there is often an imbalance between internship demand and supply in a higher institution context. Considering this, we argue that while it remains essential to train the core skills specific to interpreting, integrating translation training can endow interpreting students with a more comprehensive skill set and broaden their career prospects.

2.1.5 Role-based competences

Along with translation and interpreting competence models, there has been a rise in literature regarding role-specific competency models to shape syllabus design of specialized courses in T&I education.

Terminology competence

Terminology management is an important part of translation (Dunne K. 2007). Terminologists working in the field of translation are often tasked with the extraction, description, translation, storage, retrieval and updating of terms with special terminology management tools (Bowker 2002). Spanish scholars Montero Martínez and Faber Benítez (2009), based on their teaching experience, propose that terminology competence should entail the ability to recognize specialized concepts in communication, assessing, consulting, and developing information resources, identifying connections between languages based on specialized knowledge, and effectively managing and reusing accumulated knowledge in future translation work. Building on this proposal, Wang (2011) gives a heuristic model of terminology competence that contains language competence, thematic competence, instrumental competence, comprehension competence, management competence and documentation competence. These elements interact with each other and are reflected in the application competence that lies at the center. From a practical point of view, Popiolek (2015), Wang and Wang (2019), and Kageura and Marshman (2020) list steps of terminology management in the industry.

Revision competence

Revision is indispensable to translation in that it is not only a means of quality assurance but also provides an important source of feedback (Mossop 2014). Terms surrounding revision are numerous and often look like synonyms with each other. According to Brunette (2000), based on who revises the text, there is self-revision (the translator and revisor are the same people), peer revision (two or more people revise each other's translation), and editing/checking/proofreading/ fresh look/other revision (revision is done by other(s) who has never translated the text). But even in the last category, there are strict differences: Editing takes place early and focuses on comparing the translation with the source text to ensure that the intended meanings are accurately and smoothly conveyed, while proofreading occurs toward the end of the publishing process and is aimed at verifying that the typeset version aligns with the original text, without making any changes to the translation (Ko 2011). ISO 17100 (2015, 10) stipulates that "checking" is a translator's overall self-revision, "revising" is "editing by a person other than a translator," "reviewing" as "a reviewer, usually a subject matter expert, going over the content to assess the suitability of the target text" and "proofreading" as "a reading of the target text by someone but not the subject matter expert." All these terms fall under the umbrella process known as quality assurance or control.

In terms of specific models, Hansen (2009, 275, emphasis by original author) argues revision competence requires additional attributes besides translation competence, such as "*attentiveness* to pragmatic, linguistic, stylistic phenomena and errors, the *ability to abstract* or *distance oneself* from one's own and others' previous formulations, *fairness*, and *explaining* and *arguing*." More recently, Robert, Aline and Ureel (2017) came up with a hypothetical revision competence model based on PACTE (2017) and Göpferich (2009). They specifically add interpersonal competence into the mix because revisers need to have the ability to collaborate with the different actors involved in a translation. They also designed empirical experiments to validate the model, starting from the 'tools and research' sub-competence (Robert et al. 2017).

Post-editing competence

With the popularity of machine translation, it has become common for a source text to be machine-translated rather than human-translated before being revised. Consequently, post-editing courses have cropped up (O'Brien 2002; Koponen 2015; Feng and Zhang 2015; Guerberof Arenas and Moorkens 2019), giving rise to the need for modeling. O'Brien (2002) believes that knowledge of MT, terminology management skills, pre-editing/controlled language skills, programming skills, and text-linguistic skills are essential ingredients in post-editing competence. Rico and Torrejón (2012) categorize PE skills into core competences, linguistic skills, and instrumental competence, each of which is subdivided into 2–4 specific skills. Chinese scholars Feng and Liu (2018) came up with a three-tiered pyramid model to show that PE competence relies on attitude and relevant knowledge and skills. Nitzke, Hansen-Schirra, and Canfora (2019) break up their model into more minute elements and focus particularly on the risk assessment aspect. Coincidentally, all the models stress the knowledge of MT and programming skills, which are missing in most multi-componential translation competence models.

Project management competence

Project managers are the people who are assigned to oversee the progression of a project (Wang and Wang 2013; Walker 2023). ISO 17100 (2015, 7) believes the competence of translation project managers includes "a basic understanding of the industry, a thorough knowledge of the translation process and good management skills, in particular, the appropriately documented competence to support the translation service provider (TSP) in delivering services to meet client and other project specifications." Based on surveys of localization project managers' job postings in the USA, Brandt (2019) lists a total of 20 required management skills, namely, bilingualism, translation, evaluation, decision-making, coaching, emotional intelligence & influence, cultural competency, multi-tasking/prioritization, technology, research, subject matter expertise, processes and best practices, communication, terminology, quality control, scope, change and risk management, financial management, leadership, training and public speaking.

Clearly, project management competence has gone beyond qualities associated with translation, revision, and terminology competence to include many generic competence and business and organization skills. There have been calls to set up project management courses in translation curriculum, most of which adopt a PMBOK® Guide perspective (Wang, Yan, and Zhang 2011; Rico 2002; Wang and Wang 2013; Lu and Yan 2014; Wang 2014; Cui and Luo 2016; Yue 2019). A few programs have even established streams that teach students managing complex multilingual projects using integrated management tools (e.g. Zhang 2015). Industry surveys have shown a growing demand for competent project managers (Cui 2015), indicating, didactically, room for further growth in this area.

In summary, like translation competence models, role-based competence models exhibit a naturally multifaceted nature. Each of them incorporates the fundamental qualities of translation competence while also bearing its own distinctive elements. Like the evolution experienced by translation competence models, these role-based competence models have undergone continual reinterpretations. Collectively, they increasingly emphasize the significance of interpersonal and technological skills (Jakobsen 2019; Konttinen, Salmi, and Koponen 2021; Robert, Ureel, and Schrijver 2022). The evolving boundaries of these diverse competences hearken back to Kiraly's (2016) observation that it is challenging to pinpoint how each type of competence develops in students. Even when following the same curriculum and instructional approach, as students take on different tasks and roles, a myriad of competences comes into play. It is thus unfeasible to adequately evaluate a student's change in competence in PjBL using a single translation competence model.

2.1.6 Situating PjBL in T&I education

When a translation program is organized into modules or courses corresponding to each component of competence, there can be a lack of coordination and coherence between these modules (Kelly 2007; Kelly and Martin 2009). This disjointed approach may prevent students from gaining a holistic understanding of the entire professional process (Olvera-Lobo et al. 2009), working in virtual networks (Durban 2009), or integrating translation technology seamlessly in all stages of work (Bowker 2015). PjBL arises out of the need to foster the links. In a project, students are engaged with each other in a way that mimics the process and roles adopted by professionals. When they work toward the same goal, the actions of one participant are bound to have an impact on another. Every tool and every procedure will also have a consequence, either cost-wise, time-wise, or quality-wise. This interconnectedness will make students feel a higher stake in adopting a cost-effective workflow. It will also create incentives for learning as members start to evaluate and seek ways to fine-tune the process. Authentic projects often involve unforeseen challenges, helping students to learn adaptability and resilience. The products they create may have a positive impact on their communities, fostering a sense of civic duty and empathy.

Regarding the timing of PjBL, there is a consensus that all learning activities should be structured in order of increasing difficulty and complexity (González Davies 2004a; Kelly 2005; Liu 2011). In curriculum and syllabus design, it is important to differentiate between language learning and translation learning (Kelly 2005; Mu 2008; Schäffner 2000), as well as between undergraduate and postgraduate translation programs (González Davies 2004b). In terms of specific training approaches, it is highly recommended to adopt the task-based approach at the first stage of translator education (Colina 2003; González Davies 2004a; Colina and Venuti 2017). Once students have developed some functional translation competence, they should be given the opportunity to tackle more complex and real-world challenges as a team within an integrated technological environment. They should also have greater control in setting up their teams and designing workflows. This is where PjBL comes in. Initially, projects can be structured as simulations, progressing to authentic projects that foster a higher sense of responsibility and motivation.

For the scaffoldings offered during the entire course of training, Lee-Jahnke (2009) advocates for the adoption of anchored instruction. In the beginning, teachers should give a lot of modeling, coaching, and monitoring in the form of precise instructions and immediate informative feedback. As students gain more experience in translation, teachers should gradually fade their assistance and let students self-regulate their own translating activities. In addition to the formal curriculum instruction, the program provider should also arrange opportunities for students to meet and work with practitioners and experts from the wider field. This continuum of competence development moves learning "from transmissionist to transactional and finally to transformationist" (González Davies 2004b: 14). But visually speaking, perhaps the most apt illustration comes from Kiraly (2016). In his co-emergent competence model, the big vortex represents a student's overall translator competence development. It comprises numerous strands of mini vortices, representing unspecified contents of competences. As training gets more authentic and complex, they interact and grow ever more interlinked. Kiraly also recommends that PjBL should have a sustained presence in T&I education. However, given the inherent challenges of incorporating real translations into classrooms, students are likely to have limited opportunities for such learning experiences. This lack of exposure necessitates that trainers and program providers explore alternative options beyond occasional class projects. We will revisit this point as we gain more insight into how authentic PjBL is implemented in real settings.

2.2 Industry project workflows

The term "process" carries multiple meanings in T&I studies. Chesterman (2015) divides the process into the cognitive process of a translator's mind, which is not directly visible, and a social process that can be observed and recorded directly. Muñoz Martín (2016b) adds another process sandwiched the two. The first level corresponds to translation acts and comprises mental states and operations. The second level contains a series of recursive, goal-oriented, conscious tasks, such as reading, online searching, typing, and revising. The third level starts from the moment a client contacts a translator and ends when the translation is delivered. As a networked activity, the progression of a translation project encompasses all three levels of process, but it is the third level—a series of interrelated activities represented by the stepwise workflow—that is most relevant to the industry. Every activity taking place at this level shall follow fixed procedures (Wang 2014; Cui 2015; Zhang 2015; Yue 2019; Konttinen, Veivo, and Salo 2020). A predefined workflow increases clarity and accountability by holding whoever fills up the same position to the same criteria; otherwise, individuals may work in a way that is convenient for themselves but which may not be in the best interest of the project. It also provides a basis for documentation and record-keeping so that project managers can easily track progress, manage resources, and ensure compliance with project requirements. When new members join the project, a well-designed workflow serves as a training tool to help newcomers quickly understand how the group operates and what their role entails. Over time, analyzing the workflow can lead to continuous process improvements.

2.2.1 Sequential workflows

The classic protocol used in a translation project is known as the translation-editing-proofreading (TEP) model, which means the translated material should first be reviewed by an editor/reviser other than the translator(s), followed by a review by a third individual. Also known as the "four-eye principle," the TEP process captures the most essential steps of workflow and becomes the prototype of later models.

Gouadec (2007) is one of the early pioneers to show a comprehensive view of the translation process. He divides the workflow into pre-translation, translation and post-translation. Each stage is further divided into specific tasks. Nevertheless, with the benefit of technological advances, his model appears to be more suitable for self-employed translators rather than industrialized translation. At the post-transfer stage, Gouadec lumps checking, proofreading and revision together. At the post-translation stage, the model does not include the work related with the maintenance and management of the translation memory, terms and the knowledge gained from the task. This is actually an important step because legacy translations, or the previously translated materials, can have a cumulative effect by providing automatic suggestions for each new occasion of usage. Fourthly, in his model, the formatting work starts after validation, but in real life, the reverse is more likely to be the case. There might even be a loop of validation, formatting, and revision rather than the explicitly linear order that is presented in the model.

In parallel with Gouadec's model, standards have been developed at national and regional levels to govern the quality of translation products and processes. China, for example, rolled out its national standard for translation service *GB/T 19363. 1–2003* (China Association for Standardization 2003). Implemented nationwide on all translation service providers in 2004, it gives clear definitions and qualification requirements on a wide range of quality features, although it does not provide specifications on workflow. Europe, for another example, introduced the *Translation Services—Service Requirements,* known shortly as *EN 15038 Standard,* in early 2006. As the first pan-European standard, it makes revision by a second person an obligatory part of the workflow (European Committee for Standardization 2006) and specifies the education and experience requirements that translators, revisers, and reviewers should meet to work in the market.

The ISO 17100 (International Organization for Standardization 2015), released in 2015 to replace the EN 15038, is the current worldwide industry standard. Similar to Gouadec (2007), ISO 17100 also divides the whole process into three stages, but the line of division is different. Whereas Gouadec's pre-translational activity is about linguistic preparation, ISO 17100 believes preparations should also include administrative and technological aspects. ISO 17100 also takes a more differentiated view of "check/revision/review/proofreading" as activities carried out by different participants. It shades "review and proofreading" in a different color than "check and revision " to denote the former are optional value-added premium services requested by a client. In post-translation, ISO 17100 incorporates client feedback and translation data/asset maintenance into the design for continuous improvement.

TAUS's workflow diagram (Choudhury and McConnell 2013), which was released a bit earlier than the ISO 17100, is also worth mentioning. It gives an immediate bird's-eye view of when and how various players are contributing to the production of a joint product and can be easily used to benchmark role specifications in a translation project.

While these models have all stressed the importance of revision by a second person after translation by the original translator, they remain uniformly vague about the specific procedure revisers should take. Robert (2013) points out four possible ways seen in the revision: (1) a single monolingual re-reading; (2) a single bilingual re-reading; (3) a comparative re-reading followed by a monolingual re-reading; and (4) a monolingual re-reading followed by a comparative re-reading. There have been empirical efforts to determine which procedure produces the highest quality (e.g., Robert and Van Waes 2014; Ipsen and Dam 2016), but the experiments were all designed in laboratory settings. Mossop (2014) recommends that if time permits, it is best for translators to read the target text first, followed by a comparative reading of the source and target text. This personal observation still needs to be tested on a larger scale.

The common denominator of the above models is that they are carried out in a linear order. Beninatto and DePalma (2007) believe that since each phase must be completed before the subsequent phase begins, linear models are plagued by an inordinate amount of wait time and inefficiency. Keira Dunne (2011) describes the sequential workflows as "change-intolerant" because it would be costly to fix an error detected at the end of a project.

Another theme that runs through these models is that they have failed to describe with what kind of tools each step is carried out. This point is perceptively noted by Pym (2013: 446): "Strangely, though, these industrial standards have little to say about the use of translation technologies as such. Most notably, the post-editing of MT output has no explicit place in ISO17100, even though the development of the technologies would seem to have been one of the main historical reasons for the development of new standards."[4] In response, Kruger (2016, 122) has tried to fill this gap by establishing a link between various subtasks in the workflow and different CAT tools. His model is useful in gauging the degree and the type of CAT tools embedded in the workflow.

Overall, these models present a diachronic perspective on the changes taking place in the industry and on our understanding of the macro process of translation. If they are used as benchmarks to examine the workflow used in a translation project, we would easily judge the timeframe of the practice of said project. At the same time, it is important to bear in mind that technological innovations tend to occur faster than industry standards and even faster than they are reflected in training. The students undertaking training in school should not only build knowledge of the prevailing standards but also need to be more forward-looking. As AI-driven neural machine learning picks up pace, today's reality is to merge terminology management, translation memory and machine translation in a more integrated fashion (Zhang et al. 2018). Students, therefore, should embrace more of an integrated "PE (pre-editing)/Machine tuning/TM (translation memory)/MT (machine translation)/PE (post-editing)" workflow to close the gap between the academia and the industry (Mellinger 2017).

2.2.2 Collaborative workflow

To address the potential defects of linear models, Keira Dunne (2011) proposes two adjustments. The first is an incremental model, under which a task is partitioned into many chunks, each of which is undertaken according to the original client's requirements. The smaller a project is split, the quicker each file is translated and reviewed, and the better a team can identify changes to requirements. The key is to involve many translators, but the workflow of each smaller chunk of translation is still sequential. The other is an iteration model, which consists of a series of iterations. At the completion of each iteration, the client evaluates what has been accomplished and provides feedback to the team. A new planning activity is then conducted for the next cycle. The iterative model relieves the pressure on a reviewer to edit many translations at a short duration of time, and the iterative feedback could help the team continually improve its efficiency. But the downside is that it may lead to project delays and each iteration is also sequential in nature.

With the emergency of cloud computing, a new collaborative model comes out (Désilets and van der Meer 2011; Kelly, Ray, and DePalma 2011; Massion 2013; Muegge 2012a,b). In this model, a project manager does not have to partition files and send them to different translators. Instead, they simply upload the files to be translated to a browser-based CAT tool and invite people to join the community with specified roles. Since all the translation memories, glossaries and quality assurance checks are built and saved in the centralized web-based server, the team can work in a distributed way and save time from sharing resources. All the translators and reviewers work in the same interface and can see the work in progress and all the changes and edits, thereby raising the possibility to produce an accurate translation at a shorter timeframe. The cloud-based system has fee-based application programming interface (API)) to machine translate the text on the go. The confirmed translation is then fed back into the memory for future use. Cost wise, it operates a software as a service model (SaaS) and charges for the use of the language data sold on the platform. It can also allow the feedback from the people down the chain to flow at an earlier point in the process.

The collaborative model also presents significant drawbacks. According to Massion (2013), translators must exercise greater caution regarding the source, privacy, and ownership of data; another noteworthy issue is that the quality of translation memory (TM) and terminology base (TB) may vary since they are contributed by different translators. This necessitates additional manpower to carry out retroactive revisions in the TM. While the team may save time during the translation process, it underscores the ongoing necessity for updating and maintaining translation assets (Kageura and Marshman 2020).

Collaborative tools have been widely used in crowd-based community translations, such as in fan stubbing, Wikipedia, and the Google Translator Toolkit (Jiménez-Crespo 2017). By comparison, the take-up of cloud-based translation tools in school environment, and the pace of research thereof, appears rather slow.

As González Davies and Enrique Raído (2016, 4) point out in a special issue on situated learning in *The Interpreter and Translator Trainer*:

> That we have received almost no contributions addressing the role of ICT and/or translation/interpreting technologies in situated learning—especially in relation to new, digital work placements and schemes facilitated by crowdsourcing technologies and global social media platforms—highlights the fact that this relatively unexplored area has yet to be underpinned by systematic research.

2.3 Inter-disciplinary roots of PjBL

While authentic translation PjBL emerges from the necessity of bridging the gap between diverse competencies, its foundation is also firmly rooted in research and insights drawn from learning sciences, cognitive science, and expertise studies.

2.3.1 Learning sciences

Learning, as defined by Shi (2001), encompasses the continuous evolution of one's behaviors, competencies, and psychological inclinations through accumulated experiences. The field of learning sciences delves into various instructional methods, with the objective of comprehending the cognitive and social processes that lead to effective learning outcomes and applying the understanding in redesigning learning environments (Sawyer 2014).

Gao (2008) reviews the most common metaphors of learning throughout the 20th century. In the early 1900s, when behaviorism held sway, learning was likened to reinforcement. Educators at the time emphasized rote memorization of facts over the transfer of knowledge. By the mid-1950s, the prevailing metaphor shifted to learning as acquisition. Students were depicted as empty vessels to be filled with information dispensed by teachers. In the 1980s and 1990s, the metaphor of learning evolved to represent knowledge construction, heavily influenced by Piaget's view of learning, which posits that individuals learn through the processes of assimilation and accommodation as they integrate new knowledge. While this metaphor shifted the focus away from teachers, it still centered on the individual mind and what it absorbs. It wasn't until the last decade of the twentieth century that a new metaphor emerged, portraying learning as participation.

The Vygotskian view of learning holds that students need to consciously negotiate learning through individuals' perceptions and experiences in the social world (1978). Building on the social constructivist approach to learning, situated learning is then catapulted into the limelight. Resnick (1987) identifies four differences between the way people learn in school and in the real world. Compared to the knowledge and skills acquired through real-life experiences, Brown, Collins, and Duguid (1989) discover that in a school setting, teachers often transform knowledge into explicit rules, which offer only a limited perspective on knowledge. Gassmann (1997, as cited in Lee-Jahnke 2013) uses a segmented pyramid to represent the various types of knowledge one can acquire in life. Similar to an iceberg, the visible portion represents knowledge that has been distilled through rationalization, followed by documented knowledge obtained through physical and digital sources. Concealed from sight is the extensive reservoir of experiential and social knowledge that can only be obtained through lived experiences. Furthermore, Brown, Collins, and Duguid (1989) propose that learning is a type of social enculturation. When individuals observe and engage in the behaviors of a particular culture within its context, they naturally acquire relevant terminology, emulate behaviors, and gradually conform to the norms of that culture. Coincidently, another important breakthrough in social learning is through an anthropological lens. Lave and Wenger (1991) propose the notion of Communities of Practice (CoP) and legitimate peripheral participation to describe the trajectory on which apprentices move to full participation in a social practice. They posit that learning is not only about building up reified skills and knowledge but also about gradual identity formation as one becomes part of a greater entity (Wenger 1998).

PjBL is a situated learning approach that springs from these developments. Specifically, it is grounded in active construction, situated learning, social interactions, and the use of cognitive tools (Krajcik and Shin 2014). While there is no universally agreed-upon definition of PjBL, it is generally understood as "a systematic teaching method that engages students in acquiring knowledge and skills through an extended inquiry process centered around complex, authentic questions and carefully designed products and tasks" (Pecore 2015,159). A project can take the form of a single-class exercise or an extended endeavor spanning a semester (Morgan 1983). Its key features include the presence of a driving question or problem that organizes and guides activities, resulting in a set of artifacts that address the driving question. In addition, the practices employed should be consistent with the performance of experts in the field; students should be supported by experts and technology; and a focus on learning goals is essential.

In terms of research design and tools, PjBL research typically aims at assessing its impact on students' learning. Guo et al. (2020) review 76 studies and find that empirical investigations into PjBL predominantly concentrate on various aspects of student outcomes, encompassing emotional, cognitive, and behavioral results, as well as artifact performance. The instruments commonly employed, in order of frequency of use, include questionnaires, interviews, observations, self-reflection journals, rubrics, tests, artifacts, and log data. They emphasize the need for future research to delve deeper into students' learning processes and final outcomes while also enhancing the quality of measurement tools and data analysis techniques.

2.3.2 Cognitive science

Translation has long been recognized as a cognitive task. Like learning sciences, the field of cognitive science is also in a state of flux, with different paradigms seeking to better understand how the mind works when people are translating.

The first paradigm compares the mind to a computer that can be programmed (Newell and Simon 1961). Since cognition is the manipulation of symbols according to internal rules (programs), translation is seen as code-switching and symbol manipulation. However, the biggest drawback of this approach is that "while even the smallest change in the task or system causes the model to break down, humans can still master and understand even incomplete and grammatically incorrect information with apparent ease (Risku 2013: 4)." Therefore, the human mind-as-computer view is gradually replaced in the 1980s by the paradigm of connectionism. Connectionism derives its name from the multitude of connected nerve cells in our brain which are activated to process information in parallel. These mental representations are stored in the form of "scripts, frames, or schemata" and are continuously modified through experience (McClelland, Rumelhart, and the PDP Research Group 1986). In the case of translation, this is proved by translators who can use prior knowledge to give interpretations to suit a particular context, even when the source text in unclear.

In both symbolic and connectionist approaches, all cognition is centralized in the brain to the exclusion of the body and the outside world. However, in real life, people can always lean on the social and environmental support to memorize things and make decisions. As a result, a new paradigm known as the "4EA" cognition (embodied, embedded, extended, enacted, affective cognition) rises to prominence (Muñoz Martín 2016a). The implications of this paradigm are that in an authentic translation event, such as PjBL, instead of the traditional focus on an individual's mind or competence growth, we also need to pay attention to the interaction of the actors involved and their environment. In addition to the traditional empirical focus on the workflow, which captures human–human collaboration, we should also heed the cultural, organizational, and technologies aspect of the context and the social learning accrued by the team.

Regarding research design, investigations into cognitive processes can be conducted either in a controlled laboratory setting or within a natural environment (Göpferich and Jääskeläinen 2009). Lab-based studies are known for their high replicability and the ability to carefully isolate variables of interest. However, they may fall short in terms of ecological validity. On the other hand, studies conducted in natural environments allow researchers to observe cognitive processes in the complexity of their real-life context. However, these studies can be challenging to replicate due to the inherent variability of everyday situations.

With respect to research tools, a substantial body of literature recommends the utilization of integrated research tools (e.g. Hansen 2010; Muñoz Martín 2010; Risku 2014) to allow for cross-validation of findings obtained through different methods. There has been a growing interest in studying cognitive processes in the workplace to understand how individuals perform tasks, make decisions, and interact in their natural work environments (e.g. Kuznik and Verd 2010; Ehrensberger-Dow 2014; Teixeira 2014; Kuznik 2016; Risku and Rogl 2022). Similarly, PjBL scenarios, with their numerous uncontrollable factors, may lend themselves more readily to naturalistic study as they unfold in real-world scenarios.

2.3.3 Expertise studies

A key question in expertise studies is to find out how experts differ from novices. Researchers have found common indicators of expertise irrespective of field

(Committee on Developments in the Science of Learning 2000). In translation studies, researchers have tried to find specific indicators of translation expertise (Englund Dimitrova 2005; Angelone 2015). These findings hold implications to the design of PjBL, because when students have a chance to work alongside experts, they could use their performance as a benchmark to improve and monitor their progress. Collins, Brown, and Holum (1991) call on the pedagogical practices to make key aspects of expertise visible to students.

Secondly, although expertise denotes an exceptionally high degree of performance, in a group enterprise, expertise becomes a relative concept and thus is not concentrated in a single individual. People with various degrees of expertise can have a chance to reach zones of proximal development through mutual appropriation and negotiations (Vygotsky 1978). Even students can argue for their points of view in front of an expert if they can provide proper justifications.

Third, according to Hatano and Inagaki (1986), adaptive expertise and routine expertise are two different types of expertise that play important roles in training and skill development. Routine expertise refers to the ability to perform well-learned tasks or solve familiar problems efficiently and effectively. It is often associated with well-established procedures and techniques. Adaptive expertise, on the other hand, involves the ability to respond effectively to new and changing situations. In a translation project, although the client may have specified a request at the beginning, there are still many undefined problems inherent in translation. This open-endedness may promote higher-order thinking skills and gives student opportunities to apply knowledge in unfamiliar situations (Angelone 2023).

Fourth, expertise is built through deliberate practice (Ericsson 2010; Shreve 2006). Going through the activity of translation alone does not necessarily lead to learning. Learning is achieved only when students are empowered to engage in dialogical interactions, examine their own understanding in detail (Andriessen and Baker 2014) and through repetition. Moreover, they should be given opportunities to correct errors and test the learning gained in new situations. In PjBL, students are motivated because they are given responsibilities to solve real problems, nevertheless, teachers or the commissioner of the project must find ways to sustain their motivation and interest. Clear communication of rewards and compensation is also essential. It demonstrates transparency, sets expectations, and helps students understand what they will receive in exchange for their work, time, and effort.

To sum up, these interdisciplinary developments allow us to make connections to deepen our understanding of authentic collaborative PjBL. According to Elena Dunne (2011), since every translation is unique, participants can always expect something new to learn. When everyone brings to the task varied skill sets, there is always a chance to bridge the gap of knowledge and skill asymmetry. Ultimately, if we want students to have closer contact with the market and to maximize the benefits, it falls upon the shoulders of trainers and program providers to find ways to increase the frequency and the totality of students' project-based exposure.

Notes

1 Neubert hails from the Leipzig School, a school of thought that regards translation as a deliberate, cognitive process aimed at addressing language-related challenges rather than purely focusing on communication. For a review, see Muñoz Martín (2016a). The comparison made by Hague and his colleagues exemplifies how scholars' perceptions of translation competence evolve over time, particularly in response to technological advancements.
2 Coincidently, Austermühl (2013, 331) also believes that "revising is the new translating."
3 For a comprehensive review of four competence models proposed by academic associations, including EMT's wheel of competence, and CIUTI statutes, Transcert, and ISO 17100 translation competence model, see Krajcso (2018).
4 A separate international guideline for post-editing is released by ISO not until 2017. For details, see ISO (18587: 2017).

References

Albl-Mikasa, M. 2013. "Developing and Cultivating Expert Interpreter Competence." *Interpreters Newsletter* 18: 17–34.
Albl-Mikasa, M. 2020. "Interpreters' Roles and Responsibilities." In *The Bloomsbury Companion to Language Industry Studies*, edited by E. Angelone, M. Ehrensberger-Dow, and G. Massey, 91–114. Bloomsbury: Bloomsbury Academic.
Alves, F. (Editor). 2003. *Triangulating Translation: Perspectives in Process Oriented Research*. Amsterdam and Philadelphia: John Benjamins.
Andriessen, J., and M. Baker. 2014. "Argue to Learn." In *The Cambridge Handbook of the Learning Sciences*, 2nd ed., edited by R. Sawyer, 476–497. Cambridge: Cambridge University Press.
Angelone, E. 2015. "The Impact of Process Protocol Self-Analysis on Errors in the Translation Product." In *Describing Cognitive Processes in Translation: Acts and Events*, edited by M. Ehrensberger-Dow et al., 105–123. Amsterdam and Philadelphia: John Benjamin.
Angelone, E. 2023. "Weaving Adaptive Expertise into Translator Training." In *The Human Translator in the 2020s*, edited by G. Massey et al., 60–73. Abingdon: Routledge.
Angelone, E., and Á. Marín García. 2017. "Expertise Acquisition Through Deliberate Practice." *Translation Spaces* 6 (1): 122–158. doi: 10.1075/bct.105.07ang.
Austermühl, F. 2013. "Future (and Not-So-Future) Trends in the Teaching of Translation Technology." *Revista Tradumàtica: tecnologies de la traducció* 11: 326–337. doi: 10.5565/rev/tradumatica.46.
Beninatto, R. S., and D. A. DePalma. 2007. "Collaborative Translation." *Multilingual, Annual Resource Directory* 49–51.
Biel, Ł. 2011. "Training Translators or Translation Service Providers? EN 15038: 2006. Standards of Translation Services and Its Training Implications." *The Journal of Specialised Translation* 16: 61–76.
Bowker, L. 2002. *Computer-Aided Translation Technology: A Practical Introduction*. Ottawa: University of Ottawa Press.
Bowker, L. 2015. "Computer-Aided Translation: Translator Training." In *Routledge Encyclopedia of Translation Technology*, edited by S. Chan, 88–104. London: Routledge.

Brandt, A. 2019. "Training Translation and Localization Professionals in the Era of AI." Presentation delivered WITTA TTES 2019 Annual Assembly. https://ttv.cn/archives/4943.

Brown, J. S., A. Collins, and P. Duguid. 1989. "Situated Cognition and the Culture of Learning." *Educational Researcher* 18 (1): 32–42. doi: 10.3102/0013189X018001032.

Brunette, L. 2000. "Towards a Terminology for Translation Quality Assessment." *The Translator* 6 (2): 169–182. doi: 10.1080/13556509.2000.10799064.

Chesterman, A. 2015. "Models of What Processes?" In *Describing Cognitive Processes in Translation. Acts and Events*, edited by M. Ehrensberger-Dow et al., 7–20. Amsterdam and Philadelphia: John Benjamins.

China Association for Standardization. 2003. *Specification for Translation Service: Part 1: Translation (GB T 19363.1-2003)* [翻译服务规范 第1部分：笔译.].

Choudhury, R., and B. McConnell. 2013. TAUS Translation Technology Landscape Report 2013. TAUS. www.taus.net/think-tank/reports/translate-reports/taus-translation-technologylandscape-report.

Colina, S. 2003. *Translation Teaching, from Research to the Classroom: A Handbook for Teachers*. New York: McGraw-Hill.

Colina, S., and L. Venuti. 2017. "A Survey of Translation Pedagogies." In *Teaching Translation: Programs, Courses, Pedagogies*, edited by L. Venuti, 203–215. London and New York: Routledge.

Collins, A., J. S. Brown, and A. Holum. 1991. "Cognitive Apprenticeship: Making Thinking Visible." *American Educator* 15 (3): 6–11.

Committee on Developments in the Science of Learning. "How Experts Differ from Novices." In *How People Learn: Brain, Mind, Experience, and School: Expanded Edition*, edited by J. D. Bransford et al., 31–50. Washington, DC: National Academy Press.

Cui, Q. 2015. "Localization Project Management Course Teaching Practices [本地化项目管理课程教学实践.]." *Shanghai Journal of Translators* 2: 8–62.

Cui, Q., and H. Luo. 2016. *Translation Project Management [翻译项目管理.]*. Beijing: Foreign Languages Press.

Dawrant, A. C., B. Wang, and H. Jiang. 2022. "Conference Interpreting in China." In *The Routledge Handbook of Conference Interpreting*, edited by M. Albl-Mikasa and E. Tiselius, 182–196. London and New York: Routledge.

Désilets, A., and J. van der Meer. 2011. "Co-creating a Repository of Best-Practices for Collaborative Translation." *Linguistica Antverpiensia* 10: 27–45. doi: 10.52034/lanstts.v10i.276

Dreyfus, S. E., and H. L. Dreyfus. 1980. *A Five-Stage Model of the Mental Activities Involved in Directed Skill Acquisition*. Berkeley: University of California Berkeley Operations Research Center.

Drugan, J. 2013. *Quality in Professional Translation: Assessment and Improvement*. London: Bloomsbury Academic.

Dunne, E. S. 2011. "Project as a Learning Environment: Scaffolding Team Learning in Translation Projects." In *Translation and Localization Project Management. The Art of the Possible*, edited by K. J. Dunne and E. S. Dunne, 265–288. Amsterdam and Philadelphia: John Benjamins.

Dunne, K. J. 2007. "Terminology: Ignore It at Your Peril." *Multilingual* April/May: 32–38.

Dunne, K. J. 2011. "From Vicious to Virtuous Cycle: Customer-Focused Translation Quality Management Using ISO 9001 Principles and Agile Methodologies." In *Translation and Localization Project Management. The Art of the Possible*, edited by K. J. Dunne and E. S. Dunne, 153–188. Amsterdam and Philadelphia: John Benjamins.

Durban, C. 2009. "Battling the Black Hole in Space Mentality." In *CIUTI FORUM 2008. Enhancing Translation Quality Ways, Means, Methods*, edited by M. Forstner et al., 397–405. Frankfurt am Main: Peter Lang.

Ehrensberger-Dow, M. 2014. "Challenges of Translation Process Research at the Workplace." *MonTI Special Issue—Minding Translation*, 355–383.

EMT Board. 2017. *EMT Competence Framework*. European Commission.

EMT Expert Group. 2009. *Competences for Professional Translators, Experts in Multilingual and Multimedia Communication*. European Commission.

Englund Dimitrova, B. 2005. *Expertise and Explicitation in the Translation Process*. Amsterdam and Philadelphia: John Benjamins.

Ericsson, K. A. 2010. "Expertise in Interpreting: An Expert-Performance Perspective." In *Translation and Cognition*, edited by G. M. Shreve and E. Angelone, 231–262. Amsterdam and Philadelphia: John Benjamins.

European Committee for Standardization. 2006. *EN 15038 Translation Services—Service Requirements*. Brussels.

Fang, M. 2011. *A Dictionary of Translation Studies in China [中国译学大辞典.]*. Shanghai: Shanghai Foreign Language Education Press.

Feng, Q., and H. Zhang. 2015. "Training of Post-Editors in the Context of Global Language Service Industry [全球语言服务行业背景下译后编辑者培养研究.]." *Foreign Language World* 1: 65–72.

Feng, Q., and M. Liu. 2018. "Post-Editing Competence: A Three-Dimensional Model [译后编辑能力三维模型构建.]." *Foreign Language World* 3: 55–61.

Fu, J. 2015. "Translation Competence Research: Review and Outlook [翻译能力研究:回顾与展望.]." *Foreign Language Learning Theory and Practice* 4: 80–86.

Gao, W. 2008. "Innovations in Learning Theories for the New Millennium [面向新千年的学习理论创新.]." In *Constructivist Education Research [建构主义教育研究.]*, edited by W. Gao, Y. Xu, and G. Wu, 65–75. Beijing: Educational Science Publishing House.

Gassmann O. 1997. "F&E-Projektmanagement und Prozesse Länderübergreifender Produktentwicklung." In *Globales Management von Forschung und Innovation*, edited by A. Gerybadze, G. Regetr and F. Meyer-Krahmer, 133–173. Stuttgart: Schäffer-Poeschel.

Gile, D. 1995. *Basic Concepts and Models for Interpreter and Translator Training*. Amsterdam and Philadelphia: John Benjamins.

González, J., and R. Wagenaar (Editors). 2003. *Tuning Educational Structures in Europe. Final Report. Phase One*. Bilbao: Universidad de Deusto.

González Davies, M. 2004a. *Multiple Voices in the Translation Classroom: Activities, Tasks and Projects*. Amsterdam and Philadelphia: John Benjamins.

González Davies, M. 2004b. "Undergraduate and Postgraduate Translation Degrees: Aims and Expectations." In *Translation in Undergraduate Degree Programmes*, edited by K. Malmkjær, 67–82. Amsterdam and Philadelphia: John Benjamins.

González Davies, M., and D. Kiraly. 2006. "Translation: Pedagogy." In *Encyclopedia of Language & Linguistics*, 2nd ed., edited by B. Keith, 81–85. Amsterdam and Philadelphia: Elsevier Science.

González Davies, M., and V. Enríquez Raído. 2016. "Situated Learning in Translator and Interpreter Training: Bridging Research and Good Practice." *The Interpreter and Translator Trainer* 10 (1): 1–11. doi: 10.1080/1750399X.2016.1154339.

Göpferich, S. 2009. "Towards a Model of Translation Competence and Its Acquisition: The Longitudinal Study TransComp." In *Behind the Mind: Methods, Models and Results in Translation Process Research*, edited by S. Göpferich et al., 11–37. Copenhagen: Samfundslitteratur Press.

Göpferich, S. 2013. "Translation Competence: Explaining Development and Stagnation from a Dynamic Systems Perspective." In *Interdisciplinarity in Translation and Interpreting Process Research*, edited by M. Ehrensberger-Dow et al., 62–78. Amsterdam and Philadelphia: John Benjamins.

Göpferich, S., and R. Jääskeläinen. 2009. "Process Research into the Development of Translation Competence: Where Are We, and Where Do We Need to Go?" *Across Languages and Cultures* 10 (2), 169–191. doi: 10.1556/Acr.10.2009.2.1.

Gouadec, D. 2007. *Translation as a Profession*. Amsterdam and Philadelphia: John Benjamins.

Guerberof Arenas, A., and J. Moorkens. 2019. "Machine Translation and Post-Editing Training as Part of a Master's Programme." *The Journal of Specialised Translation* 31: 217–238.

Guo, P., N. Saab, L. S. Post, and W. Admiraal. 2020. "A Review of Project-Based Learning in Higher Education: Student Outcomes and Measures." *International Journal of Educational Research* 102: 2–13. doi: 10.1016/j.ijer.2020.101586.

Hague, D., A. Melby, and Z. Wang. 2011. "Surveying Translation Quality Assessment." *The Interpreter and Translator Trainer* 5 (2): 243–267. doi: 10.1080/1750399x.2015.1010359.

Hansen, G. 2009. "The Speck in Your Brother's Eye—The Beam in Your Own: Quality Management in Translation and Revision." In *Efforts and Models in Interpreting and Translation Research: A Tribute to Daniel Gile,* edited by G. Hansen et al., 255–280. Amsterdam and Philadelphia: John Benjamins.

Hansen, G. 2010. "Integrative Description of Translation Processes." In *Translation and Cognition*, edited by G. M. Shreve and E. Angelone, 189–211. Amsterdam and Philadelphia: John Benjamins.

Hatano, G., and K. Inagaki. 1986. "Two Courses of Expertise." In *Children Development and Education in Japan*, edited by H. Stevenson, H. Azuma, and K. Hakuta, 262–272. New York: Freeman.

Holmes, J. 1972. "The Name and Nature of Translation Studies." Unpublished manuscript, Amsterdam, Translation Studies section, Department of General Studies. Reprinted in G. Toury (Editor). 1987. *Translation Across Cultures*. 9–24. New Delhi: Bahri Publications.

Holz-Mänttäri, J. 1984. *Translatorisches Handeln: Theorie und Methode*. Helsinki: Suomalainen Tiedeaktemia.

Hurtado Albir, A. 2007. "Competence-Based Curriculum Design for Training Translators." *The Interpreter and Translator Trainer* 1 (2): 163–195. doi: 10.1080/1750399X.2007.10798757.

Hurtado Albir, A., and F. Alves. 2009. "Translation as a Cognitive Activity." In *Routledge Companion to Translation Studies*, edited by J. Munday, 54–73. London: Routledge.

International Organization for Standardization. 2015. *ISO 17100: 2015—Translation Services—Requirements for Translation Services.*

International Organization for Standardization. 2017. *ISO 18587: 2017—Translation Services—Post-Editing of Machine Translation Output—Requirements.*

Ipsen, H., and H. V. Dam. 2016. "Translation Revision: Correlating Revision Procedure and Error Detection." *HERMES—Journal of Language and Communication in Business* 55: 143–156. doi: 10.7146/hjlcb.v0i55.24612.

Jääskeläinen, R. 2010. "Are All professionals Experts? Definitions of Expertise and Reinterpretation of Research Evidence in Process Studies." In *Translation and Cognition*, edited by G. M. Shreve and E. Angelone, 213–227. Amsterdam and Philadelphia: John Benjamins.

Jakobsen, A. L. 2017. "Translation Process Research." In *Handbook of Translation and Cognition*, edited by J. W. Schwieter and A. Ferreira, 21–49. Hoboken: John Wiley & Sons.

Jakobsen, A. L. 2019. "Moving Translation, Revision, and Post-Editing Boundaries." In *Moving Boundaries in Translation Studies*, edited by H. V. Dam et al., 64–80. London and New York: Routledge.

Jiménez-Crespo, M. 2017. *Crowdsourcing and Online Collaborative Translations*. Amsterdam: John Benjamins.

Kageura, K., and E. Marshman. 2020. "Terminology Extraction and Management." In *The Routledge Handbook of Translation and Technology*, edited by M. O'Hagan, 61–77. London and New York: Routledge.

Kalina, S. 2002. "Interpreting Competence as a Basis and Goal for Teaching." *The Interpreters' Newsletter* 10 (3): 3–26.

Kautz, U. 2002. *Handbuch Didaktik des Übersetzens und Dolmetschens*. Munich: Iudicium/Goethe-Institut (München).

Kelly, D. 2005. *A Handbook for Translator Trainers*. Manchester: St. Jerome Publishing.

Kelly, D. 2007. "Translator Competence Contextualized Translator Training in the Framework of Higher Education Reform: In Search of Alignment in Curricular Design." In *Across Boundaries: International Perspectives on Translation*, edited by D. Kenny and K. Ryou, 128–142. Newcastle upon Tyne: Cambridge Scholars Publishing.

Kelly, D., and A. Martin. 2009. "Training and Education." In *Routledge Encyclopedia of Translation Studies*, 2nd ed., edited by M. Baker and C. Saldanha, 294–300. London: Routledge.

Kelly, N., R. Ray, and D. A. DePalma. 2011. "From Crawling to Sprinting: Community Translation Goes Mainstream." *Linguistica Antverpiensia* 10: 45–76. doi: 10.52034/lanstts.v10i.278.

Kiraly, D. 2003. "From Instruction to Collaborative Construction: A Passing Fad or the Promise of a Paradigm Shift in Translator Education?" In *Beyond the Ivory Tower*, edited by B. J. Baer and G. S. Koby, 3–27. Amsterdam and Philadelphia: John Benjamins.

Kiraly, D. 2016. "Beyond the Static Competence Impasse in Translator Education." In *Translation and Meaning. New Series*, edited by B. Lewandowska-Tomaszczyk et al., Vol. 1, 129–142. Frankfurt am Main: Peter Lang.

Ko, L. 2011. "Translation Checking: A View from the Translation Market." *Perspectives* 19 (2): 123–134. doi: 10.1080/0907676X.2010.514348.

Konttinen, K., L. Salmi, and M. Koponen. 2021. "Revision and Post-Editing Competences in Translator Education." In *Translation Revision and Post-Editing: Industry Practices and Cognitive Processes*, edited by M. Koponen et al., 187–202. London and New York: Routledge.

Konttinen, K., O. Veivo, and P. Salo. 2020. "Translation Students' Conceptions of Translation Workflow in a Simulated Translation Company Environment." *The Interpreter and Translator Trainer* 14 (1): 79–94. doi: 10.1080/1750399X.2019.1619218.

Koponen, M. 2015. "How to Teach Machine Translation Post-Editing? Experiences from a Post-Editing Course." Paper presented at the 4th Workshop on Post-Editing Technology and Practice.

Krajcik, J. S., and N. Shin. 2014. "Project-Based Learning." In *The Cambridge Handbook of the Learning Sciences*, 2nd ed., edited by K. Sawyer, 304–328. Cambridge: Cambridge University Press.

Krajcso, Z. 2018. "Translators' Competence Profiles Versus Market Demand." *Babel* 64 (5/6): 692–709. doi: 10.1075/babel.00059.kra.

Kruger, P. 2016. "Contextualising Computer-Assisted Translation Tools and Modelling Their Usability." *trans-kom* 9 (1): 114–148.

Kußmaul, P. 1995. *Training the Translator*. Amsterdam and Philadelphia: John Benjamins.

Kuznik, A. 2016. "Work Content of In-House Translators in Small and Medium-Sized Industrial Enterprises. Observing Real Work Situations." *The Journal of Specialised Translation* 25: 213–231.

Kuznik, A., and J. M. Verd. 2010, "Investigating Real Work Situations in Translation Agencies. Work Content and Its Components." *HERMES—Journal of Language and Communication in Business* 44: 25–43. doi: 10.7146/hjlcb.v23i44.128882.

Lave, J., and E. Wenger. 1991. *Situated Learning: Legitimate Peripheral Participation*. Cambridge: Cambridge University Press.

Lee-Jahnke, H. 2009. "Doppelter Praxisbezug und Kompetenzvermittlung als Problem der Qualitätssicherung Translatorischer Studiengänge." In *CIUTI FORUM 2008. Enhancing Translation Quality Ways, Means, Methods*, edited by M. Forstner et al., 133–195. Frankfurt am Main: Peter Lang.

Lee-Jahnke, H. 2013. "Heterogeneous Cooperation or Networking Between Disciplines: The Significance for Translation Studies." In *CIUTI-Forum 2012. Translators and Interpreters as Key Actors in Global Networking*, edited by M. Forstner and H. Lee-Jahnke, 23–46. Frankfurt am Main: Peter Lang.

Lefevere, A. 1992. *Translation, Rewriting and the Manipulation of Literary Fame*. London and New York: Routledge.

Lesznyák, M. 2007. "Conceptualizing Translation Competence." *Across Languages and Cultures* 8 (2): 167–194. doi: 10.1556/Acr.8.2007.2.2.

Li, D. 2000a. "Needs Assessment in Translation Teaching: Making Translator Training More Responsive to Social Needs." *Babel* 46 (4): 289–299. doi:10.1075/babel.46.4.02li.

Li, D. 2000b. "Tailoring Translation Programs to Social Needs." *Target*, 12 (1):127–149. doi: 10.1075/target.12.1.07li.

Li, R. L. 2011. "From Translation Competence to Translator Competence: Shifting Goals in Translation Education [从翻译能力到译者素养：翻译教学的目标转向.]." *Chinese Translators Journal* 1: 46–51.

Li, X. 2022. "Identifying In-Demand Qualifications and Competences for Translation Curriculum Renewal: A Content Analysis of Translation Job Ads." *The Interpreter and Translator Trainer* 16 (2): 177–202. doi: 10.1080/1750399X.2021.2017706.

Liu, F. M. C. 2021. "Translator Professionalism in Asia." *Perspectives* 29 (1): 1–19. doi: 10.1080/0907676X.2019.1676277.

Liu, H. 2011. "Stages of Translation Competence Development and Research on Teaching Methods [翻译能力发展的阶段性及其教学法研究.]." *Chinese Translators Journal* 32 (01): 37–45.

Lu, L., and S. Yan. 2014. *Translation Project Management [翻译项目管理.]*. Beijing: National Defense Industry Press.

Massey, G. 2017. "Translation Competence Development and Process-Oriented Pedagogy." In *Handbook of Translation and Cognition*, edited by J. W. Schwieter and A. Ferreira, 496–518. Hoboken: John Wiley & Sons.

Massey, G. 2021. "Transitioning from Interdisciplinarity to Transdisciplinarity in Applied Translation Studies: Towards Transdisciplinary Action Research in Translators' Workplaces." *The Journal of Translation Studies* 1 (2):51–78.

Massion, F. 2013. "Translating in the Cloud: Is This the Future of the Translation Industry?" In *CIUTI-Forum 2012. Translators and Interpreters as Key Actors in Global Networking*, edited by M. Forstner and H. Lee-Jahnke, 249–262. Frankfurt am Main: Peter Lang.

McClelland, J. L., D. E. Rumelhart, and the PDP Research Group. 1986. "The Appeal of Parallel Distributed Processing." In *Parallel Distributed Processing: Explorations in the Microstructure of Cognition*, Vol. II, edited by D. E. Rumelhart et al., 1: 3–40. Cambridge: The MIT Press.

Mellinger, C. D. 2017. "Translators and Machine Translation: Knowledge and Skills Gaps in Translator Pedagogy." *The Interpreter and Translator Trainer* 11 (4): 280–293. doi: 10.1080/1750399X.2017.1359760.

Miao, J. 2007. "Translation Competence Research as Foundation for Translation Didactic Models [翻译能力研究——构建翻译教学模式的基础.]." *Foreign Languages and Their Teaching* 4: 47–50.

Montero Martínez, S., and P. Faber Benítez. 2009. "Terminological Competence in Translation." *Terminology* 15 (1): 88–104. doi: 10.1075/term.15.1.05mon.

Morgan, A. 1983. "Theoretical Aspects of Project-Based Learning in Higher Education." *British Journal of Educational Technology* 14 (1): 66–78.

Mossop, B. 2014. *Revising and Editing for Translators*. London: Routledge.

Mu, L. 2008. "On Building a Comprehensive Translation Training System [建设完整的翻译教学体系.]." *Chinese Translators Journal* 1: 41–45.

Muegge, U. 2012a. "The Silent Revolution: Cloud-Based Translation Management Systems." Tcworld, July: 17–21. http://works.bepress.com/uwe_muegge/57/.

Muegge, U. 2012b. "Cloud-Based Translation Memory Tools Are Changing the Way Translators Work and Train." *The Big Wave of Language Technology*, 1 (3). http://works.bepress.com/uwe_muegge/76/ 2012.

Muñoz Martín, R. 2009. "Expertise and Environment in Translation." *Mutatis Mutandis* 2 (1): 24–37.

Muñoz Martín, R. 2010. "On Paradigms and Cognitive Translatology." In *Translation and Cognition*, edited by G. M. Shreve and E. Angelone, 169–187. Amsterdam and Philadelphia: John Benjamins.

Muñoz Martín, R. 2016a. "Reembedding Translation Process Research: An Introduction." In *Reembedding Translation Process Research*, edited by R. Muñoz Martín, 1–20. Amsterdam and Philadelphia: John Benjamins.

Muñoz Martín, R. 2016b. "Processes of What Models? On the Cognitive Indivisibility of Translation Acts and Events." *Translation Spaces*, 5 (1): 145–161. doi: 10.1075/bct.101.08mun.

Neubert, A. 2000. "Competence in Language, in Languages, and in Translation." In *Developing Translation Competence*, edited by C. Schäffner and B. Adab, 3–18. Amsterdam and Philadelphia: John Benjamins.

Newell, A., and H. A. Simon. 1961. "Computer Simulation of Human Thinking. A Theory of Problem Solving Expressed as a Computer Program Permits Simulation of Thinking Processes." *Science* 134 (3495): 2011–2017.

Newmark, P. 1988. *A Textbook of Translation*. Hoboken: Prentice-Hall International.

Nitzke, J., S. Hansen-Schirra, and C. Canfora. 2019. "Risk Management and Post-Editing Competence." *Journal of Specialised Translation* 31: 239–259.

Nord, C. 1997. *Translating as a Purposeful Activity: Functionalist Approaches Explained*. Manchester: St. Jerome.

Nord, C. 2005. *Text Analysis in Translation: Theory, Methodology, and Didactic Application of a Model for Translation-Oriented Text Analysis*, 2nd ed., translated by C. Nord and P. E. Sparrow. Amsterdam and Philadelphia/Atlanta, GA: Rodopi.

O'Brien, S. 2002. "Teaching Post-Editing, A Proposal for Course Content." *Proceedings of the 6th International Workshop of the European Association for Machine Translation*.

Teaching Machine Translation. Manchester. European Association for Machine Translation.

O'Brien, S. 2012. "Translation as Human–Computer Interaction." *Translation Spaces* 1: 101–122. doi: 10.1075/ts.1.05obr.

Olvera-Lobo, M. D., B. Robinson, J. A. Senso, R. Muñoz-Martín, E. Muñoz-Raya, M. Murillo-Melero, E. Quero-Gervilla, M. Castro-Prieto, and T. Conde-Ruano. 2009. "Teleworking and Collaborative Work Environments in Translation Training." *Babel* 55 (2): 165–180. doi: 10.1075/babel.55.2.05olv.

PACTE Group. 2017. *Research Translation Competence*, edited by A. H. Albir. Amsterdam and Philadelphia: John Benjamins.

Pecore, J. L. 2015. "From Kilpatrick's Project Method to Project-Based Learning." In *International Handbook of Progressive Education*, edited by M. Y. Eryaman and B. C. Bruce, 155–171. Frankfurt am Main: Peter Lang.

Piotrowska, M. 2016. "Revisiting the Translator Competence in the 21st Century." In *Constructing Translation Competence*, edited by P. Pietrzak and M. Deckert, 13–25. Frankfurt am Main: Peter Lang.

Pöchhacker F. 2007. *Dolmetschen. Konzeptuelle Grundlagen und deskriptive Untersuchungen.* Tübingen: Stauffenburg.

Popiolek, M. 2015. "Terminology Management Within a Translation Quality Assurance Process." In *Handbook of Terminology: Volume 1*, edited by H. J. Kockaert and F. Steurs, 341–359. Amsterdam and Philadelphia: John Benjamins.

Pym, A. 2003. "Redefining Translation Competence in an Electronic Age." *Meta*, 48 (4): 481–97. doi: 10.7202/008533ar.

Pym, A. 2013. "Translation Skill Sets in a Machine-Translation Age." *Meta*, 58 (3): 487–503. doi: 10.7202/1025047ar.

Qian, C. 2012. "Analysis of the Components of Translation Competence and Their Interrelationships [翻译能力构成要素及其驱动关系分析.]." *Foreign Language World* 3: 59–65.

Reiss, K. 2000. *Translation Criticism: The Potentials & Limitations*. Manchester/Shanghai: St Jerome Publishing/Shanghai Foreign Language Education Press.

Resnick, L. B. 1987. "Learning in School and Out." *Educational Researcher* 16: 13–20. doi: 10.2307/1175725.

Rico, P. C. 2002. "Translation and Project Management." *Translation Journal*, 6 (4). https://translationjournal.net/journal/22project.htm.

Rico, P. C., and E. Torrejón. 2012. "Skills and Profile of the New Role of the Translator as MT Post-Editor." *Revista Tradumàtica: tecnologies de la traducció* 10: 166–178. doi: 10.5565/rev/tradumatica.18.

Risku, H. 2002. "Situatedness in Translation Studies." *Cognitive Systems Research* 3: 523–533. doi: 10.1016/S1389-0417(02)00055-4.

Risku, H. 2013. "Cognitive Approaches to Translation." In *The Encyclopedia of Applied Linguistics*, edited by C. A. Chapelle,1–10. Hoboken: Blackwell Publishing.

Risku, H. 2014. "Translation Process Research as Interaction Research: From Mental to Social-Cognitive Processes." *MonTI Special Issue—Minding Translation* 331–353.

Risku, H., and R. Rogl. 2022. "Praxis and Process Meet Halfway: The Convergence of Sociological and Cognitive Approaches in Translation Studies." *Translation & Interpreting* 14 (2): 32–49.

Robert, I. 2013. "Does the Revision Procedure Matter?" *Tracks and Treks in Translation Studies: Selected Papers from the EST Congress, Leuven 2010*, edited by C. Way et al., 87–102. Amsterdam and Philadelphia: John Benjamin.

Robert, I., and L. Van Waes. 2014. "Selecting a Translation Revision Procedure: Do Common Sense and Statistics Agree?" *Perspectives* 22 (3): 304–320. doi: 10.1080/0907676X.2013.871047.

Robert, I. S., A. R. Terryn, J. J. J. Ureel, A. Remael, and TricS Research Group. 2017. "Conceptualising Translation Revision Competence: A Pilot Study on the 'Tools and Research' Subcompetence." *The Journal of Specialised Translation* 28: 293–316.

Robert, I. S., J. J. J. Ureel, and I. Schrijver. 2022. "Translation, Translation Revision and Post-Editing Competence Models: Where Are We Now?" In *The Human Translator in the 2020s*, edited by G. Massey, E. Huertas-Barros, and D. Katan, London and New York: Routledge.

Robert, I. S., R. Aline, and J. J. J. Ureel. 2017. "Towards a Model of Translation Revision Competence." *The Interpreter and Translator Trainer* 11 (1): 1–19. doi: 10.1080/1750399X.2016.1198183.

Sawyer, K. R. 2014. "The New Science of Learning." In *The Cambridge Handbook of the Learning Sciences*, 2nd ed., edited by K. R. Sawyer, 22–39. Cambridge: Cambridge University Press.

Schäffner, C. 2012. "Translation Competence: Training for the Real World." In *Global Trends in Translator and Interpreter Training*, edited by S. Hubscher-Davidson and M. Borodo, 30–44. London: Continuum.

Schäffner, C. 2020. "Translators' Roles and Responsibilities." In *The Bloomsbury Companion to Language Industry Studies*, edited by E. Angelone, M. Ehrensberger-Dow, and G. Massey, 63–89. London: Bloomsbury Academic.

Schäffner, C., and B. Adab. 2000. "Developing Translation Competence: Introduction." *Developing Translation Competence*, edited by C. Schäffner and B. Adab, vii–xvi. Amsterdam and Philadelphia: John Benjamins.

Setton, R., and A. C. Dawrant. 2016. *Conference Interpreting—A Complete Guide*. Amsterdam and Philadelphia: John Benjamins.

Shi, L. 2001. *Learning Theories [学习论.]*. Beijing: People's Education Press.

Shreve, G. M. 2002. "Knowing Translation: Cognitive and Experiential Aspects of Translation Expertise from the Perspective of Expertise Studies." In *Translation Studies. Perspectives on an Emerging Discipline*, edited by A. Riccardi, 150–171. Cambridge: Cambridge University Press.

Shreve, G. M. 2006. "The Deliberate Practice: Translation and Expertise." *Journal of Translation Studies* 9 (1): 27–42.

Shreve, G. M. 2020. "Professional Translator Development from an Expertise Perspective." In *The Bloomsbury Companion to Language Industry Studies*, edited by E. Anglone et al., 153–177. Bloomsbury: Bloomsbury Academic.

Shreve, G. M., E. Angelone, and I. Lacruz. 2018. "Are Expertise and Translation Competence the Same? Psychological Reality and the Theoretical Status of Competence." In *Innovation and Expansion in Translation Process Research*, edited by I. Lacruz and R. Jääskeläinen, 37–54. Amsterdam and Philadelphia: John Benjamins.

Snell-Hornby, M. 2006. *The Turns of Translation Studies: New Paradigms or Shifting Viewpoints?* Amsterdam and Philadelphia: John Benjamins.

Tao, Y. 2016. "Translator Training and Education in China: Past, Present and Prospects." *The Interpreter and Translator Trainer* 10 (2): 204–223. doi: 10.1080/1750399X.2016.1204873.

Teixeira, C. S. C. 2014. "Data Collection Methods for Research the Interaction Between Translators and Translation Tools: An Ecological Approach." In *The Development of Translation Competence: Theories and Methodologies from Psycholinguistics and Cognitive Science*, edited by J. W. Schwieter and A. Ferreira, 269–286. Newcastle upon Tyne: Cambridge Scholars Publishing.

Tirkkonen-Condit, S., and R. Jääskeläinen (Editors). 2000. *Tapping and Mapping the Processes of Translation and Interpreting: Outlooks on Empirical Research*. Amsterdam and Philadelphia: John Benjamins.

Vermeer, H. J. 2000. "Skopos and Commission in Translational Action." Translated by Andrew Chesterman. In *The Translation Studies Reader*, edited by L. Venuti, 221–232. London and New York: Routledge.

Vygotsky, L. S. 1978. *Mind in Society: The Development of Higher Psychological Processes*. Massachusetts: Harvard University Press.

Walker, C. 2023. *Translation Project Management*. London and New York: Routledge.

Wang, C., S. Yan, and Y. Zhang. 2011. "Translation Project Management and Professional Translator Training [翻译项目管理与职业译员训练.]." *Chinese Translators Journal* 32 (1): 55–59.

Wang, H. 2014. "Translation Project Management Curriculum Development [MTI翻译项目管理"课程构建.]." *Chinese Translators Journal* 35 (4): 54–58.

Wang, H., and H. Wang. 2013. "Practical Approaches in Translation Project Management [翻译项目管理实务.]." Beijing: China Translation & Publishing House.

Wang, H., and S. Wang. 2019. "Terminology Management: Processes, Tools, and Trends [翻译场景下的术语管理:流程、工具与趋势.]." *China Terminology* 3: 9–14.

Wang, S. 2011. "Terminology Competence for Translation: Concepts, Modeling, and Development [面向翻译的术语能力:理念、构成与培养.]." *Foreign Language World* 5: 68–75.

Wang, S., and R. Wang. 2008. "Components of Translation Competence and Their Development Pace [翻译能力的构成因素和发展层次研究.]." *Foreign Language Research* 5: 80–88.

Wang, W., Y. Xu, and L. Mu. 2018. "On the Interpreting Competence of China's Standards of English [中国英语能力等级量表中的口译能力.]." *Modern Foreign Languages* 41 (167): 111–121.

Wang, X., and X. Li. 2020. "The Market's Expectations of Interpreters in China: A Content Analysis of Job Ads for In-House Interpreters." *The Journal of Specialised Translation* 34: 118–149.

Weinert, F. E. 2001. "Concept of Competence: A Conceptual Clarification." In *Defining and Selecting Key Competencies*, edited by D. S. Rychen and L. H. Salganik, 45–65. Boston: Hogrefe & Huber Publishers.

Wen, J. 2004. "A Curriculum Model Centered on Developing Translation Competence [论以发展翻译能力为中心的课程模式.]." *Foreign Languages and Their Teaching* 8: 49–52.

Wenger, E. 1998. *Communities of Practice. Learning, Meaning, and Identity*. Cambridge: Cambridge University Press.

Yue, F. 2019. *Translation Project Management: Practical Application, Cases, and Research /翻译项目管理：实操、案例与研究.]*. Beijing: Peking University Press.

Zhang, A., Z. Yang, C. Liu, and S. Li. 2018. "An Initial Exploration of the Coupling Mechanism and Path of the Development of Artificial Intelligence Technology and Professional T&I Practice [人工智能技术发展与专业口笔译实践耦合机制路径初探.]." *Technology-Enhanced Foreign Language Education* 181: 88–94.

Zhang, Y. 2015. "Cultivating Practical Awareness in Translation Project Management: A Case Study of MIIS [论翻译项目管理课程教学中实战意识的培养——以蒙特雷国际研究学院相关课程为例.]." *Chinese Translators Journal* 36 (5): 60–64.

Zhang, Z., and Y. Wang. 2020. "Project-Based Translation Teaching and Translation Competence Development: Theory and Practice [MTI 项目化翻译教学与翻译能力培养：理论与实践.]." *Foreign Language World* 2: 65–72.

3 Meta-analysis of authentic cases of project-based learning[1]

3.1 Scope and criteria of selection

Cross-case analysis derives from multiple-case study design (Yin 2003). Each case serves as a unit of analysis and is studied for comparative and contrastive purposes (Stake 2006; Susam-Sarajeva 2001, 2009). The analysis can take various forms, including qualitative methods such as narrative reviews or quantitative methods that involve the use of statistical techniques (Koricheva and Gurevitch 2013). We adopted the case-oriented qualitative method, which is an iterative method that involves gathering multiple original accounts, deciding upon the criteria of selection, reading each case repeatedly, identifying key recurring features as themes, extracting meaning, grouping each unit of meaning, and drawing up generalizations (Miles and Huberman 1994; Khan and VanWynsberghe 2008).

The first step of the review is to set up a start and an end time to identify relevant publications. Authentic PjBL was put on the map of translator education in the 1990s, but it was not until Kiraly's monograph, "*A Social Constructivist Approach to Translator Education. Empowerment from Theory to Practice* (2000)," that it gained traction. It is thus assumed that relevant publications did not appear in large numbers until 2000. The period between 2000 and 2018, the year in which the present research began, is bracketed as the timespan of bibliometric data. Two rounds of separate queries were manually conducted to filter out relevant research. English keywords such as "project-based learning" and "projects in translator education" were typed in John Benjamin's Translation Studies Bibliography. Likewise, similar Chinese keywords were typed in CNKI, China's most comprehensive indexed journals and academic degree thesis database. All the publications generated this way were subsequently read, and the references were used to widen the scope of the selections. In addition, some niche publications and journals also exist that represent more well-exemplified research on PjBL. The latter category, including *Intralinea, Lebende Sprachen, trans-kom, Linguistica Antverpiensia*, and *CIUTI Forum*, was subsequently added to the review pool.

The publications surveyed take on the following features.

Many scholars make the case for PjBL by contextualizing it in learning sciences, curriculum design, and industry developments (e.g. Durban et al. 2003; Biel 2011; Dunne 2011; Huertas Barros 2011; Zhang 2011; Mitchell-Schuitevoerder 2013;

Hurtado Albir 2015; Calvo 2015; González Davies 2017; Massey and Ehrensberger-Dow 2017; Rodríguez de Céspedes 2017; Nitzke, Tardel, and Hansen-Schirra 2019). They may have mentioned the projects they had run as illustrations, but the intention is not to go into details of any single project.

The empirical studies are dominated by simulated projects. The designs range from one-off projects (e.g. Aula.int 2005; Alcina, Soler, and Granell 2007; Olvera-Lobo et al. 2009) to simulated translation companies (e.g. Thelen 2009; Buysschaert, Fernández-Parra, van Egdom 2017; Hansen-Schirra, Hofmann, and Nitzke 2018; Kiraly, Massey, Hofmann 2018; Konttinen, Veivo, and Salo 2020; van Egdom et al. 2020). Notably, the latter aims to develop not only student translation competence but also service provision and entrepreneurial competence.

Some simulated projects focus on using information and communication technologies (ICTs) to train students in multimodal working environments (Robinson, López-Rodríguez, and Tercedor-Sánchez 2008; García González and Veiga Díaz 2015; Prieto-Velasco and Fuentes-Luque 2016).

Although PjBL was originally suggested for advanced students (Kelly 2005), if the content is of appropriate difficulty and the learning carefully scaffolded, PjBL can also be enacted successfully for novice students (Li 2017) or for students accustomed to transmissionist training (Moghaddas and Khoshsaligheh 2019).

Content-wise, while PjBL was proposed from translation training (Gouadec 1991; Vienne 1994), it has also been applied to research-oriented projects (Li, Zhang, and He 2015; Risku 2016) and in transcreation (Huertas Barros and Vine 2019).

Regarding participant features, the locus of PjBL is traditionally a cohort of students. In China, however, there is a trend underway for authentic projects to be conducted at the program level in collaboration with an external partner as internships. If the client wishes to have continuous content translated, the team may even sustain for a long time (e.g. Chai 2015; Chen 2013).

Lastly, most Chinese research on PjBL turns out to be written by students of China's Master of Translation and Interpreting (MTI) programs as their graduation theses. Based on the requirements issued by China's T&I program regulator (Mu 2011), students can choose among the five formats for their degree thesis, one of which is to reflect on their experience in an authentic project. But the reason we cannot include this kind of research is that they may focus more on linguistic aspects than the process of translation practice, which is the focus of our interest. Therefore, they are excluded from the review.

These features helped us draw up three criteria for selection. The project should first be about translation as a practice-based activity. Second, by focusing on authentic projects, we exclude all simulated PjBL (but their designs have sensitized us to some new developments, which we discuss later in the article). Third, we need a case to have rich contextual information on which to base the comparison. A modest list of 11 studies was eventually generated, with seven in the European context and four in China:

Kiraly, Donald (2000)
Kiraly, Donald (2005)

Varney, Jennifer (2009)
Zhang, Zheng and Zhang, Shaozhe (2012)
Xu, Bin and Guo, Hongmei (2012)
Gong, Rui (2012)
Kiraly, Donald (2013)
Li, Defeng (2013)
Chen, Shuiping (2013)
Marco, Josep (2016)
Massey, Gary and Brändli, Barbara (2016)

3.2 Meta analysis framework

The above studies feature different argumentation styles to suit their research purpose. Before proceeding to analyze the cases, it is essential to use a uniform framework to extract relevant information coherently.

According to Ayres, Kavanaugh, and Knafl (2003, 880), "themes may enter the analysis a priori; others are developed during the study." We noted early on that Massey and Brändli (2016) had used headings to organize the research, which we adopted as the initial analysis framework. As our knowledge of the field increased, we added new themes and categorized all of them into research and practice features. We read each case back and forth, wrote summaries, and drew up their respective workflows before noting down and reorganizing each unit of meaning. We also tabulated some information for easy comparison.

In the following section, we will summarize how each of them is conducted as academic research and how it is implemented before we report the findings of the cross-case examination.

3.3 Summary of the projects sampled

3.3.1 *Kiraly (2000)*

Kiraly (2000) describes a translation project at Johannes Gutenberg University in Germersheim. Designed as participatory action research, this project had three main objectives:1) to explore effective strategies for PjBL, 2) to evaluate student performance, and 3) to leverage the insights gained to enhance the future course design. To assist in data collection, Kiraly invited three student assistants to record class sessions, conduct direct observations, and administer a post-event questionnaire to students.

The project was integrated into a third-year German-English general translation course in late 1995. Prior to the course, Kiraly was tasked by a book publisher to translate a travel book from German, the student's first language (L1), to English, the second language (L2). He assigned two chapters, without specifying the word count, for his class to translate within a ten-week timeframe.

During the first week, the students focused on preparation. They discussed the stylistic approach and compiled a list of reference materials. Students then formed groups of three to four members, with each group assigned an equal portion of the text. Weeks two to seven were dedicated to individual group work with no prescribed procedures. Some groups divided the text into smaller sub-sections, with members translating individually at home and coming together to discuss their work in class. Others opted for face-to-face translation and problem-solving during class sessions. Regardless of their chosen approach, each group produced a joint draft and proofread at least three drafts from other groups before making revisions. Kiraly, as the coordinator, moved between groups to provide language assistance and invited English native exchange students to regularly attend class as language counselors. In the eighth week, a third English native student joined to provide feedback as a first-time reader. In the ninth week, they involved a small group translation test that was unrelated to the project but required by the program. The final week was designated for test review and joint project assessment. In the end, the client praised the translation quality, and students collectively donated their fees to charity.

Kiraly identified five types of learners, highlighting the challenge of balancing these learner types within groups. To meet deadlines, he had to motivate slower-progressing groups. Many students were motivated by their participation in the project and rated the overall experience positively.

The course revolved primarily around this large project, which Kiraly carefully tailored to fit the class schedule. Human-to-human collaboration, scaffolding, and feedback were prominent features within and between groups, as well as between students and language experts. The project followed the basic translation-editing-proofreading (TEP) model, although specific roles and human–machine collaboration were not included.

3.3.2 Kiraly, Donald (2005)

Kiraly (2005) reports a subtitling project in an advanced translation class in a first-person narrative style. The task was to translate 250 subtitles for a documentary from German to English in 16 weeks, commissioned by a film production company. The client stipulated the use of free software with prescribed settings and a maximum length of 32 characters per line. At the outset, none of the participants possessed prior knowledge of subtitling norms or software. Consequently, for the initial two sessions, a tutor was brought in to teach the fundamentals of the chosen software.

Over the next three weeks, even as the tutor continued to offer guidance, the students took it upon themselves to experiment in pairs. They individually subtitled segments of the documentary at home and reviewed their work in class with their partners. Once the tutor's involvement concluded, Kiraly arranged for a professional expert to attend a single session. Throughout these sessions, Kiraly actively moved around to offer language assistance. The translations produced by each pair first underwent peer review and then a comprehensive group review.

All students diligently followed this process. However, when they electronically submitted a sample to the client, the file could not be imported into the client's system. The client also requested that each subtitle be shortened to a maximum of 26 characters, as opposed to the initial 32 characters. The students embraced this new challenge and devised a method to adapt to the company's system, subsequently teaching the client how to convert the format. Ultimately, the client was highly impressed by the students' performance and the quality of the final product.

This case serves as a testament to the importance of flexibility in response to evolving demands for PjBL. As Kiraly reflects, it shifted the focus of student learning from mere acquisition of knowledge to a socio-cognitive reflective process, fostering the emergence of competence through embodied cooperation. He also encourages the research community to employ qualitative case studies to explore the enactive nature of cognition and learning.

The organization of this project bears strong similarities to Kiraly (2000). The workflow, which involved students dividing the work, translating individually at home, discussing their work in class, and engaging in peer and group reviews, aligns with the fundamental principles of the TEP model. There was no predefined role specification, collective terminology management, or translation memory management before commencing the translation task. Apart from the use of free software and the client's software, no additional technologies were employed. Diverging from Kiraly (2000), where students began working on the task immediately, this project was marked by more scaffolding at the beginning and a gradual reduction of such support. Kiraly himself also played a role as a language consultant. The individual workload did not appear particularly burdensome (250 subtitles divided by 14 students over 16 weeks). Due to the absence of a formative assessment method, Kiraly used a test-based evaluation to assess student performance at the end.

3.3.3 Varney, Jennifer (2009)

Influenced by Kiraly's socially constructive approach, Varney (2009) implemented a project in her class at Bologna University. After the project's completion, she asked students to reflect on the project's design, the competencies they had improved, those that needed further development, the instructor's role, and potential improvements for future courses in the form of an open-ended questionnaire.

The project spanned an entire semester of ten weeks. A total of 33 third-year bachelor-level students participated, including Erasmus students from the UK and other parts of Europe. All the students had completed two years of translation classes. The task was to translate various texts for an NGO's official website from Italian to English.

In the first week, the class collectively identified the necessary resources. Following Varney's guidance, they formed six groups, each comprising five or six students, with at least one native English speaker in each group. Each group appointed a leader, researcher, parallel text analyst, terminologist, text reviser, and proofreader. All group members were responsible for translating assigned texts. Some groups chose to work in pairs, while others collaborated on all sections of the text. Every week, each group submitted a completed section to Varney, who would review the text and meet with the group to discuss revisions. Since there was only one computer available in the classroom, different groups took turns working in the faculty computer room during their sessions. Communication tools were not explicitly mentioned, presumably because most discussions occurred in face-to-face interactions. Ultimately, the class delivered a joint translation that satisfied the client, and everyone agreed to forgo payment due to the altruistic nature of the project.

Most students found the experience motivating. They reported improvements not only in translation skills but also in various generic competencies. They appreciated the valuable feedback provided by native English speakers and the instructor's revisions. However, some students found the lack of technology and the large group size to be hindrances to effective discussions. Some lamented the lack of opportunity to develop skills related to other roles. One student felt that after a semester of PjBL, it was incongruous to take an individual translation test at the end of the semester.

In comparison to Kiraly's earlier projects, Varney introduced role specifications, basic terminology management, and documentation preparation before beginning the translation work. Nevertheless, technology played a limited role in the project. Due to the diverse genres of the source text, each group submitted its work to the teacher without editing or proofreading the work of other groups. This suggests that collaboration and feedback were limited to each group.

3.3.4 Zhang, Zheng and Zhang, Shaozhe (2012)

Zhang and Zhang (2012) detail a project within a master-level course on Computer-Assisted Translation (CAT) at Beijing Normal University. The course was divided into three main components. The initial four sessions focused on teaching knowledge in Natural Language Processing (NLP), followed by five sessions teaching the use of CAT tools. The final 15 sessions revolved around a project translating the tenth edition of an information management book of 800,000 words. 20 students participated in the project. One of the authors served as the course instructor, while the other as the project's student project manager (PM).

The workflow, designed by the instructor, adhered to the following structure:

In the pre-translation stage, a student project manager was appointed by the teacher to oversee the running of the whole project, and the rest of the students were grouped into pairs as translators. The book was partitioned and assigned to each pair of translators (50,000 words per person), and the submission time was marked up. The PM managed to obtain the eighth and the ninth editions of the book and other reference materials, which he scanned and converted into a Word document and distributed to all members as parallel texts. The PM also compiled a style guide as a reference. A QQ chat group was set up for communication.

During translation, all the terms were extracted from the assigned texts and translated by each translator. After being validated by the PM and an outside expert, an integrated term list was created in an Excel spreadsheet. This new file was then imported into Trados Multi-term and shared among the group. Within each pair, translators first individually translated his or her part and revised the translation of their partner. On each date of submission, translators sent their peer-reviewed translations to the PM, who then passed them on to the teacher for review.

Post the translation, the instructor first reviewed the translation by marking out the mistakes or by offering comments; students then made revisions based on the teacher's markings and comments; a subject matter expert was invited to proofread the finalized translation before the integrated translation was sent to the client at the mutually agreed time.

At the completion of the project, all student participants were requested to assess their progress of translation competence using a 5-point Likert scale questionnaire and writing an individual reflective report, which they subsequently shared with the class. The responses indicated that all believed their translation competence had significantly improved. Many highlighted enhancements in their teamwork, adaptability, and critical thinking skills. The use of reflective reports, as opposed to traditional tests used in previous cases, allowed students to reassess their growth. However, because students were required to share their reflections publicly, we identify concerns about potential restrictions on content and expression that may undermine the credibility of the research (Boud 2001).

The two authors also identified shortcomings in their approach. Firstly, insufficient attention was given to terminology management, leading to inefficiencies as some students struggled with repetitive terminology during translation. Secondly, the book featured an identical introductory section in each chapter, which was not translated in advance, leading to repetitive labor. In terms of performance, the teacher noticed varying levels of commitment among students, with some consistently delivering high-quality translations on time while others frequently missed deadlines and produced subpar work. The teacher participant reported feeling overwhelmed, juggling responsibilities as the sole point of contact with the client, the designer of the workflow, and the reviser of all translations.

The team primarily relied on SDL Trados and Nuance PDF Converter 7.0 as their production tools. They adopted an incremental translation-editing-proofreading (TEP) workflow and introduced clearly defined roles. Notably, the PM assumed multiple roles, indicating a higher level of competence compared to fellow classmates. The authors failed to mention the repetitive nature of the book in comparison to previously published versions and the extent to which the latter was utilized as a translation memory (TM) to aid in their translation efforts.

3.3.5 Gong, Rui (2012)

Unlike previous class projects, the project in Gong (2012) involved three years of master level students and trainers at the Graduate Institute of Interpretation and Translation, Shanghai International Studies University. Gong, as one of the participating teachers, aimed to assess the competencies developed by the students after the project. Her data sources included her own observations and reflective reports submitted by the student participants.

The project was commissioned by a governmental organization requiring English subtitles of a series of documentaries totaling 68 episodes. The client requested that the translations be reviewed by native English speakers and proofread by Chinese native speakers. They provided all the scripts in document files, totaling 350,000 words, along with the original videos as reference material. The translations must be completed within a tight six-week timeframe and returned in document format, not integrated into the video.

Given the workload and the deadline, a total of 72 students were recruited. All of them were native Chinese speakers with English as their second language. The project also took dozen teachers from the institute on board as revisers, including both native Chinese and native English-language teachers. One of them assumed the role of the project lead. The workflow proceeded as follows:

First, all students were divided in Group A, Group B and Group C based on their year of class, with Group A and Group C composed of first-year students, and Group B of second- and third-year translation students. A student was selected from each group as the PM. Each group was given different tasks. Group A extracted and translated all terminologies by using an online cloud-based office software. Group B translated all subtitles and sent their completed translations on each date of submission. The Chinese teacher participants first edited Croup B's translations, followed by native English teachers who revised the Chinese teacher-edited translation. Group C then proofread the version by native English instructors. Finally, the lead teacher read through the entire translation as a final step of quality assurance.

The team established a QQ chat group for communication. All teacher participants were required to upload their revised translations using the tracked change function to the chat group. To ensure accurate contextual understanding, Group A and Group B must watch the videos. Gong provided many examples illustrating that a translation may appear acceptable in isolation but seemed out of place when viewed in the video, which was identified as a significant challenge faced by the team.

Gong also offered a rationale for appointing Group C, who appeared to be the weakest among all groups, as proofreaders. This could introduce fresh perspectives and encourage critical analysis when reviewing the tracked changes, potentially aiding in the development of strategies for addressing similar issues.

This project emphasized well-defined roles and terminology management. The primary technologies employed were QQ for communication, Microsoft Word for documentation, and an online cloud-based office software for terminology coordination. Feedback was exchanged among the various groups and at different stages of the workflow. Despite the pressing deadline, the revisers provided direct corrective feedback on the translations, while the students had the opportunity to engage in discussions and post queries in the chat group. The project exhibited self-scaffolding (e.g., video analysis), peer scaffolding (real-time online communication and contributions from different student groups), and expert scaffolding (revisions by teacher participants). However, Gong did not mention any cost management or assessment methods employed.

In conclusion, Gong linked various aspects of translation competence and generic competence to the project's specific design. Each group seemed to have acquired distinct competencies: Group A developed information literacy, Group C honed critical thinking and logic analysis skills, and Group B improved error analysis, transfer competence, and knowledge of writing conventions. Gong did not specify which model she used as a reference for translation competence, and the way she correlated the enhancement of each competence type appeared arbitrary.

Xu, Bin and Guo, Hongmei (2012)
Xu and Guo (2012) document a travel guide translation project at the Master of Translation (MT) program of Shandong Normal University. Their objective was not to discuss the pedagogical values of PjBL. Instead, they wanted to demonstrate

that CAT technologies, when employed effectively, could streamline the translation process and desktop publishing, thereby saving valuable time.

Both authors were university instructors of CAT tools and professional freelance translators. They were approached by a publisher to translate two travel guides from English into Chinese (L2-L1). The books had 700 pages each, including images, maps, illustrations, and text, and had to be completed within four months. To tackle this mammoth task, they brought in 20 students who were enrolled in their CAT course, assigning ten to each book. The two instructors took on multiple roles, including workflow designers, project managers, and revisers.

Traditionally, translating guidebooks of this nature began by extracting text from a PDF file into a doc. document. However, considering the potential time that may get wasted on file type conversion, they adopted an alternative approach. They persuaded the publisher to give them the original InDesign files of the books. This allowed them to export the text directly into CAT software, eliminating the need for formatting. Consequently, completed translations could be effortlessly reimported into InDesign. The workflow they implemented encompassed several specific procedures:

Step 1: The two teachers created a wordlist from the source text based on statistical frequency. They translated the list into Chinese and shared it among all team members as a basic term base.
Step 2: The two teachers held a training session where the students were briefed on the guidelines used in this translation and provided with reference materials.
Step 3: The teachers paired the students up based on their perceived competence and assigned the equal amount of text to work on to each pair.
Step 4: The student used multiple sources to validate newly identified terms and added them to the integrated term base.
Step 5: Students first translated the allotted work and revised each other's translation. They then sent the peer-revised translations to the teachers for a final review at each submission date using Dropbox.
Step 6: After all the translations were assembled in the CAT tool, the PM ran a final review using the built-in quality assurance (QA) functions of the tool.
Step 7: The finalized translation was exported from the CAT tool into InDesign and sent to the publisher for final formatting.

Xu and Guo (2012) stand out for their extensive use of translation technologies. With regard to peer support, they deemed it crucial to pair more proficient students with less experienced ones. Peer revision within this project was confined to small groups rather than involving the entire class.

Despite prior instruction on how to add terms to the terminology base, Xu and Guo found that some students skipped validation steps and displayed a lack of accountability, often relying on the instructors to rectify their mistakes. Students generally appeared unfamiliar with the conventions commonly employed in the publishing industry. It was precisely these shortcomings that underscored their belief in the importance of exposing students to authentic PjBL. To better prepare for future projects, they emphasized the significance of communication with the client and the need for increased attention to students' technical competence and their familiarity with textual conventions and terminology management.

3.3.6 Kiraly, Donald (2012, 2013)

Kiraly (2012, 2013) describes how a real translation project has evolved into a complex phenomenon due to changing *skopos*. He collected data from several sources, including notes on in-class interaction, email correspondence over the course of the project, audio recordings of in-class activities, and results of a questionnaire he distributed upon the completion of the project.

The project was carried out at ESIT of the University of Paris III. Seven first-semester MA students registered for the course, and all participated in the project. Two of them were native speakers of English, while the rest had English as their L2 language. They met every two weeks for ten weeks to complete the project.

Initially, Kiraly was told by the contact person that the class needed to translate from French into English the screenplay of a short film, which comprised 35 pages, including stage directions and a note on the background of the story. He suspected that it might be the wrong *skopos* because he knew the film had already been produced in French, but he accepted the task anyway, thinking it might be a good opportunity for the students to learn to deal with the vagaries in the market.

The class discussed preparations in the first session. One of them was appointed as the point of contact with the client. They divided themselves into teams of two or three and agreed to each translating two pages of the task before they meet next time for discussion. They also prepared a list of questions for the client to clarify. But before the questions were sent out, they were informed that the *skopos* had been modified and the initial contact person was also changed. What needed translation was the subtitles (214 in total) not the screenplay. At the second session, Kiraly gave students instruction on the norms of translation and provided PPT slides for students to learn after class. Students also discussed in class translations of the screenplay they had already done. To familiarize the students with the subtitling software, Kiraly asked them to subtitle a segment of another film as homework. At the third session, the class reviewed and revised their homework. Each student was given one seventh of the subtitles and was asked to work in teams and to upload their translations within a week. The fourth and fifth weeks were spent reviewing and revising each subtitle, with each team checking the work of one other team. Students met last time in the semester to take a test, which was not related to the project but was given due to school assessment requirement.

As the instructor, Kiraly provided significant instruction at the beginning, particularly in terms of familiarizing the students with the use of the subtitling software and relevant conventions. From the third week afterward, he played more of a facilitating role as students took control of their learning process. Except for the subtitling software, no other translation technologies were used. The main line of communication was the email correspondence that flowed between students, Kiraly and the client.

So far, the three Kiraly projects are all one-off practicum that last an entire semester. The instructions given by himself or by the external experts are all for the preparation of the project. Students work on one big project throughout a semester. They are given the freedom to form their own groups, choose their own workflow and manage the pace of their own progression. Each group edited and proofread the translation of other groups, thus subjecting the product to many eyes. The workflows adopted follow the sequential TEP model. All three projects are from L1-L2, with Kiraly providing scaffolding as native language counselors. There is little terminology management or asset management. There is no specification of roles: the students seem to work as the terminologist, the project manager, the translator, and the editor all at once. They keep each other in the loop during class hours or through email. There is little use of formative assessment. All three cases resort to testing to assess the student's performance for the course.

3.3.7 Li, Defeng (2013)

Li (2013) presents a project from his Advanced Business Translation class to exemplify the advantages of employing a task-based approach in teaching. Li was approached by a hotel operator in need of English-to-Chinese (L2-L1) translations for a collection of investment papers, totaling 100,000 words and encompassing various genres. Recognizing this as a valuable learning opportunity for his students, he accepted the task with a turnaround time of just four weeks.

During the initial week, students organized themselves into ten pairs, each tasked with translating 10,000 words from texts of their choosing. Li designated one student as the primary point of contact with the client. In the second week, they collectively analyzed the texts, scoured for parallel materials, and discussed queries pertaining to the project. By the conclusion of the second week, each group had produced a preliminary draft. The third week was dedicated to a class-wide discussion of their translations, followed by comprehensive revision and proofreading. In the fourth week, students convened to address lingering issues and submitted their translations to the student coordinator, who oversaw the final round of quality control and formatting before delivering the whole piece to the client. Following the delivery, the student coordinator invoiced the client, and the class dedicated an additional session to reflect upon and assess their performance.

Throughout this process, Li positioned himself as an adviser and facilitator rather than a direct guide. He observed class discussions during the first three weeks, offering suggestions but refraining from providing definitive answers. He also consistently emphasized the importance of meeting the deadline. In the fourth session, Li led the discussion on translating various registers and encouraged students to make presentations backed by examples they had addressed. In contrast to prior studies where teacher participants revised student translations, Li intentionally waited until students had completed all revision, editing, and proofreading tasks before adopting a more prominent teaching role during the reflection phase.

This project did not expressly mention any technologies or communication tools. Aside from the student project coordinator, who also assumed the role of final quality controller and formatting expert, there were no specified roles. Given the diverse genres of the task, students work cooperatively rather than collaboratively. They relied predominantly on self-scaffolding, primarily involving class discussions and paired work, to complete the task. As anticipated by Li, some students encountered difficulties in achieving the appropriate register, and the student coordinator felt the pressure of the deadline. Li, in his role as the instructor, acknowledged the challenge of not providing direct answers when students clearly expected them.

This project is the only one of the eleven projects sampled where students were entrusted with managing the financial aspect. However, Li did not delve into the specifics of this arrangement, presumably due to confidentiality constraints. The assessment method employed in this project is also commendable, as it eschews a traditional summative test. Instead, Li instructed students to maintain notes during the translation process and allocated two subsequent sessions for reflection, encompassing not only the final product but also the intricacies of the translation process.

3.3.8 Chen, Shuiping (2013)

Chen (2013) reports a news translation internship project at the Department of Foreign Languages at Hengyang Normal University in China. 45 third-year students and five teachers participated in the project to provide translated English content for the local government's official English website. Chen, who led the project, used closed questionnaires with students and interviews with teachers to gain insights into this experience.

The team first convened a plenary meeting to discuss requirements and criteria since the project was not linked to any specific course. To accommodate participants' schedules, students were organized into groups of nine, each led by a teacher, and they took turns working on translations.

Each week, the group on duty selected 3–5 pieces of local Chinese news as source material for the website and sent them to the teacher for content approval. This group then translated the approved content into English, forming subgroups of three, with each subgroup translating 1–2 pieces of news. They then sent their translations to the teacher for comments. Afterward, the teacher sent the revised translations back for the students to incorporate the changes. The students submitted their revised versions to the teacher again, who uploaded the finalized translations to the client website for final review.

Several key aspects of the workflow were not clearly defined. For instance, there were no specified roles, terminology guidelines, or memory management practices, and no translation technologies were employed. Chen did not address the selection criteria for Chinese news items, the specific translation strategies (faithful complete translation, trans-editing, gisting), or the assessment methods used. To motivate students, the project adopted performance-based incentives, including financial rewards, and required students to submit reflective journals regularly.

Chen's questionnaire revealed that most students welcomed the opportunity to work on real projects and felt that their competencies had improved. In terms of collaboration patterns, 72.5% of students divided the news, translated separately, reviewed each other's work, and then presented a joint product to the teacher, while 27.5% simply divided the work and assembled it together. This highlights the importance of clear role specification and workflow procedures in promoting effective collaboration.

In the interview, the teacher participants all believed they provided support through reviewing Chinese news content, revising translations, offering reference materials, technical assistance, and conflict resolution within groups. However, only 32% of students confirmed that all these forms of support were consistently provided. Some teachers expressed concern that the increased workload was not properly recognized.

Regarding feedback, 32% of students received direct corrective feedback on their translations, 45% received comments inserted alongside their work, and 32% engaged in discussions with the teachers. This variation in teacher scaffolding suggested challenges in achieving consistency in revision and feedback when multiple teachers were involved.

The primary obstacle to implementing authentic projects, as Chen reflects, is securing tasks with the appropriate level of difficulty. Some clients may not want students to handle their tasks, and aligning project timelines with teaching plans can be challenging. Chen thus proposes greater flexibility in curriculum design. He also suggests that institutional-level decisions should facilitate connections between students, teachers, and stakeholders in need of language services.

At the time of publication, this project had been running for two years and took in over one hundred participants. It is unique in that it allows the students to select source material and use a rotational approach to translate the task.

3.3.9 Marco, Josep (2016)

Based on a literary translation project, Marco (2016) demonstrates the conflicts between the key principles of situated learning, legitimate peripheral participation, and social constructivism theories, with personal observations and reflections as the main data elicitation tools.

The project was situated in the bachelor translation program at Universitat Jaume I. The program required students in the literary translation track to engage in a work placement. Since opportunities to work with publishing houses were limited, Marco took on the responsibility of securing a commission and guiding his students through the process. Six fourth-year students were on board. The task was to translate a book on an American Cartoonist from English into their native Spanish within ten weeks. The source text spanned various genres, each written by a different writer, totaling 90,000 words. They adopted an iterative model, with each cycle consisting of six steps.

Step 1: A plenary kick-off meeting to discuss the *skopos* and background of the commission and to divide the work for the first cycle of the project.
Step 2: Students translate individually the passages assigned to them.
Step 3: Each translator uploads their work to a shared platform, revise each other's work and make revisions based on peer feedback.
Step 4: Translators upload their revised translation to the shared platform again.
Step 5: The teacher downloads and revises each translation and uploads them again.
Step 6: A final meeting to bring differing positions together for a final version.

By the project's end, all participants had translated various types of texts. This distinguishes it from Varney (2009) and Li (2013), who assigned the same genre to the entire group, limiting exposure to different textual varieties.

The team made minimal use of translation technologies, primarily relying on Microsoft Word's track-change function and a cloud-based platform for file sharing. This technology-light approach aligned with the literary nature of the task. Regarding financial arrangements, the group received a fee from the publisher, equitably distributed among the students and the trainer. Furthermore, their names were featured on the copyright page of the published book.

Marco served as both the project initiator and the liaison with the client, taking complete responsibility for the product quality. He provided three types of feedback to students: direct corrective revisions (via track changes), suggestions for improvement in comments, and alternative phrasing recommendations. The publisher expressed satisfaction with the overall quality and delivery speed, even soliciting feedback from students to address any remaining issues. No formative or summative assessment methods were reported in the research.

In the end, Marco identified three key aspects that did not align well with the principles of situated learning and social constructivism: excessive revisions made to student translations, varying levels of competence among his students, and the distinction between a one-off project and the lifelong learning associated with the translation profession.

The first point has been discussed by Zhang and Zhang (2012) and Xu and Guo (2012). Excessive revisions in the initial peer review indicate that the complexity of the task may have exceeded the average student's translation skills. On the second point, while project-based learning is generally motivating and beneficial, as noted by Zhang and Zhang (2012) and Kiraly (2000, 2012, 2013), student motivation levels may vary. Implementing a recruitment/elimination mechanism that allows voluntary participation might be a solution to mitigate this risk.

3.3.10 Massey, Gary and Brändli, Barbara (2016)

Massey and Brändli (2016) describe a project that took place in an English-German translation course at IUED, Zurich University of Applied Sciences, in 2013. Given the importance of feedback in professional as well as pedagogical contexts, the two authors hypothesize that the advanced master-level student should be able to provide feedback like those provided by other, more competent professionals. One of them was the instructor of the course; the other was the researcher. They use a combination of qualitative and quantitative methods to bring the content and the flow of feedback to the surface.

The class in which the project was embedded had 16 second-semester MA translation students, all of whom had German as their native language. They were commissioned to translate a best-practice guideline (150,000 words) from English to German for a Swiss health organization in four weeks (L2-L1). They were asked to use SDL TRADOS Studio 2011, which they had been trained to use before, but which had no pre-existing TM. Their translation was neither paid nor graded, but they would receive a certificate from the client confirming their contribution.

The class first held an initial plenary session for preparation. The students decided among themselves to have a project manager and a deputy to oversee the project, a chief terminologist to coordinate project-wide terminology and to be the single point of contact with the client, a translation-memory trouble-shooter, a quality controller during the final revision phase, and a designer to create a project style guide and to oversee the final layout. In addition to these roles, student also formed their own sub-groups of four students and discussed among themselves how to assign workload. Each sub-group had the freedom to decide their own work procedure. When they finished their translation, they exchanged and reviewed translations of other groups before submitting their revised texts to the teacher for a final review. They can arrange face-to-face meetings or hold discussions through an e-learning platform set up for the project for communication. The teacher provided help through these channels only when requested. Four weeks after submission of the target text, the class held a session to discuss the teacher's corrections and the client's revisions of the published product.

In the end, the client was extremely satisfied with the product submitted. The teacher acknowledged the quality of student work but found different levels of motivation. Using the pre- and post-self and peer assessment questionnaire with the European Master's in Translation (EMT) wheel of competence as the reference, all students reported good learning effects, particularly the improvement of their interpersonal competence.

The two authors found that as the project progressed, the focus of student feedback shifted from technology and project management to translation problems and quality assurance issues. In terms of the usefulness of feedback by source, over two-thirds of the useful feedback reported came from peers, and less than one-fifth from the teacher and client combined. However, the teacher's and the client's feedback on the product was also considered very useful. With respect to the usefulness of feedback by mode, the classroom discussions were not regarded as very effective. Useful feedback seemed to be happening in online forums and bilateral written and oral exchanges rather than in classic multilateral or teacher-moderated learning settings. To conclude, the authors believed that feedback worked best when it was bilateral, dialogical, interactive, unmediated, timely and task related.

Massey and Brändli (2016) adopt the most elaborate research design of all the studies reviewed. While all the other research relies on typical qualitive methods, they add the use of quantitative methods and the comparison of pre- and post-results as well as post-project peer-assessed questionnaire to make the degree of improvement in student's self-perceived competence more explicit. This study is also the only one that brings in an outside researcher in the design to raise the rigor of the findings.

3.4 Results

In the following, we report our cross-analysis results. Please note that they only represent some broad traits and cannot do justice to the particulars of each context.

3.4.1 Research features

3.4.1.1 Research design and foci

All the studies involve qualitative research, with some designed as action research to gather more knowledge on PjBL as a training approach, and others as case studies for reflection or illustrative purposes. While each has a specific aim, eight of them have, in one way or another, correlated the use of PjBL with improvement in students' translation competence. The constructs used include the co-emergent competence model (Kiraly 2005; Kiraly 2013), PACTE model (Zhang and Zhang, 2012; Li 2013), some multi-componential models that the authors came up on their own (Varney 2009; Gong, 2012; Chen 2013) and the wheel of competence proposed by EMT in 2009 (Massey and Brändli 2016).

3.4.1.2 Participant recruitment/sampling

Nine projects are class projects in that the students who sign up for the class automatically become participants. The trainer(s) assume(s) the multiple roles of being the instructor of the course, the initiator and supervisor of the translation, and the researcher.

Two are program-level internship projects. In Gong (2012), participants are recruited from all three years of master-level students and from the trainers teaching in the program. In Chen (2013), participation is open to all third-year undergraduate students, with five teachers appointed as the revisers. Both mention the use of screening methods but neither provide details on the selection criteria.

3.4.1.3 Emic/etic perspective

Massey and Brändli (2016) is the only study in which one author acts as the researcher and the other as the teacher reviser. The authors of the remaining studies are all fully engaged in their project as supervisors.

Being an insider gives the researcher a superior understanding of the event and the ability to interact naturally with the group (Bonner and Tolhurst 2002), but it may lead to loss of objectivity (Breen 2007). Ethical concerns would also arise if the students felt they must comply with the requirement to provide information. Except for Kiraly (2000), who brings in research assistants to collect and transcribe the data, the studies that use the emic angle do not clearly indicate the measures taken to overcome the inherent personal bias.

3.4.1.4 Data elicitation methods

Questionnaires are used in five projects. According to type, two adopt open-ended questionnaires (Kiraly, 2000; Varney 2009), while three use Likert-scale questionnaires (Zhang and Zhang 2012; Chen 2013; Massey and Brändli 2016). Based on the timing and the assessor, Massey and Brändli (2016) design one pre-project questionnaire (self-assessment) and two post-project questionnaires (self-assessment and peer-assessment); the remaining four all use one self-assessment questionnaire at the end of the project.

Individual reflective reports are used in four projects. Two ask students to record their reflections when the translation is completed (Zhang and Zhang 2012; Gong

2012); the other two require writing along the course of the project (Li 2013; Massey and Brändli 2016).

Interviews are employed in two projects. Chen (2013) interviews all the teacher participants one year after their participation. Massey and Brändli (2016) organize two focus group interviews (midway and post-project).

In Kiraly (2000), all the live class interactions are recorded and transcribed for analysis.

Other projects mainly rely on the trainer's personal observation for data. Overall, most projects use "offline" data, which is produced after translations are completed, rather than data generated in real-time when participants are engaged in the very act of translating (Krings 2005). Due to the time lag, the offline data is susceptible to memory failure and emotion (Hansen 2005), and risks being constrained due to assessment concerns (Boud 2001).

3.4.1.5 Data analysis schemes

Of these projects, the text-based data from the open-ended questionnaires, interviews and reflective reports are all content-analyzed according to principles of grounded theory, with key themes identified by the researcher(s). Only Massey and Brändli (2016) describe their coding scheme (feedback by foci, and by source and by focus).

The quantitative data obtained from the projects using the Likert-scale questionnaires is all analyzed descriptively by identifying the average (mean) tendency in responses. Massey and Brändli (2016) also analyze the changes in the mean, median, and mode of pre- and post-project self-assessed questionnaires.

3.4.1.6 Argumentation and presentation of data

Most projects are experience-based, presented anecdotally by first describing the setting, followed by an account of the progression of the translation, and ending with the reflections (key themes or results from the data) reported at the end of the research. Only Massey and Brändli (2016) provide illustrations of each set of data.

Of the narrative techniques used, Kiraly (2000) lists snippets of student-recorded conversations; Kiraly (2013) provides examples of the participant's email correspondence; both Gong (2012) and Xu and Guo (2012) back the description with examples of the artifacts produced in different stages.

3.4.2 Practice features

Practices encompass all steps, techniques, procedures, and activities that are necessary for a team to go through to produce a translation(s) that is/are fit for purpose.

3.4.2.1 Client and requested translation

Table 3.1 illustrates the client and the translation requested in each project. The purpose is to determine how the selected projects are different from each other in terms of the source, genre, and subject matter of the work commissioned.

Just as in the market, the requested translations span a wide range of fields and text genres. Excluding Gong (2012) and Chen (2013), all are sourced from the teacher participants. Except for Chen (2013), in which translators are commissioned

Table 3.1 Client and the content of translation

Type of client	Context	Study	Type of translation
NGOs	Conflict and disaster relief	Varney (2009)	Information about the client to be posted on its home page
	Health care	Massey and Brändli (2016)	A healthcare booklet
Private market	Film studios	Kiraly (2005)	Subtitles of a documentary
		Kiraly (2013)	Screenplay/subtitles of a documentary
	Business corporation	Li (2013)	A series of investment papers
	Book publisher	Kiraly (2000)	2 chapters of a travel guidebook
		Zhang and Zhang (2012)	A book on information management systems
		Xu and Guo (2012)	Two travel guidebooks
		Marco (2016)	A comic book including preface and interview with the author
Governmental organizations	National level	Gong (2012)	Subtitles of a series of documentaries
	Local level	Chen (2013)	3–5 news reports per week

to provide continuous content, the remaining studies all describe single projects, which means the teams will disband when the product is delivered.

3.4.2.2 Cost management

Cost management is essential in an authentic project (Project Management Institute 2013). Of the two NGO projects, the students in Varney (2009) agreed not to ask for payment given the client's nature of work. In Massey and Brändli (2016), the students were not paid, but all received a certificate proving their contribution.

Of the projects from the private market, a student coordinator was tasked to invoice the client in Li (2013); in Kiraly (2000), the team was given a fee, but all agreed to donate it to a charity; Marco (2016) discussed payment terms with the client on behalf of the students. The fees were divided equally among the team, and all had their names recognized in the published translation.

In Chen (2013), performance-based financial incentives were used to motivate the students to produce quality work.

In others, the reticence on the matter may well arise from confidentiality reasons. Overall, negotiating fees and cost management do not appear to be an area for which the students are trained.

3.4.2.3 Workload /Number of Participants/Turnaround time

Meeting the deadline of a project with an acceptable level of quality is an important training purpose of PjBL. Calvo (2015, 315) notes that generally the average speed is 300 words per hour in the market. Although, in reality, there are many practical

Table 3.2 Workload/participants/turnaround time

Study	Total workload	Average translation rate
Kiraly (2000)	2 chapters (no wordcount mentioned)/ 24 students/1 teacher/10 weeks	0.008 chapter/student/week
Kiraly (2005)	250 subtitles/14 students/1 teacher/ 16 weeks	1.1 subtitle/student/week
Varney (2009)	text for a website (no wordcount mentioned)/33 students/1 teacher/ 10 weeks	information not available
Zhang and Zhang (2012)	800,000 text /20 students/1 teacher/ 20 weeks	2,000 words/student/week
Gong (2012)	350,000 subtitles/72 students/multiple teachers/6 weeks	810 subtitles/student/week
Xu and Guo (2012)	1400 pages of richly illustrated text/ 20 students/2 teachers/16 weeks	4.4 page/student/week
Kiraly (2013)	35 pages of screenplay/unspecified number of subtitles/7 students/1 teacher/10 weeks	0.5 page/student/week
Li (2013)	100,000 words/20 students/1 teacher/ 4 weeks	1,250 words/student/week
Chen (2013)	3–5 news reports (no wordcount mentioned)/9 students/1 teacher/1 week	information not available
Marco (2016)	90,000 text /6 students/1 teacher/10 weeks	1,500 words/student/week
Massey and Brändli (2016)	150,000 text/16 students/1 teacher/4 weeks	2,344 words/student/week

factors to consider, such as the difficulty of the task, the translator(s)' familiarity with the task domain, whether the translation may be repetitive, and what tools are used in relation to the level of quality expected. In university settings, as students are still under training and must balance various commitments, we are even more curious about their productivity in real translation tasks.

Table 3.2 lists the workload, number of participants, and turnaround time in each project. Based on the crude calculation of the average words a student has to translate a week, the rate can be as high as 2000 word/student/week (e.g. Xu and Guo 2012, Massey and Brändli 2016). In some projects (e.g. Kiraly 2005, 2013), the output does not appear to be high, mainly because the trainer has to spend substantial time brushing up student knowledge and skills of particular text conventions and tools.

3.4.2.4 Temporal and spatial features

When the length of a class project is related to the length of the course it is embedded in, sub-varieties emerge. Some projects last an entire semester and focus on a single subject matter. The instructional activities, if any, are specifically arranged for the project. The other projects are only a component of the syllabus, and there are teaching activities targeting other domains/knowledge/skills.

Neither internship project is tied to the curriculum. Gong (2013) is completed in 6 weeks in one semester. Chen (2013) is ongoing and carries on even during vacations. Both give the participants freedom to work at their own pace as long as they complete their assigned work on time.

In terms of spatial features, except for Kiraly's (2000), which is done face-to-face, and Marco's (2016) which is carried out entirely online, all the class projects are translated in class and outside the classroom. The two internship projects are both implemented in an online distributed manner.

3.4.2.5 Participants' prior knowledge

Four projects target third- or fourth-year undergraduate students and five master-level students. Kiraly (2005) and Li (2013) do not specify the level of studies but do point out that the projects are carried out at the advanced level. Overall, this trend is in line with the consensus that authentic PjBL should be introduced at the advanced stage of training (Kelly 2005; Kiraly 2013, 2016; González Davies 2017). Three of them (Gong 2012; Marco 2016; Massey and Brändli 2016) specifically mention the students' familiarity with the PjBL format.

3.4.2.6 Grouping and role specifications

In terms of the way participants are grouped, pair work and four-person groups appear to be the most popular. The exceptions include Marco (2016), where only six students are involved, with each translating individually before editing and reviewing each other's work; Chen (2013), where 45 participants are divided into five groups, with each group taking turns to handle the weekly tasks; and Gong (2012), where 72 students are involved, with the first-year students as terminologists and proofreaders, and the second and third-year students as translators.

While most projects give students the choice to form their own group, Xu and Guo (2012) believe that to ensure the quality of a draft translation, it is important to pair a student with a lower level of competence with a student having a higher level of competence. Kiraly (2000) identifies different styles of learners and finds that the students with a dominant personality may control group interactions. Chen (2013) notes that some groups simply divide the work among themselves, and piece the artifacts together without reviewing each other's work.

In terms of how the roles are assigned, substantial differences exist among the studies. Not every project assign roles and those that do show differences. In Varney (2009) and in Massey and Brändli (2016), students translate but are also given specific roles (project managers, terminologists, tech support etc.). Kiraly (2013), Li (2013), and Zhang and Zhang (2012) all appoint one student as the project-manager to coordinate all activities. In Gong (2012) and Xu and Guo (2012), the students translate, and peer review each other's work, while the roles of project manager and reviser are filled by the teacher. Varney (2009) finds that when roles are defined, the students lament not being able to be trained in a specific role. Massey and Brändli (2016) believe the participants often assume multiple roles, despite role specifications.

3.4.2.7 Terminology management

In a project, having key terms consistently translated substantially improves the quality and efficiency of work (Dunne 2007; Muegge 2020). However, this aspect is not given a detailed description. Of those that mention the practices, both Varney (2009) and Massey and Brändli (2016) assign specific person(s) to manage terminology but do not describe how; Xu and Guo (2012) use the statistical approach to extract high-frequency words from the source text; In Zhang and Zhang (2012), key bilingual terms are extracted from some bilingual reference material, and are managed in Trados Multiterm; Gong (2012) uses a collaborative spreadsheet documentation software to coordinate and translate terminology.

It should be noted terminology management does not only happen at the beginning of a project. As a project progresses, the initial set of terms may get expanded and refined; when the product is delivered, the term base should also be updated (Popiolek 2015). Sometimes, it is also necessary to keep standardized metadata for each term entry by including the source, usage details, and grammatical properties. All these steps require ongoing negotiation of meaning, but the studies included in this review do not provide any information about how this issue was addressed in the projects.

3.4.2.8 Workflow

Workflow procedures increase accountability by defining when and who should do what work in the process. Using both sequential and collaborative models discussed in Chapter 2 as benchmarks, the types of workflows in the reviewed projects are shown in Table 3.3. All opt for the linear model, with Marco (2016) adopting the iteration, and the remaining using the incremental model. None choose the collaborative model, which harks back to González Davies and Enrique Raído's (2016) observation that the use of cloud-based translation tools remains to be investigated in situated learning methods.

3.4.2.9 Technology

There are different ways to classify translation technologies. Building on the previous ways of categorization, Alcina (2008) and Flórez and Alcina (2011) put technologies related to translation into six groups (see the left column of Table 3.4). In terms of technology trends, TAUS (Choudhury and McConnell 2013) contends that translation tools have evolved from desktop to client/server to cloud based services, from licensed software to subscription business models, and from isolated to integrated translation management systems. Cost-wise, translation technology comprises both proprietary and free/open-source software (Bowker, McBride, and Marshman 2008; Flórez and Alcina 2011).

With this knowledge in mind, the tools that are used most in the reviewed studies are communication and documentation tools, followed by editing and desktop

Table 3.3 Workflows in reviewed projects

Type of workflow	*Subtype*	*Study*
Linear model	Incremental	Kiraly (2000), Varney (2009), Kiraly (2005, 2013), Gong (2012), Chen (2013), Li (2013), Xu and Guo (2012) Zhang and Zhang (2012) Massey and Brändli (2016)
	Iteration	Marco (2016)
Collaborative model		None

Table 3.4 Types of technologies in reviewed projects

The translator's computer equipment	Except Kiraly (2000), where the project is paper based, the remaining projects all use word-processors
Communication and documentation tools	Dropbox (Xu and Guo 2012) Google drive (Marco 2016) OCR tool (Zhang and Zhang 2012) QQ (Zhang and Zhang 2012; Gong 2012) Mobile phone messages (Zhang and Zhang 2012; Xu and Guo 2012) Google Calendar (Xu and Guo 2012) Video call software (Marco 2016) Emails (Kiraly 2005; Kiraly 2013; Xu and Guo 2012; Li 2013; Marco 2016; Massey and Brändli 2016) Online forum via the university's e-learning platform (Massey and Brändli 2016)
Text editing and desktop publishing	Nuance PDF converter (Zhang and Zhang 2012) InDesign (Xu and Guo 2012) Unnamed Free subtitling software (Kiraly 2005, Kiraly 2013) Zoho projects (Gong 2012)
Language tools and resources	None
Translation tools	SDL Trados (Zhang and Zhang 2012; Massey and Brändli 2016); Déjà vu (Xu and Guo 2012)
Management tools	None

publishing tools. Not a single project uses project management tools nor translation resources in the form of corpora. Of the three that use CAT tools, all such tools are those the students use in their taught module; all are proprietary software; and all are desktop/server-based versions.

3.4.2.10 Scaffolding

Scaffolding comprises assistance and support provided by others (e.g., teachers, peers, invited experts) and self-scaffolding (e.g., through technologies and artifacts) (Holton and Clarke 2006). All projects provide details on the scaffolds that are either explicitly sought or implicitly provided (see Table 3.5).

Some projects emphasize the importance of having students justify their translation choices in response to feedback (Varney 2009; Zhang and Zhang 2012; Gong 2012; Marco 2016; Massey and Brändli 2016). Although reference materials are used in some cases, there is little discussion on how repetitive they are compared to the source text, and in what way they serve the norm-referencing function. Only Li (2013) points out the ethical hazards associated with plagiarizing the existing translation.

3.4.2.11 Challenges encountered

The challenges experienced in these projects are particularly illuminating. Many implicitly or explicitly admit that the difficulty first comes from the amount of

Table 3.5 Types of scaffoldings in reviewed projects

Pre-project instruction	Kiraly (2005, 2013), Zhang and Zhang (2012), Xu and Guo (2012)
Parallel texts in the form of books, maps, documents, and online resources	Kiraly (2000), Varney (2009), Zhang and Zhang (2012), Gong (2012), Xu and Guo (2012), Li (2013)
Style guide, glossaries and term bases, technology troubleshooting, desktop publishing	Varney (2009), Zhang and Zhang (2012), Gong (2012), Xu and Guo (2012), Massey and Brändli (2016)
Native language experts when translating into L2	Kiraly (2000), Varney (2009), Gong (2012), Kiraly (2013)
Subject matter experts	Kiraly (2005), Zhang and Zhang (2012)
Face-to-face/video/email discussions when the translation is underway	All projects
Teacher's direct corrective feedback on the artifacts	All projects except Li (2013)
Feedback in the form of teacher comments and suggestions on the artifacts	Kiraly (2000, 2005, 2013), Varney (2009), Marco (2016), Chen (2013)
Feedback in the form of class discussion and project debriefing at the completion of project	Kiraly (2005), Varney (2009), Li (2013), Marco (2016), Massey and Brändli (2016)
Client feedback on the final artifact	Kiraly (2000, 2005), Xu and Guo (2012), Chen (2013), Marco (2016); Massey and Brändli (2016)

market connections a trainer has, and the pressure to meet the deadline. In authentic projects, since the problems a team may encounter are ill-defined and only become progressively clear, it is not easy to assess their difficulty in relation to student's prior competence in advance. In Massey and Brändli (2016), the supervising teacher felt that she was not consulted often. In contrast, Xu and Guo (2012) became aware of many blind spots in student knowledge and skills only when the project was in mid-way. Zhang and Zhang (2012) also found that, even though the translations had been peer-reviewed, some errors remained, and correcting them for timely delivery substantially increased teacher workload.

The design of the workflow is critical to team efficiency. Zhang and Zhang (2012) argue that, when the students focused on their allotted work without an overview of the whole task, they wasted time translating repetitive parts and ended up spending more time to achieve consistency later.

Many studies note that the students appreciate the learning gained from the feedback and the chance of argumentation (Gong 2012; Marco 2016; Massey and Brändli 2016). For the whole project to be successful, the team must share and work toward the same goal, but not every student is equally motivated and engaged in the project (Kiraly 2013; Zhang and Zhang 2012). In Chen (2013), some teacher participants complained about lack of a scheme to recognize their contribution. Unsurprisingly, several student participants also pointed out the inconsistency in the scaffolding provided by multiple teachers.

The duration and transferability of the learning effects is also a point worth careful design in PjBL. Competence is domain-specific and requires repetition and continuity of practice (Shreve 2006; Li 2019). Both Xu and Guo (2012) and Marco (2016) allude to this by arguing that, while beneficial, a one-off practicum is far from enough for students to become proficient in a particular field.

Note

1 Parts of Chapter 3 and Chapter 4 have been previously published in Li, R. 2022. "Convergence and Gaps: A Cross-case Analysis of Authentic Translation Projects Implemented in Translator Education." *The Interpreter and Translator Trainer* 16 (4): 484–502. doi: 10.1080/1750399X.2022.2082813. The Journal can be found at the web site www.tandfonline.com/.

References

Alcina, A. 2008. "Translation Technologies Scope, Tools and Resources." *Target* 20 (1): 79–102. doi: 10.1075/target.20.1.05alc.

Alcina, A., V. Soler, and J. Granell. 2007. "Translation Technology Skills Acquisition." *Perspectives* 15(4): 230–244. doi: 10.1080/13670050802280179.

Aula.int. 2005. "Translator Training and Modern Market Demands." *Perspectives* 13 (2): 132–142. doi: 10.1080/09076760508668982.

Ayres, L., K. Kavanaugh, and K. A. Knafl. 2003. "Within-Case and Across-Case Approaches to Qualitative Data Analysis." *Qualitative Health Research* 13 (6), 871–883. doi: 10.1177/1049732303255359.

Biel, Ł. 2011. "Professional Realism in the Legal Translation Classroom: Translation Competence and Translator Competence." *Meta* 56 (1): 162–178. doi: 10.7202/1003515ar.

Bonner, A., and G. Tolhurst. 2002. "Insider/outsider Perspectives of Participant Observation." *Nurse Researcher* 9 (4): 7–19. doi: 10.7748/nr2002.07.9.4.7.c6194.

Boud, D. 2001. "Using Journal Writing to Enhance Reflective Practice." In *Promoting Journal Writing in Adult Education. New Directions in Adult and Continuing Education*, edited by L. M. English, and M. A. Gillen, 9–18. Hoboken: John Wiley & Sons.

Bowker, L., C. McBride, and E. Marshman. 2008. "Getting More Than You Paid For? Considerations in Integrating Free and Low-Cost Technologies into Translator Training Programs." *Redit* 1 (1): 26–47.

Breen, L. J. 2007. "The Researcher 'In the Middle': Negotiating the Insider/Outsider Dichotomy." *The Australian Community Psychologist* 19 (1): 163–174.

Buysschaert, J., M. Fernández-Parra, and G. W. van Egdom. 2017. "Professionalising the Curriculum and Increasing Employability through Authentic Experiential Learning: The Cases of INSTB." In *Current Trends in Translation Teaching and Learning E* 4, 78–111.

Calvo, E. 2015. "Scaffolding Translation Skills through Situated Training Approaches: Progressive and Reflective methods." *The Interpreter and Translator Trainer* 9 (3): 306–322. doi: 10.1080/1750399X.2015.1103107.

Chai, M. 2015. "The Internship Mechanism of the MTI Program in GIIT, SISU." In *CIUTI-Forum 2014. Pooling Academic Excellence with Entrepreneurship for New Partnerships*, edited by M. Forstner, H. Lee-Jahnke, and M. Chai, 277–291. Frankfurt am Main: Peter Lang.

Chen, S. 2013. "Project-based Training in Translator Education: Implications, Problems, Solutions." [项目翻译教学模式：意义、问题与对策——项目翻译教学的行动研究.] *Foreign Language Learning Theory and Practice* 4: 82–87.

Choudhury, R., and B. McConnell. 2013. *TAUS Translation Technology Landscape Report 2013*. De Rijp, The Netherlands: Translation Automation Users Society (TAUS).

Dunne, E. S. 2011. "Project as a Learning Environment: Scaffolding Team Learning in Translation Projects." In *Translation and Localization Project Management. The Art of the Possible*, edited K. J. Dunne, and E. S. Dunne, 265–288. Amsterdam: John Benjamins.

Dunne, K. J. 2007. "Terminology: Ignore It at Your Peril." *Multilingual* 18 (3): 32–38.

Durban, C., T. Martin, B. Mossop, R. Schwartz, and C. Searles-Ridge. 2003. "Translator Training & the Real World." *Translation Journal* 7 (1). https://translationjournal.net/journal/23roundtablea.htm.

Flórez, S., and A. Alcina. 2011. "Free/Open-Source Software for the Translation Classroom." *The Interpreter and Translator Trainer* 5 (2): 325–357. doi: 10.1080/13556509.2011.10798824.

García González, M., and M. T. Veiga Díaz. 2015. "Guided Inquiry and Project-Based Learning in the Field of Specialised Translation: A Description of Two Learning Experiences." *Perspectives* 23 (1): 107–123. doi: 10.1080/0907676X.2014.948018.

Gong, R. 2012. "Reflections on the Format of Authentic Project: A Case Study." [MTI专业笔译实战项目教学模式探讨——以国新办宣传片项目为例.] *East Journal of Translations* 6: 25–31.

González Davies, M. 2017. "A Collaborative Pedagogy for Translation." In *Teaching Translation: Programs, Courses, Pedagogies*, edited by L. Venuti, 118–131. London: Routledge.

González Davies, M., and V. Enríquez Raído. 2016. "Situated Learning in Translator and Interpreter Training: Bridging Research and Good Practice." *The Interpreter and Translator Trainer* 10 (1): 1–11. doi: 10.1080/1750399X.2016.1154339.

Gouadec, D. 1991. "Autrement Dire … Pour une Redéfinition des Stratégies de Formation des Traducteurs." *Meta* 36 (4): 543–557. doi: 10.7202/002947ar.

Hansen, G. 2005. "Experience and Emotion in Empirical Translation Research with Think-Aloud and Retrospection." *Meta* 50 (2): 511–521. doi: 10.7202/010997ar.

Hansen-Schirra, S., S. Hofmann, and J. Nitzke. 2018. "Acquisition of Generic Competencies through Project Simulation in Translation Studies." In *Positive Learning in the Age of Information: A Blessing or a Curse?*, edited by O. Zlatkin-Troitschanskaia, et al., 266–280. Wiesbaden: Springer VS.

Holton, D., and D. Clarke. 2006. "Scaffolding and Metacognition." *International Journal of Mathematical Education in Science & Technology* 37 (2): 127–143. doi: 10.1080/00207390500285818.

Huertas Barros, E. 2011. "Collaborative learning in the translation classroom: preliminary survey results." *The Journal of Specialised Translation* 16: 42–60.

Huertas Barros, E., and J. Vine. 2019. "Training the Trainers in Embedding Assessment Literacy into Module Design: A Case Study of a Collaborative Transcreation Project." *The Interpreter and Translator Trainer* 13 (3): 271–291. doi: 10.1080/1750399X.2019.1658958.

Hurtado Albir, A. 2015. "The Acquisition of Translation Competence. Competences, Tasks, and Assessment in Translator Training." *Meta* 60 (2): 256–280. doi: 10.7202/1032857ar.

Kelly, D. 2005. *A Handbook for Translator Trainers*. Manchester: St. Jerome Publishing.

Khan, S., and R. VanWynsberghe. 2008. "Cultivating the Under-Mined: Cross-Case Analysis as Knowledge Mobilization." *FQS* 9 (1): Art. 34. doi: 10.17169/fqs-9.1.334.

Kiraly, D. 2000. *A Social Constructivist Approach to Translator Education. Empowerment from Theory to Practice.* Manchester: St. Jerome Publishing.

Kiraly, D. 2005. "Project-Based Learning: A Case for Situated Translation." *Meta* 50 (4): 1098–1111. doi: 10.7202/012063ar.

Kiraly, D. 2012. "Skopos Theory Goes to Paris: Purposeful Translation and Emergent Translation Projects." mTm. Minor Translating Major—Major Translating Minor—Minor Translating Minor, Special issue: In memoriam Hans J. Vermeer, 4: 119–144.

Kiraly, D. 2013. "Towards a View of Translator Competence as an Emergent Phenomenon: Thinking Outside the Box(es) in Translator Education." In *New Prospects and Perspectives for Educating Language Mediators*, edited by D. Kiraly, S. Hansen-Schirra, and K. Maksymski, 197–224. Narr Francke Attempo.

Kiraly, D. 2016. "Beyond the Static Competence Impasse in Translator Education." In *Translation and Meaning. New Series*, edited by B. Lewandowska-Tomaszczyk, et al., Vol. 1. 129–142. Frankfurt am Main: Peter Lang.

Kiraly, D., G. Massey, and S. Hofmann. 2018. "Beyond Teaching Towards Co-Emergent Praxis in Translator Education." In *Translation-Didaktik-Kompetenz*, edited by B. Ahrens et al., 11–64. Berlin: Frank Timme.

Konttinen, K., O. Veivo, and P. Salo. 2020. "Translation Students' Conceptions of Translation Workflow in a Simulated Translation Company Environment." *The Interpreter and Translator Trainer* 14 (1), 79–94. doi: 10.1080/1750399X.2019.1619218.

Koricheva, J., and J. Gurevitch. 2013. "Place of Meta-Analysis among Other Methods of Research Synthesis." In *Handbook of Meta-analysis in Ecology and Evolution*, edited by Julia Koricheva et al., 3–13. Princeton: Princeton UP.

Krings, H. P. 2005. "Wege ins Labyrinth—Fragestellungen und Methoden der Übersetzungsprozessforschung im Überblick." *Meta* 50 (2), 342–358. doi: 10.7202/010941.

Li, D. 2013. "Teaching Business Translation. A Task-Based Approach." *The Interpreter and Translator Trainer* 7 (1): 1–26. doi: 10.1080/13556509.2013.10798841.

Li, D., C. Zhang, and Y. He. 2015. "Project-based Learning in Teaching Translation: Students' Perceptions." *The Interpreter and Translator Trainer* 9 (1): 1–19. doi: 10.1080/1750399X.2015.1010357.

Li, L. 2017. "Training Undergraduate Translators: A Consciousness-Raising Approach." *The Interpreter and Translator Trainer* 11 (4): 245–258. doi: 10.1080/1750399X.2017.1359757.

Li, X. 2019. "Material Development Principles in Undergraduate Translator and Interpreter Training: Balancing between Professional Realism and Classroom Realism." *The Interpreter and Translator Trainer* 13 (1): 18–43. doi: 10.1080/1750399X.2018.1550039.

Marco, J. 2016. "On the Margins of the Profession: The Work Placement as a Site for the Literary Translator Trainee's Legitimate Peripheral Participation." *The Interpreter and Translator Trainer* 10 (1): 29–43. doi: 10.1080/1750399X.2016.1154341.

Massey, G., and B. Brändli. 2016. "Collaborative Feedback Flows and What We Can Learn from Them: Investigating a Synergetic Experience in Translator Education." In *Towards Authentic Experiential Learning in Translator Education*, edited by D. Kiraly, et al., 177–199. Gottingen and Mainz: V&R Unipress/Mainz UP.

Massey, G., and M. Ehrensberger-Dow. 2017. "Machine learning: Implications for translator education." *Lebende Sprachen* 62 (2): 300–312. doi: 10.1515/les-2017-0021.

Miles, M. B., and A. M. Huberman. 1994. *Qualitative Data Analysis: An Expanded Sourcebook*, 2n ed. Thousand Oaks: Sage.

Mitchell-Schuitevoerder, R. 2013. "A Project-Based Methodology in Translator Training." In *Tracks and Treks in Translation Studies: Selected Papers from the EST Congress, Leuven 2010*, edited by C. Way et al., 127–142. Amsterdam: John Benjamin.

Moghaddas, M., and M. Khoshsaligheh. 2019. "Implementing Project-Based Learning in A Persian Translation Class: A Mixed-Methods Study." *The Interpreter and Translator Trainer* 13 (2): 190–209. doi: 10.1080/1750399X.2018.1564542.

Mu, L. 2011. "Formats and Patterns of MTI Master's Degree Thesis. [翻译硕士专业学位论文模式探讨.]." *Foreign Language Learning Theory and Practice* 1: 77–82.

Muegge, U. 2020. "Why You Should Care about Terminology Management—Even If You Never Translate a Single Term." *The ATA Chronicle* March/April: 22–25.

Nitzke, J., A. Tardel, and S. Hansen-Schirra. 2019. "Training the Modern Translator – The Acquisition of Digital Competencies through Blended Learning." *The Interpreter and Translator Trainer* 13 (3): 292–306. doi: 10.1080/1750399X.2019.1656410.

Olvera-Lobo, M. D., B. Robinson, J. A. Senso, R. Muñoz-Martín, E. Muñoz-Raya, M. Murillo–Melero, E. Quero-Gervilla, M. Castro-Prieto, and T. Conde-Ruano. 2009. "Teleworking and Collaborative Work Environments in Translation Training." *Babel* 55 (2): 165–180. doi: 10.1075/babel.55.2.05olv.

Popiolek, M. 2015. "Terminology Management within a Translation Quality Assurance Process." In *Handbook of Terminology Volume 1*, edited by H. J. Kockaert, and F. Steurs, 341–59. Amsterdam: John Benjamins.

Prieto-Velasco, J. A., and A. Fuentes-Luque. 2016. "A Collaborative Multimodal Working Environment for the Development of Instrumental and Professional Competences of Student Translators: An Innovative Teaching Experience." *The Interpreter and Translator Trainer* 10 (1): 76–91. doi: 10.1080/1750399X.2016.1154344.

Project Management Institute. 2013. *A Guide to the Project Management Body of Knowledge (PMBOK® Guide)*, 5th ed. Newtown Square: Project Management Institute.

Risku, H. 2016. "Situated Learning in Translation Research Training: Academic Research as a Reflection of Practice." *The Interpreter and Translator Trainer* 10 (1): 12–28. doi: 10.1080/1750399X.2016.1154340.

Robinson, B., C. I. López-Rodríguez, and M. Tercedor-Sánchez. 2008. "Neither Born nor Made, but Socially Constructed: Promoting Interactive Learning in an Online Environment." *TTR* 21 (2): 95–129. doi:10.7202/037493ar.

Rodríguez de Céspedes, B. 2017. "Addressing Employability and Enterprise Responsibilities in the Translation Curriculum." *The Interpreter and Translator Trainer* 11 (2–3): 107–122. doi:10.1080/1750399X.2017.1344816.

Shreve, G. M. 2006. "The Deliberate Practice: Translation and Expertise." *Journal of Translation Studies* 9 (1): 27–42.

Stake, R. 2006. *Multiple Case Study Analysis*. New York: Guilford Press.

Susam-Sarajeva, Ş. 2001. "Is One Case Always Enough?" *Perspectives* 9 (3): 167–176. doi: 10.1080/0907676X.2001.9961415.

Susam-Sarajeva, Ş. 2009. "The Case Study Research Method in Translation Studies." *The Interpreter and Translator Trainer* 3 (1): 37–56. doi: 10.1080/1750399X.2009.10798780.

Thelen, M. 2009. "Quality Management for Translation." In *CIUTI-Forum 2008. Enhancing Translation Quality: Ways, Means, Methods*, edited by H. Lee-Jahnke et al., 195–213. Frankfurt am Main: Peter Lang.

van Egdom, G. W., K. Konttinen, S. Vandepitte, M. Fernández-Parra, R. Loock, and J. Bindels. 2020. "Empowering Translators through Entrepreneurship in Simulated Translation Bureaus." *Hermes* 60: 81–95. doi: 10.7146/hjlcb.v60i0.121312.

Varney, J. 2009. "From Hermeneutics to the Translation Classroom: Current Perspectives on Effective Learning." *Translation & Interpreting* 1 (1): 27–43.

Vienne, J. 1994. "Towards a Pedagogy of 'Translation in Situation'." *Perspectives* 2 (1): 41–50. doi: 10.1080/0907676X.1994.9961222.

Xu, B., and H. Guo. 2012. "Project Management in Book Publishing Project." [出版翻译中的项目管理.] *Chinese Translators Journal* 33 (1): 71–75.

Yin, R. K. 2003. *Case Study Research: Design and Methods*, 3rd ed. Thousand Oaks: SAGE.

Zhang, J. 2011. "Project-Based Translation Practice-Empowering Both Teachers and Students." In *CIUTI-Forum 2010. Global Governance and International Dialogue: Translation and Interpreting in a New Geopolitical setting*, edited by M. Forstner and H. Lee-Jahnke, 153–163. Frankfurt am Main: Peter Lang.

Zhang, Z., and S. Zhang. 2012. "Authentic Project, Authentic Environment, Authentic Experience: A Case Study." [真项目 真实践 真环境 真体验——基于北京师范大学MTI CAT案例教学的探索与实践.] *Chinese Translators Journal* 33 (2): 43–46.

4 Revisiting facets of authentic project-based learning

In Chapter 4, we reflected on how the sample studies differed from each other in their research and practice features. It is important to note that all samples were handpicked based on our judgments of their representativeness. Any results to be drawn are first subject to the size, time of writing, geographic focus of the samples, and whether they have provided enough details. The conclusion also depends on the granularity and time frame of the criteria used. Nevertheless, with the macro view they provided, we find a few areas that need more close attention.

4.1 Degree of "authenticity"

"Authentic" is a key feature characterizing these projects. Brown, Collins, and Duguid (1989, 34) broadly define authentic activity as "the ordinary activity of the practitioners in a culture, or activity congruent with their ordinary activity." However, Kiraly (2012, 84) holds that a single criterion of authenticity is to see if a translation activity is carried out in the service of a real-world client or user. Although simulations can replicate the procedures and adopt the same tools used by professionals, they are less prone to changes in *skopos*, and they might lack client assessment of the artifact produced. Psychologically, since simulations do not fulfill a real need, they may not create as much of a strong sense of relevancy, motivation, and pressure.

From a philosophical perspective, the term "authentic" is often associated with authentic learning experiences that are unstructured and not bound by predefined challenges or learning objectives. Aguilar (2016, 21) argues that in educational settings, the traditional reliance on "learning outcomes" to shape the content and objectives of translator education may inadvertently promote a view of education as a process of "closing gaps, fulfilling needs, transmitting information, consuming commodities, and representing a static world." Authentic learning, however, transcends the mere accumulation and construction of information. It involves actively engaging in actions driven by a sense of responsibility as unique and singular beings in the world. This transformative process yields something entirely novel and unexpected, both in terms of the individual and the resulting outcomes.

DOI: 10.4324/9781003542469-4

Nonetheless, even in projects involving external users, there exists a spectrum of realism concerning professional practice. According to the PMBOK® Guide (Project Management Institute 2013, 61), a typical project encompasses time management, quality management, risk management, scope management, and communication management. However, the reviewed projects often neglect cost management, not to mention stakeholder, resource, and procurement management. The "pre-production" and "post-production" processes and activities, which offer valuable learning opportunities, tend to be assumed by the teacher and receive insufficient research attention. Undoubtedly, these overlooked areas have a direct impact on the development of service-oriented entrepreneurial competencies (Galán-Mañas, Kuznik, and Olalla-Soler 2020). Future cases of PjBL should explore these facets more comprehensively to prepare students holistically, and they also warrant further investigation in research.

4.2 Layers of "collaboration"

"Collaboration," another essential feature, proves even more difficult to define. For a start, collaboration should not be confused with collaborative translation. The latter refers to "a type of participative online activity in which an individual, an institution, a non-profit organization, or company proposes to a group of individuals of varying knowledge, heterogeneity, and number, via a flexible open call, the voluntary undertaking of a task" (Jiménez-Crespo 2017, 14). A project may adopt similar tools and workflows used in collaborative translation (Beninatto and DePalma 2007), but the origins of the two are very different.

Secondly, O'Brien (2011) recognizes collaboration not only as human–human collaboration but also as human–machine collaboration. On a broad level, collaboration exists either between translators and any one of these other agents or between two or more translators; but narrowly speaking, it refers only to the situation where two or more translators work together to produce one translated product. Both levels of human–human collaboration exist in PjBL.

Furthermore, Dillenbourg (1999) specifies that for a situation to be characterized as collaborative on a human–human level, there are three criteria to meet. The first is whether there is symmetry of action, symmetry of knowledge and symmetry of status among participants. The second criterion is whether the participants share common goals. It is the third criterion, which concerns the degree of division of labor among the group members, that is hard to pinpoint. There is a difference between collaboration and cooperation. In cooperation, participants simply split the work, solve sub-tasks individually and then assemble the partial results into a final output. The way work is divided is more fixed and explicit. In collaboration, participants do the work "together" when the work is interwoven, with one subject monitoring the other, and when the roles may shift, and their interactions are negotiable. These differences have also been elaborated by Kenny (2008) and Thelen (2016). In samples we reviewed in Chapter 3, other than the researcher's own description of the workflow, we have no way to ascertain if the participants are collaborating or cooperating, or both. If we could examine the real-time activity data (e.g. Kußmaul 1995; House 2000; Pavlović 2009; Pym 2009), we might have concrete evidence of different learning approaches.

On human–machine collaboration, Hoadley (2012) holds that technology not only links people together in a joint endeavor but also provides a shared repository of information resources. Yet compared with the description of the workflow and the human–human collaboration, research on human–machine collaboration has not been traversed to the same extent. We need to systematically gauge the extent and the range of tools deployed in PjBL and student evaluations of these technologies (Bowker 2015).

When it comes to the digital legacy created by a project, we would argue for a third dimension of collaboration. For translators, the value and ownership of a piece of work translated does not end with its delivery to the client. High-quality language data is now a commodity and an asset (Massardo and Van der Meer 2017). Members of a team need to build, negotiate, share, and leverage a common repository of knowledge and keep it up to date with client requests, not only for themselves but also for new participants. This type of collaboration requires a more forward-looking vision. It is less visible than the first two types of collaboration and is even far less a subject of research now.

4.3 Variants of authentic translation projects

The review suggests a need for a more precise typology of authentic translation projects. When we use their temporal and spatial aspects criteria, two primary variants emerge: "class projects" and "internship projects." "Class projects" refers to projects that are an integral component of a specific course, while "internship projects" are ones conducted within a T&I program but outside the formal curriculum. Their differences can be roughly summarized in Table 4.1.

Class projects, undoubtedly, stand out as the predominant form. These projects are typically initiated by individual teachers and are conducted within a defined class of students. To execute such a project successfully, teachers often rely on personal connections to secure commissions. They must also ensure that the project aligns with the curriculum, adheres to institutional policies, and matches the students' existing skills. These constraints frequently lead some educators to explore alternatives such as simulations.

On the other hand, internship projects represent a new category of authentic PjBL. These projects are commissioned by external partners in need of translation services. Their scope ranges from single commissions to multiple assignments or, in extreme cases, ongoing internships with continuous commissions (as seen in examples like Gong 2012, and Chen 2013). Hence, different forms of PjBL available in a school environment are shown in Figure 4.1.

The emergence of internship projects in T&I education, especially within the context of China, can be attributed to several factors. One primary reason is the remarkable growth of such programs over the past decade, coupled with the essential need to offer students practical exposure in their chosen field (e.g. Chai 2017; Huang 2017; Zhong, Zhao, and Xu 2020). In fact, the inclusion of internship or

Table 4.1 Comparison of class projects and internship projects

	Class projects	Internship projects
Initiator	These projects are typically initiated by trainers, who are personally held responsible for the quality of the product	These projects are organized by the program provider with an external partner
Client and requested translation	The task could be on any subject and of any textual type and may span several genres and in the trainer's view, related to course content and objective	The client tends to be (inter)governmental organizations which have demand for quality translation for important occasions or events. The translation may or may not be related to curriculum
Participant features	All the students who sign up the class automatically participate in the project. No prior selection. No elimination	Both teacher and student participants are recruited to the project. Students may come from different classes or/and from different grade level in a T&I program
Temporal features	Singular, isolated work with clearly defined scope and a set deadline	If the client is satisfied with the quality and has consistent needs, tasks may be assigned regularly, turning the project into a continuous effort. Each task has a set deadline
Spatial features	Participants work both face-face in class and after class	Participants usually work in their spare time as a distributed team on the sidelines of the formal curriculum
Legacy translations	Students must find parallel/comparable text for reference and create new terminology/style guide from scratch. The accumulated termbase (TB) and translation memory (TM) may not be used next time	There may be relevant TB, TM and style guide from previous tasks, and the TB and TM created for one task may allow for reuse and optimization in next tasks
Relationship to the curriculum	Embedded element of a course. Assessment method is subject to curriculum and syllabus policy and trainer and client agreement	Not a mandatory element of the curriculum. The assessment method used does not count toward student credit points and is subject to program provider and client

work placement experience has now become a mandatory component of T&I degree programs. Without such opportunities, students might end up securing internships unrelated to translation services (Chai 2015). Even when students do engage in translation work, they often lack immediate feedback, as the translation industry prioritizes results and performance over training (Calvo 2015; Angelone and Marín García 2017).

That is why some T&I programs in China have started to partner up with the industry to organize in-house internship projects. They recruit students to work

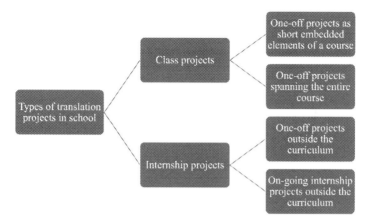

Figure 4.1 Types of translation projects in school. Image by the author.

as translators and teachers or industry experts as revisers in such projects. There are multiple benefits brought by this new form of situated learning. The text(s) translated first meets (a) the real translation need(s) of the external partner. The student participants in such projects often know their fellow team members. They trust their teachers and expect quality learning from them. The teacher participant(s), once involved, want(s) to be perceived as competent and responsible mentors in the eyes of their students. The published translations can also serve as a promotional opportunity for the program. If word of its quality service spreads out, the program provider might get an enhanced reputation, increased enrollment, and better networking opportunities. In the long term, it is not only the participants, T&I programs, vendors of language services, the clients who rely on language professionals, and suppliers of translation tools and technologies could all benefit from the synergy. As is evidenced by Chinese scholarship, there have been a lot of efforts underway to set up internship projects[1] in recent years (e.g. Zhang, Chai, and Yao 2011; Yang 2012; Yu and Zhang 2013; Cai and Zhang 2013; Dong and Zhang 2015; Sun and Dai 2016; Liu and Liang 2019).

However, it is important to acknowledge that there are significant challenges associated with implementing internship projects. Li and He (2011) identify five key challenges. Firstly, program providers must be prepared to invest in training and infrastructure, including equipment, tools, and software, not just initially but also throughout a project's lifespan as needs evolve. Secondly, establishing trust and nurturing relationships with a partner that consistently requires translation services takes considerable time and effort. Thirdly, running a project may necessitate dedicated managerial staff and financial investment, yet many institutions struggle with limited financial and personnel resources to effectively manage internship programs. Fourthly, external partner commissions tend to be irregular, while the curriculum must adhere to a fixed schedule, necessitating coordination to prevent conflicts between the two forms of learning. Lastly, teacher participants must be motivated to engage in such projects voluntarily, rather than feeling coerced. A structured scheme should be in place to acknowledge their contributions and help them balance their teaching and research responsibilities.

On top of these challenges, we believe that for an internship to run smoothly, the content of work must first stay in compliance with legal regulations and align with training objectives. Student participation should also be made on a voluntary and ethical basis. They should be fully aware of their rights and obligations before they agree to participate and have equitable access. To maintain and ensure quality, it is advisable to implement a screening process. Recognizing that student needs and interests may change, there should also be an exit mechanism in place. The team must be agile enough to adapt to evolving client needs and respond to unexpected events. Considering that, on average, a T&I program in China lasts 2–3 years at the master's level and 3–4 years at the bachelor's level, if a project spans several years, there might be a mix of experienced and new students with varying skill levels. All these issues raise intriguing questions, which existing studies have failed to address adequately.

4.4 Connections between project teams and CoP

Community of Practice (CoP) is a a concept proposed by Lave and Wenger (1991) as they move from psychological and cognitive explanation of learning to a social and situated view of learning. They define a CoP as "a collection of individuals who share mutually defined practices, beliefs, and understandings on a regular basis over an extended time frame for a shared enterprise" (Wenger 1998, 4). Learning by taking part in such a community is thus seen as a process in which newcomers move from peripheral participation to central participation in a social practice until they replace old times and select new entrants.

In fact, CoP is not a concept new to T&I education. Many have described the end goal of T&I education is to help students enter a professional community of practice (e.g. Kiraly 2003; Lee-Jahnke 2011; Berthaud and Mason 2018). Some even look upon the teams formed by a class project as identical with a CoP. In two of the reviewed studies, Marco (2016) believes that he and his students have formed a small-scale community who are gradually moving toward the center of professional practice. Kiraly (2013, 216) even explicitly acknowledges that:

> Throughout the course, I would attempt to foment the development of a micro community of practice in the classroom, where the students would take increasing responsibility for contributing to the completion of the project and for their own learning in terms of personal competence, social competence, and translation competence *per se.*

Strictly speaking, a project is different, if not always distinct, from a CoP. The basic definition of a project is "a temporary endeavor undertaken to create a unique product, service or result" (PMI 2013, 3). All the above projects, with the exception of Chen (2013), are temporary, one-off practicums that have a predetermined beginning and end and revolve around a particular task, compared with a CoP that cuts across multiple tasks and exists in a sustained manner by reproducing itself. According to Wenger, McDermott, and Snyder (2002, 42), a project team is formed by a discrete activity. They are temporary, and their knowledge is largely lost when they disband. But a CoP is marked by a cyclic rhythm that goes beyond the duration of one commission. Barab and Duffy (2000) point out that although the two learning contexts are guided by similarly situated learning principles, a CoP is additionally marked by individuals that share a common purpose and an identity, a common cultural and historical heritage that can be inherited; and a reproduction procedure in which old members are replaced by new members.

Building on Wenger's theory, Risku and Dickinson (2009, 56) further describe cultural characteristics of a CoP:

> A community needs to have had a founder (or group of founders), some kind of leadership or structure, center on a common interest (shared purpose) and focus on member-generated content. It also needs a critical mass of members who meet membership requirements (identity/boundaries), form relationships (reputation/ trust) and see the need to communicate over time (motivation/loyalty) in an appropriate manner (standards/values). Its history and dynamics are influenced by the formalization brought about by the standards and network effects.

Apparently, it takes time for these features to take shape. While they may not be all found in a single class project, we would venture to suggest that they might be cultivated in an ongoing internship project. Just imagine, if an external partner is satisfied with the translations provided and has long-term need for language services, there is a possibility that they would send tasks on a frequent basis. In this way, the original project may be sustained for a long time, possibly years. As a result, it may become a CoP, where each group of new participants can move on a centripetal learning trajectory. However, being a recent phenomenon, the number of studies that draw on the social anthropological view to study such projects has been exceedingly limited. There can be little doubt a study along these lines will shed light on new ways to enact authentic and collaborative learning in T&I education. We thus devote the remainder of this research to investigating how one such internship project is run.

Note

1 Program-level internship projects are sometimes organized inhouse in the form of "翻译实践基地" in Chinese，" or "translation practice field" if translated into English literally.

References

Aguilar, R. P. 2016. "The Question of Authenticity in Translator Education from the Perspective of Educational Philosophy." In *Towards Authentic Experiential Learning in Translator Education*, edited by D. Kiraly et al., 13–32. Göttingen: V&R Press.

Angelone, E., and Á. Marín García. 2017. "Expertise Acquisition through Deliberate Practice." *Translation Spaces* 6 (1): 122–158. doi: 10.1075/bct.105.07ang.

Barab, S. A., and T. Duffy. 2000. "From Practice Fields to Communities of Practice." In *Theoretical Foundations of Learning Environments*, edited by D. H. Jonassen and S. M. Land, 25–56. Mahwah: Lawrence Erlbaum & Associates.

Beninatto, R. S., and D. A. DePalma. 2007. "Collaborative Translation." *Multilingual, 2008 Resource Directory & Index* 2007: 49–51.

Berthaud, S., and S. Mason. 2018. "Embedding Reflection Throughout the Postgraduate Translation Curriculum: Using Communities of Practice to Enhance Training." *The Interpreter and Translator Trainer* 12 (4): 388–405. doi: 10.1080/1750399X.2018.1538847.

Bowker, L. 2015. "Computer-aided Translation: Translator Training." In *Routledge Encyclopedia of Translation Technology*, edited by S. Chan, 88–104. London and New York: Routledge.

Brown, J. S., A. Collins, and P. Duguid. 1989. "Situated Cognition and the Culture of Learning." *Educational Researcher* 18 (1): 32–42. doi: 10.3102/0013189X018001032.

Cai, H., and C. Zhang. 2013. "Exploring School-Industry Collaboration in the Training of Students in Professional Master-degree Translation and Interpreting Programs. [论翻译专业硕士培养中的校企合作.]" *Chinese Translators Journal* 34 (1): 51–55.

Calvo, E. 2015. "Scaffolding Translation Skills through Situated Training Approaches: Progressive and Reflective Methods." *The Interpreter and Translator Trainer* 9 (3): 306–322. doi: 10.1080/1750399X.2015.1103107.

Chai, M. 2015. "The Internship Mechanism of the MTI Program in GIIT, SISU." In *CIUTI-Forum 2014. Pooling Academic Excellence with Entrepreneurship for New Partnerships*, edited by M. Forstner, H. Lee-Jahnke, and M. Chai, 277–291. Frankfurt am Main: Peter Lang.

Chai, M. 2017. "Understanding the Current Situation, Enhancing Quality, and Pioneering Progress: The Future Development of Translation Studies. [认识现状 提升质量 开拓前行——翻译专业的未来发展.]" *East Journal of Translation* 6: 4–8.

Chen, S. 2013. "Project-based Training in Translator Education: Implications, Problems, Solutions. [项目翻译教学模式:意义，问题与对策——项目翻译教学的行动研究.]" *Foreign Language Learning Theory and Practice* 4: 82–87.

Dillenbourg, P. 1999. "What Do You Mean by Collaborative Learning?" In *Collaborative-Learning: Cognitive and Computational Approaches*, edited by P. Dillenbourg, 1–19. Oxford: Elsevier.

Dong, H., and Q. Zhang. 2015. "Reflections on the Model of MTI Professional Degree Internship Bases. [翻译硕士（MTI）专业学位实习基地建设模式创新思考.]" *Technology-Enhanced Foreign Language Education* 2: 30–34.

Galán-Mañas, A., A. Kuznik, and C. Olalla-Soler. 2020. "Entrepreneurship in Translator and Interpreter Training." *HERMES – Journal of Language and Communication in Business* 60: 7–11. doi: 10.7146/hjlcb.v60i0.121307.

Gong, R. 2012. "Reflections on the Format of Authentic Project: A Case Study. [MTI专业笔译实战项目教学模式探讨——以国新办宣传片项目为例.]" *East Journal of Translations* 6: 25–31.

Hoadley, C. 2012. "What Is a Community of Practice and How Can We Support It?" In *Theoretical Foundations of Learning Environments*, 2nd ed., edited by D. H. Jonassen and S. M. Land, 287–300. London: Taylor & Francis.

House, J. 2000. "Consciousness and the Strategic Use of Aids in Translation." In *Tapping and Mapping the Processes of Translation and Interpreting*, edited by S. Tirkkonen-Condit and R. Jääskeläinen, 149–162. Amsterdam and Philadelphia: John Benjamins.

Huang, Y. 2017. "Professional MTI Degree Programs: A Groundbreaking Reform with a Promising Future. [翻译硕士专业学位教育:划时代的改革,前程似锦的未来.]." *Chinese Translators Journal* 38 (3): 5–6.

Jiménez-Crespo, M. 2017. *Crowdsourcing and Online Collaborative Translations*. Amsterdam and Philadelphia: John Benjamins.

Kenny, M. A. 2008. "Discussion, Cooperation, Collaboration: The Impact of Task Structure on Student Interaction in a Web-Based Translation Exercise Module." *The Interpreter and Translator Trainer* 2 (2): 139–164. doi: 10.1080/1750399X.2008.10798771.

Kiraly, D. 2003. "From Instruction to Collaborative Construction: A Passing Fad or the Promise of a Paradigm Shift in Translator Education?" In *Beyond the Ivory Tower*, edited by B. J. Baer and G. S. Koby, 3–27. Amsterdam and Philadelphia: John Benjamins.

Kiraly, D. 2012. "Growing A Project-Based Translation Pedagogy: A Fractal Perspective." *Meta* 57 (1): 82–95. doi: 10.7202/1012742ar.

Kiraly, D. 2013. "Towards a View of Translator Competence as an Emergent Phenomenon: Thinking Outside the Box(es) in Translator Education." In New Prospects and Perspectives for Educating Language Mediators, edited by D. Kiraly, S. Hansen-Schirra, and K. Maksymski, 197–224. Tubingen: Narr Francke Attempo.

Kußmaul, P. 1995. *Training the Translator*. Amsterdam: John Benjamins.

Lave, J., and E. Wenger. 1991. *Situated Learning: Legitimate Peripheral Participation*. Cambridge: Cambridge UP.

Lee-Jahnke, H. 2011. "Trendsetters and Milestones in Interdisciplinary Process-Oriented Translation: Cognition, Emotion, Motivation." In *CIUTI-Forum 2010. Global Governance and Intercultural Dialogue: Translation and Interpreting in a New Geopolitical Setting,* edited by M. Forstner and H. Lee-Jahnke, 109–153. Frankfurt am Main: Peter Lang.

Li, R. L., and Y. He. 2011. "Researching Translation Project-Based Learning Models from the Perspective of Learning Science. [学习科学视角下的项目翻译学习模式研究.]." *Foreign Language Education* 32 (1): 4–98.

Liu, H., and S. Liang. 2019. "Teaching Translation in the Context of Artificial Intelligence. [人工智能背景下笔译的学与教.]." *East Journal of Translation* 2: 19–26.

Marco, J. 2016. "On the Margins of the Profession: The Work Placement as a Site for the Literary Translator Trainee's Legitimate Peripheral Participation." *The Interpreter and Translator Trainer* 10 (1): 29–43. doi: 10.1080/1750399X.2016.1154341

Massardo, I., and J. van der Meer. 2017. *The Translation Industry in 2022. A report from the TAUS Industry Summit*. TAUS. www.taus.net/insights/reports/the-translation-industry-in-2022.

O'Brien, S. 2011. "Collaborative Translation." In *Handbook of Translation Studies 2*, edited by Y. Gambier and L. van Doorslaer, 17–20. Amsterdam and Philadelphia: John Benjamins.

Pavlović, N. 2009. "More Ways to Explore the Translating Mind: Collaborative Translation Protocols." In *Behind the Mind: Methods, Models and Results in Translation Process Research*, edited by S. Göpferich, A. L. Jakobsen, and I. M. Mees, 81–106. Copenhagen: Samfundslitteratur.

Project Management Institute. 2013. *A Guide to the Project Management Body of Knowledge (PMBOK® Guide)*, 5th ed. Newtown Square: Project Management Institute.

Pym, A. 2009. "Using Process Studies in Translator Training. Self-Discovery through Lousy Experiments." In *Methodology, Technology and Innovation in Translation Process Research*, edited by S. Göpferich, F. Alves, and I. Mees, 35–156. Copenhagen: Samfundslitteratur.

Risku, H., and A. Dickinson. 2009. "Translators as Networkers: The Role of Virtual Communities." *HERMES – Journal of Language and Communication in Business* 42: 49–70. doi: 10.7146/hjlcb.v22i42.96846.

Sun, W., and C. Dai. 2016. "Research on the Development of Competence for MTI Students under School-Enterprise Collaboration. [校企合作下的技能型、应用型翻译人才培养模式研究.]." *Shanghai Journal of Translators* 3: 72–76.

Thelen, M. 2016. "Collaborative Translation in Translator Training." *KSJ* 4 (3): 253–269.

Wenger, E. 1998. *Communities of Practice. Learning, Meaning, and Identity*. Cambridge: Cambridge UP.

Wenger, E., R. McDermott, and W. M. Snyder. 2002. *A Guide to Managing Knowledge: Cultivating Communities of Practice*. Cambridge: Harvard Business School Press.

Yang, C. 2012. "Training Model for MTI Students from the Industrialization Perspective. [产业化视域下的翻译硕士培养模式.]." *Chinese Translators Journal* 33 (1): 24–28.

Yu, H., and Z. Zhang. 2013. "Project-Based Learning: Theory and Practice with a CAT Course as an Example. [项目化教学:理论与实践——MTI的CAT课程建设探索.]." *Chinese Translators Journal* 34 (3): 44–48.

Zhang, Y., M. Chai, and J. Yao. 2011. "Design of the MTI Program Internship Module. [翻译硕士专业学位（MTI）实习模块的设计.]." *East Journal of Translation* 5: 4–17.

Zhong, W., T. Zhao, and M. Xu. 2020. "Professional Interpreting Translation Education in the Chinese Mainland: History, Achievements, Challenges and Future Prospects." *Babel* 66 (6): 883–901. doi: 10.1075/babel.00199.zho.

5   Zooming in on a new case

5.1 Project background

The new case we set out to examine is known as the UN DGC project, which derives its name from the partnership Graduate Institute of Interpretation and Translation, Shanghai International Studies University (GIIT), Shanghai International Studies University (SISU) forms with DGC (Department of Global Communications) of the United Nations (UN). GIIT is a top-notch graduate-level T&I program in China. In August 2008, it was certified as a UN memorandum of understanding (MoU) institution, paving the way for its collaboration with all organizations of the UN family (Chai and Zhang 2013). DGC is a department of the Secretariat of the United Nations. Its News and Media Division (NMD) works to disseminate information on the United Nations and its work with its partners across its media network. As multilingualism is a core value of the United Nations, DGC finds it essential to have the materials they publish online translated into the six official languages of the UN for a global audience.

In 2014, as an extension of the UN's MoU agreement, the Director of the News and Media Division of the DGC visited SISU and signed a partnership agreement with GIIT on behalf of the DGC. Under the scheme, GIIT students were given opportunities to remotely translate DGC materials from English into Chinese on the sidelines of their curriculum and to simultaneously learn about the United Nations language service requirements and norms. As with all UN outreach programs, the students selected were not compensated financially by the UN for their translations, but in return, they would receive a certificate in recognition of their service to the UN. Those who perform well would be recommended by GIIT for internships at DGC's own premises. GIIT could also get its name recognized in print on the paper-based publications of all translations.

While DGC was responsible for the final quality control, GIIT was in charge of organizing the translation activities. The first task DGC sent in 2014 was the 41st English edition of *Basic Facts about the United Nations*, a flagship publication detailing various organizations and agencies of the UN, with 12,3968 English words. Over 50 students and faculty members from GIIT were mobilized in this task over a period of nine months. As DGC was extremely satisfied with the quality of this initial cooperation, they started to send more materials to translate,

DOI: 10.4324/9781003542469-5

underscoring the need for a more fixed team. As a result, in September 2015, a dozen second-year MT students, all of whom had taken part in the first task, formed a group. They were joined by one translation teacher from the institute, an experienced professional translator himself, to work as the reviser. Together, they explored, experimented, and set up a set of practices. At the end of that year, the initial cohort of students devised examinations to select first-year students into the team. They shared with these new members their experiences and lessons learned. When they exited the project in 2016, the younger members had grown more competent to assume the mantle.

When we heard of the DGC project in September of 2018, it had hosted four successive years of students in this way and had produced, among others, a translation of over a dozen paper-based UN publications and over 2 million words of UN website content. At the time, the head of NMD visited GIIT again and expressed, on behalf of the DGC, their appreciation of the team's quality of work and rate of turnaround. DGC used the words "you have never missed a deadline" as validation of the team's performance over the years.

This short history of the DGC project led us to believe that it has evolved into a Community of Practice (CoP). As Kilbourn (2006, 545) argues, "A fundamental assumption for any academic research is that the phenomena (data) that we wish to understand are filtered through a point of view (a theoretical perspective)." If it is a CoP, it must reflect all the key principles of such entities (e.g. domain, access, mutual engagement, joint enterprise, shared repertoire, legitimate peripheral participation, and continuity of practice, etc.) But to an outside eye, many important details remain elusive. To start with, compared with conventional one-off projects, members in a CoP interact regularly in a shared practice, yet we don't know the variety, frequency, and volume of the work the team handles. Secondly, translation in the UN has strict accuracy and consistency requirements (Cao and Zhao 2006). This presumably applies to the content the team translates for the DGC as well. But with over 20 numbers, how does the team achieve consistency? Technology-wise, what is their level of engagement with technology? Is the workflow adopted in any way different from industry standards or those of the UN translation services? Thirdly, beyond the productive process, there is an ever-macro process at play in a CoP. However, we have little idea of its recruitment, mentoring, assessment, and reproduction processes. We have yet to hear in the participants' own words how they perceive the benefits they have gained from the project.

Intrigued, we sought approval from the gatekeeper to observe the team's online and offline activities starting in October 2018. This was the time when the team was about to recruit new members from the class that had just enrolled in 2018. We decide to focus on this incoming group for investigation. We want to track how they were taken in and how they would move from being an observer to gradually taking ownership to ultimately complete the reproduction cycle and exit. We also plan to use the gleaned archival records, documents, and interviews with the previous members to piece together the practices adopted and the changes that might take place in this cycle to understand how this community has built up its heritage.

5.2 Research design

This research blends the single-case study and ethnographic study design in an overall qualitative study. The circumstances of the DGC project meet the typical conditions of case study design. First, case studies bound the research object in time and in space (Creswell and Poth 2018). The DGC project proceeds in the sequence dictated by its members. As a researcher, we simply want to follow and understand its natural development path. Secondly, a case study is particularly applicable if the main research questions are "how" or "why" questions. Thirdly, case studies can be of single-case or of multiple-case design. The single-case design is justified if the case represents an extreme or unusual circumstance. Given the little scholarly attention directed toward internship projects, much less on a continuous one, the DGC project would doubtlessly serve as an exemplary unique case.

There is also a strong ethnographic element to our investigation. Ethnography is an in-depth study of a group of people to find out "how they view the situations they face, how they regard one another and how they see themselves" (Hammersley and Atkinson 2007, 3). It has been increasingly used to study translators *in situ* (e.g. Koskinen 2008; Asare 2011; Risku and Windhager 2013; Risku, Milošević, and Rogl 2021). Through the narrative of everyday details and routine text production, an ethnographic study can provide explanations and descriptions of a culture in all its richness, complexity, and specificity. It could also be used to explain the evolution of the group and explain why any changes have taken place.

While case studies and ethnographic studies are both qualitative, there are indeed some differences. "Ethnographic researchers do not look for causality look for links between real world events in their study results" (Fusch, Fusch, and Ness 2017, 926), but case studies can. Ethnography is based on thick description and multiple forms of data, with the researcher as the filter of observation. In all, the two methods combined could mitigate the limitations of each to achieve the research purpose.

5.2.1 Participants, time, and space boundaries

At the time when the present research was taken, the DGC project had taken in approximately 100 students and undergone six cycles of replacement. The group we tracked was the fifth one, which stayed in the project between November 2018 and April 2020. At the start of this cycle, 22 students were admitted through a selective process. Some of them were later removed from the team due to competitive evaluation. Eventually, 16 of them gained formal membership and completed the cycle.

In terms of the space boundaries of the case, the DGC project has been operating as a distributed team since the very beginning, with every task received, assigned, prepared, translated, revised, proofread, and delivered online. The participants rely on various tools to share knowledge and produce artifacts. By accessing the community, we were accessing the information and communications technology (ICT) tools and the cloud-based translation tool the team uses, the archival records, files and artifacts saved in the tools, and the member's real-time dialogues logged by these tools. In addition, the participants organized several offline plenary meetings to review and discuss ways to optimize their practices. We learned of these events from the announcements on the team's chat group and were allowed to attend and keep notes as a participant observer.

5.2.2 Unit of analysis and sub-unit of analysis

A case study can employ holistic design to explore the broader aspects of a unit or utilize embedded design to investigate its smaller components. The examination of sub-units can frequently contribute significantly to in-depth analysis, thereby enriching our understanding of a single case (Yin 2003). It is for this reason that we find it essential to break down a single cycle into its individual stages as sub-units of analysis. Without doing so, it would be challenging to thoroughly explore the intricate nature and multitude of variables involved.

In general, each cycle of student participation lasts about one and a half years. It begins with the recruitment of the first-year students in November. From December to January, while the old members continue to work on routine DGC tasks, the new participants are trained in tasks using the materials the older members have just translated for DGC. Then, they are given opportunities to engage in real assignments as terminologists and proofreaders along with the old members. In March, all the old members exited the project, except the three project managers (PMs), who continue to manage the team as the new participants take up each task. The three of them will also assess the membership of the new recruits based on their training record and oversee the selection of new PMs. Starting in May, with the exit of the three old PMs, the new participants are truly left on their own to run the project. Over time, these new members will grow mature and become old members themselves. When November rolls in again, they hold examinations to bring in new first-year students into the fold. They will mentor them until they themselves exit in April, thus completing the cycle.

In view of these key developments and their time-sensitive features, the progression of the cycle is broken into the stages described below. While stage 1 to 5 is explicitly sequential, stage 6 and 7 are embedded in stage 5. The questions asked at each stage are listed in Table 5.1.

5.3 Data collection instruments

In process-oriented studies, process data are elicited from both online and offline sources (Krings 2005). "Online" data are generated in real-time when participants are engaged in the very act and event of translation, whereas "offline" data consist of participants' explanations of their translation activities after such activities are completed and on the translations they produce. While online data are quantitative and hard evidence, offline data can uncover what underlies the translation process. The two are often combined to form an integrative description of the process (Hansen 2010).

Table 5.1 Timeline of one cycle and questions for each stage

Stage 1	Stage 2	Stage 3	Stage 4	Stage 5
Nov. 2018: recruited as new members	Dec. 2018–Feb. 2019: trained by old members	Mar.–May 2019: exploring on their own	Apr.–May 2019: assessment of full membership and leadership transitions	May 2019–March 2020: moving to the center of production and taking ownership

		Stage 6	Stage 7
		Nov. 2019: admitting new members	Jan.–Mar. 2020: training new members and passing on the baton

Stage 1	Stage 2	Stage 3	Stage 4	Stage 5	Stage 6	Stage 7
How are applicants selected? How are recruitment tests designed and graded? Why are applicants motivated to participate? What is their prior knowledge and experience?	How are recruits initiated to the community? How are they trained? Do they have chance to work with the old members and if so, how?	How do recruits perform when given the opportunity to translate real tasks? How are they scaffolded in each task? Do they experience any changes in motivation compared to the beginning?	How is the membership assessed for recruits? How are the new PMs selected from the recruits?	What is the variety, workload, turnaround, and frequency of tasks? What are the workflow features? What are the patterns of human–human interaction? What are the technological features and patterns of human–machine interaction? How is the translation asset developed and managed collaboratively? What assessment methods are used? What do the student participants believe they have learned? How does their sense of identify and motivation change?	How are the students from the next year of class selected compared with a year before?	How are the recruits from the next year of class trained compared with a year before?

Zooming in on a new case 79

Meanwhile, Yin (2003) advises the use of six general qualitative data sources in a case study: direct observation, interviews, archival records, documents, participant observation, and physical artifacts. If they are mapped to Krings' categorization, interviews, archival records, documents, and physical artifacts are offline methods, while direct observation and participant observation lie on the online side, although they both still rely on the researcher as the data collection instrument and are prone to personal bias. Of the more objective online tools advocated by Krings, computer video recording, eye tracking and brain measurement are often employed to reflect the mental processes of an individual (Göpferich and Jääskeläinen 2009), whereas dialogue protocols can more easily capture activities of a group without destroying the ecological validity of data. Therefore, in consideration of each tool's focus of strength, we decide to use the following data collection methods.

- Collaborative verbal data: ONLINE

As a distributed team, all participants use QQ, an instant messaging platform, to keep each other in the loop. They also discuss translation solutions online. All the posts are automatically recorded by their chat group and constitute a rich source of artifact-mediated discourse for analysis.

- Field notes of all group events: ONLINE

The project managers would, from time to time, run offline plenary meetings to discuss organizational matters. We were allowed to keep audio recordings of what transpired during these events. They gave us immediacy to the community and opportunities for us to know and talk to the participants face to face.

- Physical artifacts: OFFLINE

Physical artifacts encompass both final and intermediate products made by the participants in the production process. They include the terminology sheets, the style guide, the draft translations, revised translations, and proofread translations. They reveal clues on where members have collaborated with each other and the degree of technological integration of the translation activities.

- Documentation: OFFLINE

Documentations are written documents that are generated in running the project. They include but are not limited to the email correspondence, recruitment examinations paper and results, duty roster, workload calculation records, assessment record, election plans made by the members running for PMs, and the PM vote results. They provide us with details of the non-productive activities of the community.

- Informal, unstructured interviews: OFFLINE

During our investigation, we have become closer with some participants. This allows us to organize unstructured interviews with the key informants if we feel we must seek more contextual information about the project.

- Questionnaires: OFFLINE

Since the number of participants that we got to interview is limited, questionnaires can help us obtain information from more participants who are not open for interviews or direct observation. Altogether, three anonymous questionnaires have been distributed to the student participants at different time points, and one questionnaire to the teacher participant in June 2019. All the items contained in these questionnaires are phrased in Chinese, the participants' native language, for the sake of clarity. All the student questionnaires were piloted with the PMs before being distributed on QQ. The response rates were 100%, 81.8%, 87.5% and 100% respectively.

- Archival records: OFFLINE

Archival records include the files and the artifacts the participants of the previous cycles have saved on QQ; and the retrospective reflections, which some participants have chosen to write as their graduation thesis. They provide information on how the project used to run and a baseline for us to identify changes and the evolution of the practices.

5.4 Data analysis procedures

Once all the fieldwork was completed, we started organizing the collected evidence. In line with Creswell and Poth (2018), if a case unfolds in a chronological sequence of events, arranging the occurrences in chronological order enables the researcher to assess various data sources and identify evidence pertinent to each stage or phase in the case's development. Consequently, our initial action involves categorizing the evidence according to the timing of their occurrences as outlined below (see Table 5.2).

The second step is to interpret the evidence and make sense of how each stage works. Since stages 1, 2, 4, 6, and 7 had more to do with the non-productive process, the combination of different sources of evidence made it comparatively easy for us to reconstruct scenes, events, and the perspectives of participants. The iteration of stage 1 and 6 and stage 2 and 7 could also reveal changes and improvements taking place.

In comparison, stages 3 and 5 were on the productive side. Both spanned a long time, comprised different tasks and generated a substantial volume of online dialogues. This was where we used verbal analysis to examine all the posts automatically recorded by QQ, as evidence of their collaboration. According to Chi (1997, 273), verbal analysis is "a methodology for quantifying the subjective or qualitative coding of contents of verbal utterances" so that a researcher could "tabulate, count, and draw relations between the occurrences of different kinds of utterances." It is a standard methodology in complex forms of learning and problem-solving (Jeone 2013). Put simply, we wanted to code the verbal qualitative data, count the number of posts represented by different codes and examine the frequencies for patterns and trends over time. The steps taken in verbal analysis included the following:

82 *Project-based Learning in Translation and Interpreting Studies*

Table 5.2 Data structured according to when it occurs

Stage 1: Recruitment
Email instructions of the recruitment tests; test paper, marked test paper and test results; unstructured interviews with the project members; the first questionnaire distributed to recruits in December 2018

Stage 2: Training
Field trip of the orientation; email instructions of all training exercises and new members' submitted homework; unstructured interviews with the project members; collaborative verbal protocols and physical artifacts recorded during at this stage; curriculum documents of the 2018 class participants

Stage 3: Exploring on their own
Collaborative protocols and physical artifacts generated during at this stage; unstructured interviews with the project members; the second questionnaires distributed in March 2019

Stage 4: Assessment of membership and leadership successions
Email correspondence; membership assessment records; PM election plans, PM vote results; unstructured interviews with the project members

Stage 5: Moving to the center of production
Collaborative protocols and artifacts generated during this stage; the field trip to the plenary meeting; the third questionnaire distributed in July 2019; unstructured interviews with the project members; duty roster and project assessment records

Stage 6: Taking in new blood
Fieldtrip to the plenary meeting; collaborative protocols recorded during this time; email correspondence of examinations, marked recruitment texts, test results; unstructured interviews with the project members

Stage 7: Grooming new members and passing on the baton
Email instructions of all training exercises and new members' summitted homework; field trip of the orientation and celebratory event; email notifications of all training exercises; unstructured interviews with the project members; collaborative protocols and artifacts generated during this time

Preparing the verbal data

As with all online discourse, the posts written may be one-to-one, one-to-many and many-to-many. All the posts were logged by the time of their utterance. They seemed unstructured, but the person to whom a post was directed could understand it despite the delay. To perform a quantitative analysis of this verbal data, it is crucial to not only organize the raw data chronologically but also categorize it based on tasks (Dörnyei and Ushioda 2011). By doing so, we can create distinct clusters of posts, each focusing on a single task. These clusters then serve as our basis for comparisons (Chi 1997).

Two other actions were performed in preparing the verbal data. One involves removing the posts that were not related to the productive activities of each task, such as posts related to the training and organization of the plenary events. Meanwhile, when the members discussed translation solutions, they often used evidence, such as screenshots of the intermediate artifacts, to mediate their discourse. Sometimes, they also used emojis to show their feelings. All these images were converted to their word-based meanings.

Tabulating the verbal data

Each post cluster contains key attributes of each task, such as the date of its receiving, the name and type of the task, the number of participants involved, and the date of delivery. We extracted such information and tabulated it chronologically to help us understand the variety, frequency, and volume of work of the team.

Creating the coding scheme

When the posts are presented diachronically in a single task, they tell us exactly *with whom* and *for what reason the interaction takes place*. They tend to synch up with the sequence of workflow procedures. The first set of preliminary codes was thus created based on the initiator of the dialogue. But there were also posts that did not fall neatly into the routine type of interactions; for example, there were times when the participants started to discuss how to manage the resources or technical troubleshooting, so these additional two types of codes were added. After we coded through all the posts, we repeated the procedure one month later and compared the result with the previous one until no additional labels emerged. In total, we came up with 11 codes, to reflect the temporal development of interactions between the participants (See Table 5.3)

Counting the number of coded data in each post cluster

According to Kenny (2008), there is a distinction between cognitive postings in which participants engage directly with the learning material by questioning, brainstorming, and proposing solutions related to the learning task, and "organizational" or non-cognitive postings, in which participants discuss plans for non-productive activities. Seen in this way, in the above codes, the dialogues that are initiated by the teacher-reviser, the student translators and the PM are cognitive posts, while the rest are organizational posts. Post counts are thus either indicators of the level of cognitive conflict or of organizational challenges the team has experienced. Counting the number of each type of data in a post cluster makes it possible for us to know the focus of interaction and the amount of argumentative learning triggered by a task. If a task produces an inordinate number of posts, we will immediately see which specific type of post count deviates from the pattern.

Interpreting the change of post counts over time

As participants became more engaged in the practice, we hypothesized that their increasing familiarity with the workflow and improved proficiency with the tools would lead to a reduction in the number of posts they generate. By monitoring the evolution of post counts over time, we could obtain evidence of their advancing competence in managing DGC translations. This approach is grounded in the belief that we can objectively and quantifiably analyze the learners' expressions to gauge how their knowledge representation evolves during the learning process (Chi 1997).

Table 5.3 Coding scheme and post examples

Category	Description and subtypes	Post examples
PM posting tasks (PM-P)	The PM on duty posting the task(s) by specifying its type, name, wordcount, deadline, and number of translators and peer-reviewers needed on the chat group of QQ and ask the translators on duty to take up the task(s)	e.g.: PM-1: 大家早上好~来了一份国际青年日的稿子，共400词，今晚6点前完成初译和互校，需要初译、审校各一人，请本周值班的同学报名哦~@J @L@K
Assigning translators and peer-reviewers (PM-A-T)	The translators and peer-reviewers signing up the translation tasks	e.g.: Translator A: 报名初译。
Task preparation (Prep) Translation asset management (AM) Technical support and troubleshooting (Tech T/S) Time management I (TM 1) Teacher-reviser initiated dialogues during revision (TR-D)	The PM assigning translators and peer-reviewers directly	e.g.: PM-2: 各位同学，UNPDF来了一份新稿子，共1000词，需要两名同学合作初译与互校，DDL为周六（9.28）晚6点。这周同学手上任务都比较多，请上周@D @H 认领.
	The PM reminding translators who may have failed to ready the post to sign up	e.g.: PM-3: 这篇今晚交，大家尽快认领尽快做起来哦我知道大家现在都很忙，希望可以自己协调一下哈，有任务的时候还是要积极接任务@J @F @C
	PM thanking the translators and peer-reviewers for signing up the task	e.g.: Translator B: 好滴！谢谢！
	Translators on duty apologizing for not reading the post/signing up the task immediately	e.g.: Translator C: 啊不好意思上午没看到消息 报名审校。 e.g.: Translator D: 我也刚看到 抱歉…
	Coordinating the role of translators and peer viewers	e.g.: Translator E: 那我审校吧哈哈。 e.g.: Translator F: 哈哈 我刚也想说
Time management II (TM 2) Teacher's feedback and evaluation (TR-F) Student translator-initiated dialogues with teacher reviser (ST-D)	The PM importing tasks to the tool and sending source text to the assigned translators and peer-reviewers	e.g.: PM-1: 文件已经导入Yicat啦 文件已导入平台 "网页翻译"下 e.g.: PM-3: 辛苦各位！我去建项目。请两位查收邮件~辛苦啦 e.g.: PM-2: 稍后给各位发分工文件。
	Translators and peer-reviewers confirming the assignment and the receival of the text	e.g.: Translator F: 收到 e.g.: Translator G: 好的，收到

Table 5.3 (Continued)

Category	Description and subtypes	Post examples
	The PM/teacher reviser sending tips, reminders, reference materials, to translator(s)	e..g.: PM-2: 六份往期文件供参考~ e.g.: Teacher: 提示一下，如果三个人一起翻一篇，那么，三个人都必需通读原文，掌握论点，提取梗概和思维导图
PM-initiated dialogues with teacher reviser and the translators (PM-D)	Discussions on ways to manage translation asset generated from production	e.g.: Teacher: 接活的同学请首先建语料 e.g.: Teacher: 你们有没有设置资产管理专员？术语管理和语料管理谁在做？ e.g.: Teacher: 在开始做之前，要先合并句段 e.g.: Teacher: 然后把原来的参考文件做好对齐导进去做语料 e.g.: Teacher: 每一次做完有没有更新术语库？
PM posting tasks (PM-P) Assigning translators and peer-reviewers (PM-A-T)	Translators/PM/Teacher reviser seeking technical support	e.g.: Translator J: 学姐 你好。下面这篇纪事的文档导出来有内容的缺失，yicat上已经确认了，请问这个是什么原因呢？图片。 e.g.: PM-3: 想请问一 Yicat翻译界面是不是没有像word里面的那种 撤销上一步操作？比如我不小心把一大段的译文删掉了我想恢复上一步操作 e.g.: Translator F: 学姐，请问网站出了啥问题吗？又一次取消了我快翻完了[伤心表情]
	Support offered by technical service provider/service update announcement	e.g.: Technical support: 各位同学老师，今晚十一点半-明早7:30进行系统升级。升级期间，Tmxmall所有产品将无法使用，大家及时做好安排哟~
Task preparation (Prep) Translation asset management (AM) Technical support and troubleshooting (Tech T/S) Time management I (TM 1)	Translators reminding the teacher revisor the translation has been peer-reviewed PM alerting the teacher reviser of the deadline	e.g.: Translator D: @老师，网页翻译已完成，麻烦您审校。 e.g.: PM-2: 老师，这篇也是今晚就要交的. 其中一篇ddl是11点，所以得抓紧点哈！
Teacher-reviser initiated dialogues during revision (TR-D)	Teacher revisor asking about the deadline Teacher revisor acknowledging the knowledge of the deadline	e.g.: Teacher: 我也是睡前审校吗？ e.g.: Teacher: 400字的还没好吗？ e.g.: Teacher: 在看，稍安勿躁

(*Continued*)

Table 5.3 (Continued)

Category	Description and subtypes	Post examples
Time management II (TM 2) Teacher's feedback and evaluation (TR-F) Student translator-initiated dialogues with teacher reviser (ST-D)	Teacher revisor posing questions to the translator about their translations	e.g.: Teacher: TOB是什么意思？ e.g.: Teacher: TOB要确认，不要留英语缩写，我觉得是没什么特别的意思
	Translator justifying their decisions with evidence	e.g.: Translator M: 老师TOB没有查到相关资料，在备注里写了一下，但是因为怕后面审校的时候忘记，就先留在原文了。
	PM joining the discussion	e.g.: PM-2: 片语要多参考Linguee上的译法
	Teacher reviser and student translator coming to agreement	e.g.: Translator H: 好的，谢谢老师。
PM posting tasks (PM-P) Assigning translators and peer-reviewers (PM-A-T) Task preparation (Prep)	Teacher reviser announcing the revision is completed	e.g.: Teacher: @F, 你那篇看好了。
	Translator, peer-reviewers and PM thanking the teacher reviser for the input	e.g.: Student translator: 好的，老师辛苦啦！
	PM alerting translator to start proofreading and desktop publishing	e.g.: PM-3: 请@Z @S 尽快通读讨论，提交清稿。
Translation asset management (AM) Technical support and troubleshooting (Tech T/S)	Teacher reviser offering short evaluation of the translation	e.g.: Teacher: 现在看起来可以，但整体不一定，导出来尽量整体通读一下，前后要流畅一些。 e.g.: Teacher: 翻译的非常棒，但有个词protocol应该不是协议，我认为是方案或者安排，请查证。自行车日的翻译有点随意。
	Translator, peer-reviewers and PM thanking the teacher reviser for the input	e.g.: Translator N: 好的，老师辛苦啦！
Time management I (TM 1) Teacher-reviser initiated dialogues during revision (TR-D) Time management II (TM 2)	Translator posing questions to teacher revisor if they don't understand the revision or offering other possible translations or pointing out some mistakes	e.g.: Translator K: @Teacher 在联合国相关网站上，illustrated edition of the Universal Declaration of Human Rights是处理成《世界人权宣言》漫画图册，我看册子里的插画都是漫画形式，是不是还是用漫画图册比较准确？
	Teacher revisor answering translator's queries	e.g.: Teacher: 降解的概念比较小 e.g.: Teacher: 我查过linguee e.g.: Teacher: 有不同说法 e.g.: Teacher: 考虑到下面的动词erode, 用降解不合适

Table 5.3 (Continued)

Category	Description and subtypes	Post examples
	Teacher reviser and the translator coming to agreement	e.g.: Teacher reviser: 长见识了。 e.g.: Translator C: 这个地方我赞同老师的处理，是我疏忽了！
Teacher's feedback and evaluation (TR-F)	The PM would occasionally post questions to the teacher reviser or to the translators as the final round of quality control	e.g.: PM-1: 清稿返稿图片；昨天的稿子W和L做的很好！效率也很高[开心表情] e.g.: PM-1: 其他同学有兴趣的可以打开学习一下老师的审校稿~还有一些小的格式问题 大家以后多多注意一下

Integrating qualitative analysis of verbal data

While focusing on the quantitative aspects of verbal data, we also wanted to examine the content of the dialogues. We were first curious about when and what type of scaffoldings the PMs have provided to translators during the task preparation. Second, we wanted to know the ways in which the legacy translations (translation assets, such as translation memory or terminology) were maintained and leveraged and the participants' feelings and expectations toward these practices. The third area of interest was on technical challenges the participants experienced and measures taken to cope with these problems. Lastly, because the teacher reviser sometimes provided evaluations of student translations directly on the chatgroup, we wanted to know how his overall evaluations of student translations changed over time as additional proof of the participants' growing competence.

5.5 Methods to add rigor to the research

One risk to validity is the observer effect, meaning that the individuals under observation may modify their behaviors if they feel they are being "scrutinized" (Saldanha and O'Brien 2014). The other concern is whether the research has achieved internal validity, or whether the method taken, and the resulting accounts represent the truth of the research object (Göpferich and Jääskeläinen 2009). The following methods were taken to reduce such adverse effects and to increase the precision of description:

- Minimum presence of the researcher

Since we want to keep our intervention to the normal activities of the team to the minimum, we have taken particular care not to leave any posts online during their production. At the group plenary meetings, we refrained from asking any direct questions. Therefore, we believe the participants have become generally oblivious to our presence as a researcher during their time in the project.

- Triangulation of different data sources

We collected quantitative and qualitative evidence from different sources, organized them based on their timing and maintained carefully kept files and research journals. The evidence, when examined, compared, and contrasted with one another, would allow us to move closer to clarity of what happened in each stage of the process.

- Inclusion of multiple perspectives

To ensure the answers we got from one participant interviewed were credible, we combined them with the answers from the other participants and other types of evidence to see if they confirmed and corroborated each other. In a way, this also helps us be more reflective and enhance our understanding of the complexity of the events.

- Piloting questionnaires and debriefing

All the questionnaires administered to the student participants had been piloted to the three PMs to make sure the questions were phrased in acceptable ways. The results of the questionnaires had also been shared with the participants who showed an interest in the findings.

- Member checking

As we wrote up the research, the DGC project was still ongoing, and we still maintained contact with some of the participants we have observed. This gave us a chance to double-check our interpretation with these participants and to ask for additional perspectives.

- Double coding

As Baxter and Jack (2008) suggest, in the absence of a peer examiner, to ensure verbal data could be coded consistently, researchers could implement "double coding" to establish inter-coder reliability. We first entered all post clusters into a Microsoft Excel spreadsheet, coded all verbal data and then used the software to automatically count the number of each type of dialogue. One month later, we repeated the same procedure to check if the result tallied with the previous one. In case of inconsistencies, we read the entire post cluster again, marked the codes and counted a third time to reach a final decision. We then tabulated the post counts of each type of verbal data in a clean Excel spreadsheet for analysis.

5.6 Ethical considerations

Since the sensitivity of the information might expose the identity of the participants, ethical considerations are integral to an ethnographic case study (Koskinen 2008; Risku, Milošević, and Rogl 2021). The following measures are taken to ensure protection of our research participants.

In the initial stage of the research design, we briefed the program provider about our intention to disseminate the practices of the DGC project and obtained the approval of the research. In the data elicitation stage, all the participants were informed of our research purpose the first time we met. All of them were made aware that we would join their chat group, observe, and record their dialogic interactions. There were sensitive items in the questionnaire and in the interviews, such as their motivation in participating and their views on the effectiveness of various practices, to which we wanted to hear their honest opinion. Therefore, all the student questionnaires were anonymous, and the interview notes were managed in a confidential way. Meanwhile, we have tried to interview as many participants as we can, and we make sure all the interviews and questionnaires are carried out on a voluntary basis and furnished back to the participants interested in the findings. All the evidence, including those saved on the platform, was obtained with the approval of the relevant stakeholder, with their use explained in a clear manner.

In the data analysis stage, we used proprietary software to automatically transcribe all interviews. We maintained separate files of the transcripts and replaced all the participant names with pseudonyms. However, because the field of eligible UN MoU universities is so small and news reports of the DGC project can be easily found online, it would be easy to deduce the names of the translation program provider and the external partner. We decided to keep these two names unchanged.

In writing up the research, we maintained confidentiality and privacy of all data gathered. Any reference to the identified person(s) has been deleted. However, in case we need to present the evidence and artifacts, the posts from the chat group and responses from the interviews were copied verbatim in the original Chinese to give a fuller sense of the discourse, and then translated into English in the research to make them understandable to English readers.

References

Asare, E. 2011. *An Ethnographic Study of the Use of Translation Tools in a Translation Agency: Implications for Translation Tool Design*. Kent State University, PhD dissertation.

Baxter, P., and S. Jack. 2008. "Qualitative Case Study Methodology: Study Design and Implementation for Novice Researchers." *The Qualitative Report* 13 (4): 544–559. doi: 10.46743/2160-3715/2008.1573.

Cao, A., and X. Zhao. 2006. *Translation of United Nations Documents. [联合国文件翻译.]*. Beijing: China Translation Corporation.

Chai, M., and A. Zhang. 2013. "Professionalization of Translation and Interpreting Training – Reflections Inspired by the 3rd UN Cooperation Memorandum of Cooperation Signing Meeting. [翻译职业化带来翻译专业化教育——"第三届联合国合作备忘录签约高校年会"引出的思考.]." *East Journal of Translation* 4: 4–8.

Chi, M. T. H. 1997. "Quantifying Qualitative Analyses of Verbal Data: A Practical Guide." *Journal of the Learning Sciences* 6 (3): 271–315. doi: 10.1207/s15327809jls0603_1.

Creswell, J. W., and C. N. Poth. 2018. *Qualitative Inquiry & Research Design: Choosing Among Five Approaches*, 4th ed. Thousand Oaks: SAGE.

Dörnyei, Z., and E. Ushioda. 2011. *Teaching and Research Motivation*, 2nd ed. London: Pearson.

Fusch, P. I., G. E. Fusch, and L. R. Ness. 2017. "How to Conduct a Mini-Ethnographic Case Study: A Guide for Novice Researchers." *The Qualitative Report* 22 (3): 923–941. doi: 10.46743/2160-3715/2017.2580.

Göpferich, S., and R. Jääskeläinen. 2009. "Process Research into the Development of Translation Competence: Where Aare We, and Where Do We Need to Go?" *Across Languages and Cultures* 10 (2), 169–191. doi: 10.1556/Acr.10.2009.2.1.

Hammersley, M., and P. Atkinson. 2007. *Ethnography: Principles in Practice*, 3rd ed. London and New York: Taylor & Francis.

Hansen, G. 2010. "Integrative Description of Translation Processes." In *Translation and Cognition*, edited by G. M. Shreve and E. Angelone, 189–211. Amsterdam and Philadelphia: John Benjamins.

Jeone, H. 2013. "Verbal Data Analysis for Understanding Interactions." In *The International Handbook of Collaborative Learning*, edited by Cindy E. Hmelo-Silver et al., 168–183. London and New York: Routledge.

Kenny, M. A. 2008. "Discussion, Cooperation, Collaboration: The Impact of Task Structure on Student Interaction in a Web-Based Translation Exercise Module." *The Interpreter and Translator Trainer* 2 (2): 139–164. doi: 10.1080/1750399X.2008.10798771.

Kilbourn, B. 2006, "The Qualitative Doctoral Dissertation Proposal." *Teachers College Record* 108 (4): 529–576.

Koskinen, K. 2008. *Translating Institutions: An Ethnographic Study of EU Translation*. Manchester: St. Jerome.

Krings, H. P. 2005. "Wege ins Labyrinth—Fragestellungen und Methoden der Übersetzungsprozessforschung im Überblick." *Meta* 50 (2): 342–358. doi:10.7202/010941ar.

Risku, H., J. Milošević, and R. Rogl. 2021. "Responsibility, Powerlessness, and Conflict: An Ethnographic Case Study of Boundary Management in Translation." In *Translating Asymmetry—Rewriting Power*, edited by O. Carbonell i Cortés and E. Monzó-Nebot, 145–168. Amsterdam and Philadelphia: John Benjamins.

Risku, H., and F. Windhager. 2013. "Extended Translation. A Sociocognitive Research Agenda." *Target* 25 (1): 33–45. doi: 10.1075/target.25.1.04ris.

Saldanha, G., and S. O'Brien. 2014. *Research Methodologies in Translation Studies*. London and New York: Routledge.

Yin, R. K. 2003. *Case Study Research: Design and Methods*, 3rd ed. Thousand Oaks: SAGE.

6 The DGC project under the microscope

Communities have rhythms and go through stages of development. Of the over 180 tasks handled in the cycle we observed, each was different, and each was translated by different pairs of participants connected on the web. The easy and obvious choice for us was to narrow the focus on important events that shape the overall course of the cycle (see Table 6.1). Our account is thus weaved together chronologically by two threads: the visible thread is to describe the events and practices adopted at each stage, but at the same time, an effort is made to delve into the participants' reflections on the practices to reveal the links of these events and their implications on the participants' changing sense of identity, motivation, and learning.

6.1 Gaining access to the community

6.1.1 Recruitment examinations

A community is marked by boundaries set by its members (Wenger 1998). Collectively, they decide to whom, how, and when the access can open to newcomers. In the DGC project, as we found out, recruitment is only open to first-year students once a year. Selections are exclusively based on the results of two examinations, with one graded by the formal student members and the other by the teacher reviser.

Our observation began as the students of the 2018 class had just enrolled in the Graduate Institute of Interpretation and Translation (GIIT). Three student leaders of the DGC project, known as PMs (Project Managers), who were second-year students of the Master of Translation (MT) track, first posted a recruitment announcement online in late October 2018 to all first-year MT students. They invited anyone interested in joining to submit a resume within a five-day window (from October 20 to October 25). There were no requirements regarding the format or content of the resumes, and there were no preliminary screenings conducted. The sole purpose was to provide the PMs with an estimate of applicants and assist in creating a recruitment schedule. By the application deadline, a total of 47 out of 60 MT students submitted their resumes.

On October 30, the PMs sent out the first group email informing them of a translation examination. The instructions were well-organized, with crucial information highlighted in yellow in the email. In the attachment was a Microsoft Word

DOI: 10.4324/9781003542469-6

Table 6.1 Important dates in the observed cycle

Gaining access	
Oct. 30–Nov. 7, 2018	Two examinations held for translation stream students
Nov. 14–26, 2018	Teacher reviser and old members grading exam papers
Nov. 17–23, 2018	Two examinations held for interpreting stream students
November 28, 2018	Recruitment results announced
Orientation & on-boarding	
November 29, 2018	Orientation ceremony held for the new recruits
December 20, 2018	First two training exercises sent through email
January 27, 2019	UNIA translation exercise sent through email
Working alongside old-timers	
December 26, 2018	New members starting to proofread translations of old members in real tasks
Feb. 24-March 2, 2019	New members starting to work as terminologies and proofreaders for older members
Making fledging steps	
March 13–May 15, 2019	New members translating real tasks with the old PMs managing the team
Becoming formal members and selection of new leadership	
April 13–16, 2019	Membership status assessment of the new members
April 21, 2019	Interviews held for those interested in running for PMs
April 22–26, 2019	Making votes for the new PMs
May 15, 2019	New PMs announced
Moving to the center of production	
May 16, 2019–April 3, 2020	New members translating tasks with new PMs managing the team
Taking in new members from next year of class	
November 1, 2019	Two examinations held for all new applicants from next year of class
November 14–26, 2019	Teacher reviser and members grading exam papers
November 28, 2018	Recruitment results announced
Training new members from next year of class	
December 6, 2019	Networking & Orientation for new recruits from next year of class
January 6, 2020	First training exercise sent through email
February 9, 2020	The second training exercise sent through email

document containing a complete English article (1,241 words) from the UN *African Renewal* magazine, with the article's internet link provided on top. Applicants were instructed to translate four consecutive marked-out paragraphs (233 words) instead of the whole article within a three-day timeframe. They were allowed to use any tools and resources they deemed appropriate but were required to submit their translations in Word format while adhering to specific formatting rules and the submission deadline. They were also reminded to consult the United Nations Multilingual Terminology Database (UNTERM) for terminology and other UN-related websites for background information.

The second examination, sent by email on November 3, 2018, assessed applicants' revision competence. It included eight excerpts from real tasks recently completed by formal members. Each excerpt was presented in both its original English text (averaging 200 words each) and its Chinese translation, with intentional errors introduced into the translations. These errors, referred to as "traps," encompassed a wide range of issues, such as mathematical errors, spelling mistakes, punctuation errors, inconsistent terminology, omissions, additions, and even unconventional mistakes like the misplacement of tags and hyperlinks. As the PMs revealed in the interview, these mistakes were not randomly generated but were actual errors made by formal team members. Applicants were not required to correct these errors but were expected to identify and explain them using the comment function in Word. From the perspective of the PMs, those who demonstrated a sharp eye for mistakes and inaccuracies were ideal candidates to help improve consistency and productivity.

As the two examinations came to an end in mid-November, all formal members from the 2017 class, including the teacher reviser and the program head, gathered for an in-person meeting. During this meeting, they conducted a comprehensive review of recent tasks and typical mistakes. They collectively decided to introduce peer-reviewing into their workflow and replace the use of Microsoft Word with Yicat, a cloud-based collaborative tool, for translations. The PMs also briefed the teacher reviser and the program head on the recruitment plan they made for the 2018 class. They also clarified how responsibilities would be distributed among the team for grading applicants' revision exam papers.

While discussing these matters, a new issue emerged. Over the past few years, students in the Master of Interpretation (MI) track have been expressing their desire for participation opportunities. In response to feedback from past graduates and recognizing the need to equip future interpreters and translators with a more versatile skillset for the job market, all participants unanimously agreed to open opportunities for first-year interpreting students starting from 2018. As a result, in the following week, the same two examinations were repeated to accommodate new interpreting students.

By the end of the two rounds of examinations, 42 out of the 47 translation students and eight out of the 27 interpreting students submitted their exam papers via email. All the translation papers were sent to the teacher reviser for grading. He employed a five-level letter-based system of "A," "A−," "B+," "B," and "B−" to evaluate the overall fluency and accuracy of each translation.

The formal student members, on the other hand, took charge of the grading of the revision exam. Each of the 15 current members was assigned 3–4 revision papers along with an assessment guideline and a reference answer provided by the PMs. Points were allocated for correctly identified and explained errors, with a maximum of five points for accurately identified errors. Fewer points were given for errors that were identified but not analyzed correctly. Furthermore, each student member was required to provide feedback for each item to justify their grading decisions.

The three PMs then collected all the graded papers and conducted a thorough review to ensure that the scores were accurately calculated. To determine the total score, the PMs initially converted the letter ratings into percentage grades (A: 90; A-: 85; B+: 80; B: 70; B-: 60). Subsequently, they multiplied these grades by their respective weights, assigning a 60% weight to translation and a 40% weight to revision.

On November 27, the recruitment results, along with each graded examination paper, were privately emailed to applicants. They were given a one-day window to contest the results if they identified any grading or scoring errors.

Finally, the top 22 highest-scoring applicants, with 19 from the MT track and three from the MI track, were announced by group email as the new selections for the year.

The DGC project's approach to recruiting new members highlights several noteworthy aspects. To begin with, as is revealed in interviews with the PMs, the reason that recruitment only opens to the first-year students, rather than the students from other years of class, is that the training of new members lasts half a year. Allowing second-year students to join would mean that those recruited might not have the opportunity to work independently before graduating.

Moreover, the recruitment practices—including the tone, format, and instructions of emails and the design of the two exams—were not created by the current three PMs. These practices date back to 2016 when the project's founding members began experimenting with recruitment content, exam scheduling, design, and evaluation criteria. Over the years, these practices have been refined and passed down through successive cycles of PMs, creating a deep-rooted cultural heritage within the team. This established tradition continues irrespective of the individuals currently leading it. By inheriting these well-established procedures, new members have come to appreciate their effectiveness and actively contribute to their evolution.

Thirdly, while it is common sense to use aptitude tests for enrolling new members, it is crucial to ensure these tests are designed effectively to identify prospective candidates. Surprisingly, there have been few studies assessing the effectiveness of these exams in predicting the performance of new members (Shang, Russo, and Chabasse 2023). Lafeber (2012) sheds some light on translation recruitment practices within international governmental organizations (IGOs). She suggests that not all aspects of translation competence hold the same weight within IGO translation roles. Some competencies are more vital than others, and others are frequently lacking among new recruits. Lafeber compiled a list of forty different skills and knowledge areas and sent it out to translators, revisors, and heads of IGO translation services. The first questionnaire asked them to rate the impact of various skills and knowledge types on translation effectiveness, while the second sought their opinions on the frequency with which new recruits lacked these competencies. By correlating the findings from both questionnaires, she categorized the 40 competencies into four types: highly impactful but seldom neglected, highly impactful but frequently neglected, less impactful but rarely neglected, and less impactful but often neglected. Her conclusion emphasizes that IGOs, when designing recruitment tests, should not only prioritize the most important competencies but also consider those that are currently insufficiently represented.

Interestingly, the DGC project's recruitment design seems to align with Lafeber's recommendations. While the translation examination can provide insights into a

Table 6.2 Exam scores of the top 22 applicants. Provided by the DGC project, with participant names deleted for anonymity

Ranking	Name	Major	Translation score	Weighted Trans score	Revision score	Final score
1		MT	A	90	284	168
2		MT	B+	80	277	159
3		MT	B	70	265	148
4		MI	B	70	258	145
5		MT	A	90	227	145
6		MI	B+	80	232	141
7		MT	A-	85	221	139
8		MT	A-	85	220	139
9		MT	A-	85	218	138
10		MT	B	70	238	137
11		MT	B+	80	223	137
12		MT	B+	80	222	137
13		MI	A-	85	211	135
14		MT	B+	80	217	135
15		MT	A	90	200	134
16		MT	B+	80	210	132
17		MT	B	70	224	132
18		MT	A-	85	201	131
19		MT	B	70	223	131
20		MT	B-	60	222	125
21		MT	B+	80	192	125
22		MT	B+	80	191	124
SD				6.8		53.9

candidate's overall translation competence, it should not be relied upon exclusively to predict their skillset. It appears that the revision competence is more precise in identifying specific traits that are highly valued within our community and is lacking. This distinction is further reflected in the distribution of scores between the two exams. In the translation exam, the teacher reviser only specified five bands, and candidates' scores tend to cluster around "B+" and "B" (Standard deviation= 6.8). In contrast, the scores for the revision examinations exhibit a broader spread (Standard deviation=53.9), suggesting that the latter is more effective in screening out preferred candidates (see Table 6.2).

Considering that all applicants admitted in the first questionnaire were exposed to the DGC material for the first time, the only plausible explanation is that some candidates put in more thorough preparation and demonstrated greater proficiency in analyzing the text and validating their queries with reliable sources.

The fourth aspect that stands out is the remarkable efficiency and collaboration among team members. To begin with, they are dedicated to ensuring a recruitment process that is both fair and transparent, extending opportunities to all first-year students. What sets their approach apart is their commitment to impartiality; candidates are chosen solely based on their examination results, without any influence from program providers, teacher reviewers, or current PMs. Moreover, the examination materials are drawn from the same authentic texts that the existing members have translated. There is a rigorous adherence to strict formatting and file-naming conventions for exam submissions.

In terms of grading, the involvement of all current members is a key feature. Not only do they assess the exam papers, but they also engage in a meaningful dialogue with applicants through the comment function in Word, even though they have never met each other. This approach ensures that everyone has a stake in identifying and welcoming the most promising students into the team. Each member, like a cog in a well-oiled machine, contributes in their unique way to the cohesive image of the team, making an impression on newcomers right from the start.

In an unstructured interview with the PMs of the 2017 class, we asked if they had ever identified any deficiencies in the recruitment practice. Given that two-thirds of the first-year applicants were screened out, we were wondering whether they believed the exams were a reliable indicator of applicants' translation competence. They admitted that it was indeed difficult to decide on the cutoff line of selection, which is why they increased the quota from 20, used a year ago when they were taken in, to 22 students. The weight they gave to the two exams—60% for the translation test and 40% for the revision test—did influence the final score, but as the previous PMs set them, they decided to keep the proportion unchanged. As to the reliability of the admission, they believed the exams only reflected the applicants' incipient competence toward the domain represented by the DGC, and there was no point in assessing their translation competence with other text types. Their conviction in the efficacy of the exams points back to Wenger's observation that "domain" is a shared identity that distinguishes a community from other structures.

6.1.2 Participants' prior knowledge and initial motivation

Given the competitive nature of the recruitment process, we were intrigued by the motivation of applicants and the amount of preparation they had made. From the first questionnaire distributed to the 22 recruits in mid-December 2018, which all of them answered, certain aspects of their prior knowledge stood out:

- 20 had recently graduated from their undergraduate programs and had not yet had any formal employment experience.
- Among the recruits, four held undergraduate degrees in translation, 12 had undergraduate degrees in English, and six were from non-language-related majors.
- Nine students lacked any prior experience in translation projects, while the remaining recruits had varying degrees of experience, whether through freelance work with translation agencies or participation in project-based learning (PjBL) facilitated by their translation trainers.
- 19 Recruits admitted to never having received any form of training in project management.

- When it came to formal instruction in translation technology, 16 recruits had not received any, while the remaining six had acquired fundamental training in mainstream translation tools.
- Interestingly, exactly half of our recruits used translation tools as an integral part of their translation process, while the other half opted for a more traditional approach, foregoing the use of any translation technology.

It's evident that these individuals, as recent college graduates, shared a similar background. They lacked significant experience in working as a technology-enabled team and were relatively new to the translation workflow commonly used in the industry. Their prior translation experience primarily stemmed from formal education in college, with only a few having freelanced for translation agencies.

Regarding their motivation for participating in the DGC project, the top five reasons they cited were as follows:

- A strong desire to enhance their translation skills (90.91%).
- The opportunity to gain experience in handling real translation projects (81.82%).
- The aspiration to improve their translation project management abilities (72.73%).
- The possibility of eventually interning at the UN (63.64%).
- The aim to refine their revision skills (63.64%).

Vallerand (1997) distinguishes between intrinsic and extrinsic motivation, where intrinsic motivation involves behavior driven by the desire to learn, achieve, and experience stimulation for its own sake. Extrinsic motivation, on the other hand, is driven by the pursuit of rewards or the avoidance of punishment.

Based on these criteria, it is apparent that these recruits were predominantly intrinsically motivated. They were driven by a genuine desire to enter this new field, learn, and potentially intern at the UN, rather than simply fulfilling internship requirements for their degrees. Despite their limited knowledge of what lied ahead, aside from fragmentary information gleaned from media reports and conversations with upperclassmen, they firmly believed that joining the DGC project would significantly enhance their learning experience at GIIT, expose them to real-world tasks, and provide them with invaluable insights into the translation practices of the UN.

In terms of the type of preparations they have made, 59% admitted consulting parallel texts found on UN websites, 54.55% used internet resources to build language and background knowledge, 27% read news reports of the DGC project, 27.27% even asked their contacts of the 2017 class for tips in translating the DGC materials. Curiously, one recruit claimed having never made any sort of preparations for the two exams, which we found very unlikely because all the resources were clearly listed in the examination instructions email.

To have an idea how the DGC project integrates with the formal curriculum, we examined the curriculum documents of the 2018 class (see Table 6.3 and

Table 6.3 GIIT curriculum plan for MT students (2018–2020)

	Autumn Semester	Spring Semester
Year 1	Translation I (6) Translation I (3) Interpreting I (3) Chinese Culture (2)	Translation II (6) Intro to Translation II (3) Interpreting II (3) Intro to Economics/Law (2)
Year 2	Business Translation (3) Literary Translation I (3) Legal Translation (3) Chinese Translation Theories (2) Project Management (2)	Terminology and Post-editing (3) Literary Translation II (3) Legal Translation (3) Western Translation Theories (2) Academic writing (2)

Table 6.4 GIIT curriculum plan for MT students (2018–2020)

	Autumn Semester	Spring Semester
Year 1	English-Chinese Interpreting (3) Chinese-English Interpreting (3) Translation I (3) Chinese Culture (2)	Consecutive Interpreting II (6) Document Translation for the UN (3) Translation II (3) Intro to Economics/Law (2)
Year 2	Business Interpreting (3) Sight Interpreting (3) Conference Management (3) Computer-assisted Interpreting (3) Translation Theories (2)	Consecutive Interpreting (6) Intro to Simultaneous Interpreting (3) Academic writing (2)

Table 6.4) and sat in on a few of their translation classes. For the MT track, first year students would receive 7.5 class hours of translation training every week, during which time they would be introduced to various subject matter and text genres. While the UN translation is indeed covered in the first year, according to the interviews with GIIT trainers, the syllabus focuses on formal UN conference documents and agreements, rather than the website content used for general communication. In the second year, students can choose to specialize in legal translation, literature translation, business translation and project management. Again, there is no course specifically targeted on the UN website content translation. For the MI track, students have one 2.5 class hours of mandatory translation course in the first semester of their first year, followed by an elective course in the second semester on UN document translation. Overall, the domain of the DGC project is not covered by their formal curriculum.

Thus, we have reason to believe that any learning derived from the DGC project does not overlap with the formal curriculum but complements it. According to Sawyer (2004), the term "hidden curriculum" encompasses the unspoken lessons, values, and behaviors that students acquire in school, which are not part of the formal academic curriculum. It encompasses the social, cultural, and moral aspects of education that students absorb through their interactions with teachers and peers, the school environment, and its organizational structure. In contrast, the "open curriculum" refers to the officially designed educational content and objectives, including subjects, courses, textbooks, and documented learning goals.

These two concepts are interconnected because both significantly impact a student's overall education. Sawyer (2004, 41–43) goes on to explain that a formal curriculum plan merely represents an ideal and not the curriculum as it is experienced in practice. In his words, "The only curriculum that truly exists for the learner is the curriculum as it is experienced," and this curriculum, in turn, shapes the spirit of the institution.

The DGC project is a result of deliberate institutional design and the involvement of the United Nations DGC. It is operated and managed by each year's student participants, with full support from the program administrator. It constitutes a "hidden" curriculum for students, where participants must exercise their agency to maximize their learning experience. Furthermore, it complements the goals of the open curriculum by molding students' values, attitudes, and behaviors as they function as semi-professionals for international organizations.

6.2 On-boarding new members

6.2.1 Initiation to the community

The examinations have provided access to the community; however, individuals are still positioned on the periphery (Lave and Wenger 1991). They require further training to acquire both the explicit and tacit knowledge held by the team.

Following the announcement of the recruitment results, an orientation session was conducted on November 29, 2018, with the aim of making new members feel welcome, appreciated, and facilitating their smooth transition into this new experience. The orientation brought together all existing members, new recruits, the teacher reviser and the head of the program. The ceremony was led by the three PMs from the 2017 class. One of them began by providing a brief overview of the project's history, traditions, and significant publications that the team had translated. This was followed by an explanation of the three primary types of texts that the team handled, as outlined in Table 6.5.

The first type of text involves translating various multimedia content that the DGC publishes on its website, including international day/week observances, United Nations Academic Impact (UNIA) articles, UN in pictures, and UN senior officials' bios. These tasks cover a wide range of topics and vary in length from over 100 words to up to 2,000 words. They represent the most frequent type of tasks, but they are not dispatched on a fixed schedule and often require quick turnaround (one or two days).

The second type of task entails translating subtitles for *United Nations in Action* (UNIA), a series of 3-minute short documentaries broadcast on the UN website that

Table 6.5 Types of DGC texts in need of translation

Website Content	International day observances
	UNAI (United Nations Academic Impact) web content
	UN in pictures
	UN senior official bios
	Thematic webpages and their updates
UNIA	Script for the documentary series
UN Chronicle	A quarterly paper-based publication; switching to fulling online issue in 2020

take a behind-the-scenes look at UN news. These assignments are typically sent out in batches of two or three episodes per month, with a turnaround time of three to five days. Each episode is 300–600 words.

The final type of text involves translating the *UN Chronicle*, a quarterly paper-based publication that features in-depth articles contributed by the UN officials, international experts, policymakers, NGO representatives, and civil society representatives. Each issue includes approximately a dozen articles, each ranging from 1,000 to 2,000 words. Occasionally, the quarterly issue is replaced by a special double issue, which is released every six months[1].

The PMs then briefly described the workflow of each type of task. For the first two types, all the formal members were put on a weekly rotating schedule, with one PM and four translators on each shift of duty. A typical workflow started with the PM on duty checking of the Teambition[2] for any incoming tasks regularly throughout a day. She would then announce the task on QQ and wait for the four translators on duty to take up the work as translator(s) and peer-reviewer(s). The translators assigned must produce a peer reviewed version to the teacher-reviser for revision. They also need to validate the teacher's feedback, format the translation, and send it to the PM for a final proofreading. For the *UN Chronicle*, since it came out every four to six months, the whole team was brought on board. They paired up to translate as well as to proofread each other's work. Usually, it took a month to complete the translation of an entire issue.

Using the terms that had appeared in revision examination as an example, the PMs then introduced several ways for the translators to locate and verify terminologies with the help of online resources. Specifically, the UNTERM, Linguee and an inhouse style guide developed by the previous members were listed as the most important self-scaffolds. UNTERM is a public accessible database of officially approved UN terminologies in its six official languages. Linguee is an online bilingual concordance tool. It searches the internet for appropriate bilingual texts and divides them into parallel sentences, which makes it more like a segmented corpus and a translation aid. As the PMs pointed out, the best thing about the first two resources was that the users could compare and see the sources of the listed examples and decide whether to trust their quality. The style guide was originally compiled by the founding members, but it has been added and refined in the subsequent cycles to become a 28-page booklet. It listed out all the formatting rules members must follow. In the words of the three PMs, it was the most valuable "asset" of the team.

The teacher reviser then gave a live demonstration on how to use Yicat, a collaborative cloud-based translation tool, to machine translate the article used in the examination and post-edit it. He explained sentence by sentence the most common types of mistakes the applicants have made and expressed clear expectation for every new member to use Yicat. Finally, the new members and all the 2017 class members were introduced to each other and paired up, so that help was around should any of them encounter difficulties. After the meeting, the PMs set up a new chat group on QQ for the new members and sent them the style guide, the workflow chart, and an Excel glossary file the team had accumulated to assist their self-learning.

The orientation provided these new members with a comprehensive insight into various aspects of our work. In the first questionnaire, they all indicated having gained a basic understanding of the team's practices, familiarized themselves with the range of tools and resources available, and had the opportunity to network with both seasoned and fellow new members. Additionally, it served as a rapid immersion into the team's values and culture.

During the orientation, the PMs and the teacher reviser highlighted what they believed to be the most crucial skills and knowledge areas. This encouraged the new members to identify gaps in their own expertise and skills, enabling them to establish individualized learning goals. It was explicitly emphasized that passing the recruitment examination did not guarantee automatic formal membership. An assessment scheduled for five months later would determine which members would continue.

When we asked these new members about their key takeaways from the orientation, 18 of them expressed satisfaction that it had addressed their questions regarding the recruitment examination. Interestingly, 16 of them admitted they had never used Yicat, but they all expressed a clear intention to make the most of their learning opportunities through it.

Regarding the shortcomings of the orientation, one student highlighted a valuable point during our interview. Since the highest-performing students would have the opportunity to work as interns at the UN, she suggested that the PMs provide information on the pathway to securing such internships and any associated benefits. While this wasn't her primary motivation, she believed that transparency on this front would be beneficial.

For a successful orientation, it is essential to create an informed membership. This means ensuring that new members understand not only the community's structure, work content, and procedures, but also their rights, privileges, and responsibilities. Such comprehensive knowledge not only contributes to the success of the orientation but also help retain new recruits who can make meaningful contributions to the project.

6.2.2 Decontextualized training exercises

Training and exercises play a crucial role in preparing newcomers for real-world tasks. While the 15 official members of the 2017 class were responsible for translating DGC tasks from December 2018 to January 2019, the new recruits underwent three distinct training exercises.

The first training task, sent on December 20, 2018, tasked them with aligning the 56 tasks that the 2017 class members had completed between July and December 2018 into translation memory. Each new member was assigned two to three tasks. Their objective was to first locate the official published texts for these tasks, carefully analyze the differences between the published version and the version the team submitted to the DGC, and then use an alignment tool to match the source and published translations segment by segment, ultimately consolidating them into a single ".tmx" file. All the translation memory (TM) files collected in this process would be imported into Yicat, serving as the team's shared translation memory.

According to the teacher-reviser and the PMs, this training task served a twofold purpose. Firstly, it aimed to familiarize new members with the alignment function of Yicat. Secondly, it contributed to the establishment of a reusable translation asset. If all translations were digitized, organized, and aligned, they would become more accessible and easily repurposed, thereby promoting consistency and scalability. Until this point, the DGC project did maintain a centralized term base in an Excel file. However, all translations that had previously been done in Word were in the hands of disparate translators, making centralized management and accessibility an issue. Occasionally, translators and revisers had to manually check the Excel file, which was time-consuming. As the team prepared to transition to this online, cloud-based Yicat tool, their top priority was to harness the existing content for greater efficiency gains, creating a digital legacy that can be readily reused and managed (Wenger-Trayner and Wenger-Trayner 2015).

In the second training task, all recruits were given translations made by previous members, along with their corresponding teacher-revised versions, but were not told which was which. They needed to analyze the two versions and report their findings in a reflective report. This training exercise was designed by the teacher-reviser, who found that the mistakes made by the previous members were typical and could highlight common problems. Judging by the reports the new members submitted, there were indeed issues with incorrect terminology and collocations. These mistakes could have been easily avoided if the original translators had spent more time researching and validating their translation choices using resources like UNTERM and Linguee. Comparing different versions of the same text helped new members understand that working as a team means using the same terminology, the same phrasing, and following the same style guide, rather than being overly literal with the source text and sticking to individual styles.

The third training task, given on January 27, 2019, asked new recruits to translate a UNIA video. The decision to assign this task was guided by the distinct nature of UNIA content in comparison to other text-based tasks. UNIA content presents a unique challenge, as not every word in the text requires translation. Translators must carefully watch the video and ensure that their Chinese translations do not exceed the word limit of the original English audio. To assist these new members in adapting to this specialized style, the PMs also provided them with bilingual translations of three previous episodes as self-learning resources.

During this period, the training content was collaboratively determined by the PMs in consultation with the teacher reviser. While the learning materials used were authentic, their delivery was digitized, personalized, and somewhat disconnected from real-world production, allowing learners to progress at their own pace. The objective was not to rush new members into producing high-quality translations quickly, but rather to cultivate their sensitivity to the textual conventions specific to DGC tasks and instill the habit of consulting resources like Lingue, UNTERM, and the style guide for consistent terminology and style usage.

With the explicit instructions provided for each training task, new members were encouraged to take personal initiative to enhance their learning experience. They could ask the more experienced formal members they were paired with for help if they encountered difficulties. However, no formal assessment or feedback was given on the reflective reports, translation memory, or video translations submitted by the new members. While all members completed their assigned tasks, assessing the level of effort expended proved challenging. This lack of feedback emerged as the primary concern among the new members in the interview and the questionnaire. For example, questions raised in their reflective reports remained unanswered, and the new members were uncertain whether their UNIA translations met the team's quality standards. Many expressed a desire for opportunities to engage in practical work and collaborate with old members soon.

6.2.3 Working side by side with old members

In parallel with the three training exercises, to help the new members feel ownership of the real processes, the three PMs began to involve them in real tasks, starting with the proofreading and the terminological work.

In late December 2018, one PM announced on the chat group that new members would be integrated into the production as proofreaders for each real task. To ensure fairness, opportunities were offered on a first-come, first-served basis when tasks were posted on QQ. The PMs hoped that this training approach would help new members become more attuned to the team's online activities. The texts designated for proofreading had already undergone revision by the teacher reviser and reviewed by the translator themselves. As such, the primary role of the new members was to provide fresh perspectives on terminology consistency, punctuation, capitalization, spelling, and formatting issues. They were required to use Word's comment function to highlight any errors they identified and provided justifications. As DGC sent out four translation tasks in January of 2019, four corresponding proofreading tasks were requested. Altogether five new members participated in these exercises.

The other task that involved joint work was for the special double issue of the *UN Chronicle*, which was sent in mid-February of 2019[3]. There was a total of 18 articles in this double issue, including a foreword. It was decided that the translation was to be taken up by 15 old members, each translating on average 2,000 words and reviewing the same amount of another member, but terminology checking and proofreading were delegated to the new members. The first seven new members that responded to the PM's post were recruited as terminology controller.

The first step in translating the *UN Chronicle* was to create a term list within two days based on the topic covered by the issue. The team followed a simple four-step approach in terminology management (See Table 6.6).

Here, we began to see that negotiation of understanding was deliberately encouraged between the new members and the more competent members with Shimo, a cloud-based office software. Shimo allowed members to share, edit, and track all changes in the same online interface, providing a foundation for meaningful dialogue. For example, one entry recorded different Chinese terms—"群岛国家," "岛屿国家," and "岛屿和群岛国家"—proposed for the same English term "archipelago nations." The three contributors, including a new member, each presented compelling arguments in support of their choices and attempted to distinguish it from similar concepts like "island nation." This shows that all participants contribute valuable knowledge derived from their personal backgrounds, regardless of their expertise levels. It also demonstrates that for the new members, engaging with recognized experts legitimizes learning and adds value from the perspective of the apprentice (Lave and Wenger 1991).

After the terminology work was completed, each translator was given one week to finish their own translation and review the translation of another team member. They would then send their translation directly to the teacher through the chat group. The teacher reviser made improvements to the text using Word's "track changes" feature. Occasionally, he would pose questions to the translators if further clarification or evidence was needed.

Once the teacher reviser finished reviewing a piece, he would return it to the chat group. The original translator would download the revised version, carefully study all the revisions, and then post any questions they had for the teacher reviser until all inquiries were resolved. Subsequently, the translators would send a clean

Table 6.6 Terminology management steps in DGC project

Extraction	The translators (old members) extract terms (including high frequency phrases) from his/her assigned article and record entries in the online document
Translation	The translators (old members) translate the extracted terms and adds the sources they have consulted beside each entry
Review	The translators (old members) review each other's entries and write down their comment; non-relevant terms and the repetitive terms are removed
Approval	The seven members log onto the online document, review their assigned entries and write down their comment
Final approval	The PMs log onto the online document, give the final decision and export the terms to share with all members

copy of their work to their assigned new team member for a fresh review. When proofreading, the new members were reminded to start by reading through the entire content and to pay close attention to formatting errors, numerical errors, mistranslations, omissions, and typos, including the use of quotation marks. The focus was on details without becoming overly concerned with phrasing issues. When making annotations, they had to provide reasons and evidence from authoritative websites. If they wished to suggest changes, they had to provide sufficient justification to the original translators, who would then decide whether to accept the suggestions.

Finally, the translator sent back a finalized version to the PMs, who would prepare the translations for delivery. The entire process took approximately one month to complete, and the workflow with deadlines for each stage is outlined in Table 6.7.

This marked the first and only time when both the recruits from the 2018 class and the more seasoned members from the 2017 class participated in a joint productive endeavor. As highlighted by Lave and Wenger in their observations, "A newcomer's tasks tend to be positioned at the ends of branches of work processes, rather than in the middle of linked work segments" (ibid. 1991, 110). These tasks tend to be brief and straightforward, with minimal consequences for errors, and the apprentices carry relatively little overall responsibility for the activity. When we examine the workflow chart, we can see that the tasks assigned to the new members (shaded in gray in Table 6.7) indeed occupied positions at the initial and concluding stages of the workflow. While the experienced members executed the predominant practices, the newcomers closely observed their interactions and began to grasp how discussions between the teacher-reviser and the translators influenced the evolving product. They also gained an appreciation for the team's commitment to thorough double-checking and mutual monitoring, all in pursuit of achieving the highest quality outcomes.

It should be noted that although members had decided to switch to Yicat at the plenary meeting held in mid-November of 2018, the only tool that had been used during this period was still the traditional desktop software Word. The workflow was rather linear, with the PMs coordinating various activities in each task. The new recruits, therefore, had no chance to train and test their skills of Yicat in training.

6.2.4 New members' reflections on training

Training cannot be considered complete without understanding how new members assess its effectiveness. In early March 2019, we distributed the second anonymous questionnaire, and 18 participants provided their feedback, allowing us to gain insights into their reflections. We began by asking them to share their top three takeaways from the training. Their key impression was a renewed appreciation for the significance of verifying information from reliable sources when dealing with terminologies and phrases. They also highlighted the pressure of meeting deadlines associated with each task and emphasized the importance of adhering to the workflow.

Table 6.7 DGC project workflow in translating *UN Chronicle*

Deadline	Translators (15 old members, including 3 PMs)	Terminologists (7 new members)	PMs of the 2017 class	Proofreaders (22 new members)	Teacher reviser
Feb. 15–16	Translators extract the terms and write the original term, its Chinese translation and the documentation source in a collaborative online documentation software. Then they check each other's entries and provide feedback as the first line of the check				
Feb. 18–19		Terminologists review entries submitted by the translators and write down their opinion as the second line of check. In case they do not agree with the submitted term, they have to write down their version and provide justification.			
Feb. 20	Translators make a decision in response to the peer reviewer's and terminologists feedback		PMs finalize term list and export it and share it with each translator and the teacher reviser		
Feb. 21–26	Translators complete the translation of his/her assigned article in MS Word				

Feb. 27–28	Translators peer review the translations of another member		
Mar. 1–9	Translators incorporate the changes made by their peer reviewer and send their translations to the PM by email	The lead PM collects all the translations and send all translations to the teacher reviser in a compressed file by email	The teacher reviser revise all translations using the track-change functions in Word. He would also pose questions on QQ for clarifications The teacher reviser answer translator's queries on QQ
	Translators receive revised translations, decide whether to incorporate the change and pose their queries to the teacher reviser on QQ		
Mar. 10–11	Translators send the revised version to the proofreader for a third review through private email	Proofreaders write down in the comment inconsistencies and send the proofread version to the translator by private email	
Mar. 12	Translators decide whether to incorporate the change and send to the lead PM a finalized version by email	One PM collects all finalized translations and send it in a compressed file to the DGC via Teambition	

Source: Image created by the author based on original Chinese workflow chart made by the DGC project.

When asked about the comparison between their training and the learning they gained from the formal curriculum, the prominent response mentioned was "teamwork." Collaborating with a partner allowed them to view things from a fresh perspective, and through discussions, they were able to elevate the quality of their translations. It was noted that teamwork fostered a sense of urgency in completing tasks, as opposed to working at their own pace.

Another significant difference revolved around the team's emphasis on accuracy and consistency. New members were required to adhere to specific research protocols and follow precise style guidelines and standards. This approach contrasted sharply with their formal curriculum, which encouraged students to break free from the constraints of language and foster creativity in translation. Some new members even viewed this contrast as a limitation on their creative freedom.

Nevertheless, all of them supported or strongly appreciated the exposure to authentic PjBL offered by the DGC project. Some of them had even started to take part in other internship translation projects that were underway at GIIT. Compared with their initial sense of motivation, toward the end of training, six students (22.22%) said they retained the same level of interest; eight (44.44%) found themselves more engaged, and four (33.33%) felt they had become significantly more motivated. The biggest factors holding their interest in check included a lack of opportunity for real practice and a lack of freedom in translation, although all of them still expressed a clear intention to stay in the project. When asked if any of them had plans to run for the PM position, seven indicated a clear interest, six ruled it out directly and five remained undecided.

Given that all of them had observed the artifact-mediated discourse between the teacher reviser and the older members on QQ, we asked them how they perceived the difference between the teacher reviser's feedback and those made by trainers of their formal curriculum. One third students mentioned that the feedback in the project was more prompt, detail-oriented, personalized, compared with three who didn't see any obvious difference. Half of the team appreciated the chance to talk with the teacher reviser immediately in case they didn't understand his revisions. In terms of the importance of peer feedback, all of them agreed or strongly agreed that it was crucial for members to peer review each other's work both before and after the teacher's revision because they believed the teacher reviser and the student members directed attention to different areas. The teacher focused more on whether the original understanding of the source text was correct, whereas the students focused more on whether the translations read naturally.

In terms of the effectiveness of each training task, 11 students perceived all training tasks equally beneficial because they targeted different areas; six students felt that working together with old members in translating the *UN Chronicle* was most useful; only one student regarded proofreading the UN website content beneficial. All of them agreed that the training had pushed them to consult the style guide frequently.

When asked why some of them did not sign up to be the terminologists or the proofreader in the real training tasks, 11 students regretted having not checked out the task announcement posts more promptly; six did see the posts, but due to other commitments at hand, they could not afford the time. Only one student felt he/she was not ready to take on the task. 15 Members agree or strongly agree that compared with before, the way each task was assigned made them more attentive to updates on the chat group.

As to the amount of attention directed toward the terminological work, all of them admitted having logged onto Shimo to check the terminologies, but most only read the terminologies related to their assigned articles; only one student read them all. Similarly, in terms of the attention given to the revisions and discussions online, six students only downloaded the article they were to proofread; 11 downloaded all the teacher-revised articles but only read their assigned articles. Some read every single post on the chat group, some only read the posts related to their assigned article, and four read posts related to the assigned article and the articles containing the terminologies.

Central to the Community of Practice (CoP) is the concept of "legitimate peripheral participation." Lave and Wenger (1991) use this term to describe the process newcomers must experience before becoming full members of a community. Novices start by being mentored by more experienced members. However, in the DGC project, we find that in real production, old members focused more on the completion of their allotted tasks and that they would not go out of their way to provide training. New members must demonstrate initiative, autonomy, and motivation to learn. The second anonymous questionnaire revealed that at this stage, while all gained a preliminary understanding of the workflow and the importance of uniformity, they also started to show varying levels of engagement and motivation. Compared with the decontextualized training tasks, the understanding they gained from working with the mature members was dominated by bilateral private communication and was hard to assess.

6.3 Taking fledging steps

With the completion of the translation of the final paper-based edition of the *UN Chronicle* in early March 2019, the official members of the 2017 class officially retired from the project. However, the three PMs continued to take weekly turns leading the team. Like their predecessors, they would wait till May when new leaders were selected. This marked a shift in the learning process for the new members of the 2018 class. While in the previous stage, they had primarily learned by assisting the old members with peripheral tasks, they were now able to learn through hands-on experience with real tasks.

Initially, there had been a rotating schedule for the formal members of the 2017 class when it came to translating website content. However, the three PMs decided not to implement a similar schedule for the new members right away. They wanted to assess the level of engagement among the newcomers. Tasks were still given to whoever signed up after they were posted online. Implicitly, the new members understood that their membership would soon be evaluated. They needed to seize the opportunities to make a positive impact.

Between March 12 and May 15, 2019, a total of 25 tasks, all related to the website content, were sent for translation. These tasks amounted to a total of 29,908 English words. The biggest was the translation of a thematic webpage page commemorating the 25th anniversary of the 1994 genocide in Rwanda, which consisted of 14,038 words and was presented in an Excel table format. On the other end of the spectrum, the smallest task involved only 317 words. Figure 6.1 shows the frequencies and types of tasks requested during this time.

Here, we began to see the newcomers organize group discussions on QQ just like the previous members did. Figure 6.2 presents a breakdown of the number of posts created by each task. For instance, the task focusing on the Rwanda genocide generated the highest number of posts at 354. This was primarily because it involved 17 members, making coordination challenging. Additionally, with so many translators working on Yicat together, the tool unexpectedly crashed, causing some previously unsaved translated text to disappear in the middle of production. Consequently, the team had to invest a significant amount of time in discussing solutions to the problem.

6.3.1 Embracing a new workflow

A milestone change took place at the beginning of this stage. Starting from the second task, since the new members took over, at the requirement of the teacher reviser, the team made a complete switch to Yicat in routine practice. The new workflow thus flowed in the following way:

- The PM on duty checks Teambition multiple times throughout a day to see if there are any incoming assignments.
- The PM analyzes specific requirements of each task, prepares and maintains the project log by noting down the name of task, the deadline, workload, and features.
- The PM posts the task on the chat group and waits for translators to take up the task.
- The rest of the student members take up the role the roles of translator and peer reviewer (in small tasks, two translators are assigned, with one working as a translator and the other as a peer-reviewer; in the bigger task, the text is split and with translators reviewing each other's work).
- The PM imports the text to be translated into Yicat and assigns the task to the translator and peer reviewer through email notifications.
- The student translators machine-translate their assigned texts with the help of TM and TB, post-edit the translation, and validate new terms as they go; at the same time, the PM monitors the project status and assists the translators if they experience technical glitches and seeks help from the teacher reviser or the outside technical support expert.
- The translator peer-reviews the translation on Yicat and alerts the teacher reviser once the whole text is peer-reviewed.
- The teacher reviser logs on Yicat, revises the whole translation and alerts the translators on QQ once his revision is completed.

The DGC project under the microscope 111

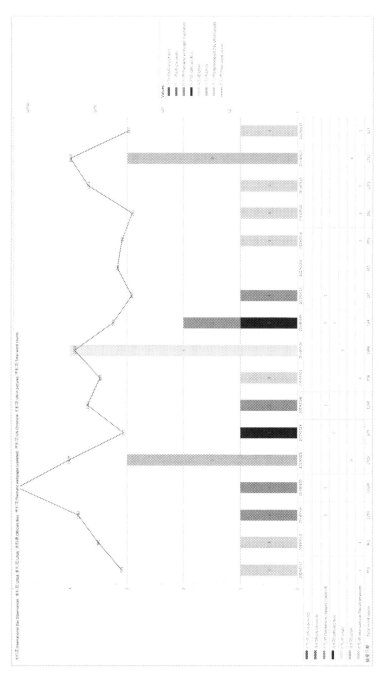

Figure 6.1 Types and volume of translation requested (March–May 2019).

Source: Image created by the author based on information provided by the DGC project.

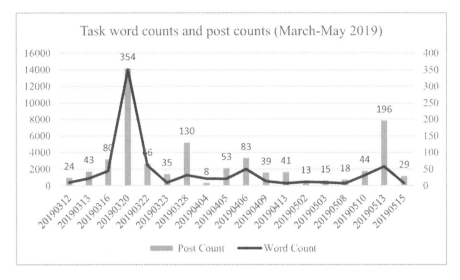

Figure 6.2 Posts generated per translation (March-May 2019).

Source: Image created by the author based on information provided by the DGC project.

- The translator logs on Yicat to study revisions and decide whether to accept them. They pose their queries to the teacher reviser online and engage in argumentative learning.
- The translator exports the revised translations into a bilingual Word document and proofreads the translation in compliance with the style guide.
- The translator sends the PM the proofread translation in a Word bilingual document and marks out all new and old terminologies.
- The PM performs a final quality check of a translation before sending it off in a bilingual Word document to DGC on Teambition.

Yicat brought immediate changes to the way translators worked with each other. In the past, old members had to wait for each other to complete and send back and forth multiple versions of the same documents on QQ to know what changes had been made. Now, the translator, the peer reviewer and the teacher reviser could not only work in the same interface but also work at the same time. Secondly, when translating using Word, the quality is purely dependent on a person's translation competence. Yicat has APIs that link to several machine translation engines, which means text can be pre-translated either by existing memory or machine-translated. The repetitive elements of the text are thus immediately translated. It also protects the translators from committing very simple mistakes, such as mathematical mistakes and omissions. Lastly, the team used to save all the terms in an Excel file after each task, but no TM for the website content. But now, with a cloud-based system, all linguistic assets are stored on a single centralized server of the cloud-based system, which makes them immediately accessible to all.

Through discussions with some members of previous cycles, we discovered that the team had previously used Software and Documentation Localization (SDL) Trados a computer-assisted translation (CAT) tool, and Icat, a lightweight tool integrated with Word. This revelation piqued our curiosity as to why the teacher reviser was advocating the use of Yicat in this cycle. When we put this question to the teacher-reviser, the simple answer was Yicat's features, including real-time monitoring throughout the process, its free nature, and the fact that there was no need to install it on personal computers or worry about compatibility issues.

Introducing new technologies that may not align with established practices can elicit varying reactions from participants. For instance, the three old PMs, likely due to their familiarity with working in Word, did not seem to share the same level of enthusiasm for Yicat as the teacher-reviser did. This contrast was evident in a post made by one of the PMs when addressing the team as they transitioned to Yicat.

E.g.:

PM: 你们想在哪里翻译，都可以。但是老师想要在平台上审校，所以你们只要确保在时间截点之前让平台上出现译文即可。初译和审校不设置硬性时间截点。所有工作在周三下午六点之前完成就可以啦。

(PM: You can translate using whatever tool you like, but the teacher wants to revising using Yicat, so just make sure that your translation appears on Yicat before the deadline. There is no preset time limit for the draft translation and peer-review, but you must complete these two steps by 6 pm on Wednesday afternoon.)[4]

This post, however, was read a couple of minutes later by the teacher reviser, to which he quickly replied:

Teacher reviser: 希望都在平台上做，以后省得专门做语料对齐。

(Teacher reviser: I hope everyone uses Yicat to produce draft translation. Doing so will automatically make our translation into TM and save effort.)

In the interview with the PMs from previous years, they revealed that the biggest disadvantage of Yicat was its formatting function. Although Yicat allowed the export of bilingually aligned text, the formatting issues were so significant that it took them longer to reformat the text than if they had translated it directly into Word from the start. As a result, they ended up manually exporting the revised translation segment by segment back to Word for delivery. However, out of respect, all new members followed the teacher's advice and used Yicat. Overall, they did not show as strong a resistance to the tool as the former PMs. This is partly because they were told to use Yicat right away and partly because they never had much experience translating DGC texts in Word anyway. As the second questionnaire showed, in terms of the time/effort they have invested in learning to use Yicat,

42.86 found Yicat very easy to use; 50% found it easy to use; the rest, 7.14%, reported no challenge. Nobody reported any difficulty.

As to the ways through which they learned the use of the tool, most (92.86%) said that they learned to use Yicat by exploring on their own through trial and error; half asked for help from their peers and from the PMs; 21.43 % asked for help from an old member they were paired with. There were also students who either sought help from trainers of their formal curriculum, attended school lectures given by Yicat staff, or watched Yicat online user tutorials. It remains to be seen what specific challenges they might encounter as they apply the tool to more tasks.

6.3.2 Scaffoldings in routine practice

Vygotsky (1978) defines scaffoldings as support given by a more competent partner to an individual to help him or her perform beyond the capability to reach the zone of proximal development. The cross-case review of sample studies in Chapter 3 demonstrates that scaffoldings may come from a variety of sources, including teachers, peers, invited experts, or self-scaffoldings through technologies and artifacts.

In the DGC project, expert scaffoldings mainly come from the teacher reviser's direct corrective feedback; self-scaffoldings are presented in the form of suggestions made by the machine translation (MT) or TM or from online resources such as Linguee and UNTERM. It is hard to specify what help they gained from their fellow collaborators if they chose to talk bilaterally, though, in the questionnaire, the majority (71.47%) believed that feedback from the teacher reviser, the PM and their fellow members was equally important, compared with 21.43% who perceived the PM and the teacher reviser as more important source of feedback. As for the benefits of peer reviewing each other's work, all believed that they could get the chance to improve their revision competence by arguing and defending their own views (92.86%), improve the quality of the translation through argumentation (78.57%), and focus on different things from teacher reviser (71.43%).

What particularly stood out at this stage is the number of scaffolding measures provided by the three PMs. Elena Dunne (2011, 278) believes "project managers can proactively engage in expert and reciprocal scaffolding to increase the efficiency of the learning process within the translation team." She identifies eight forms of PM scaffoldings, including (1) clear directions; (2) clarification of purpose; (3) keeping learners on task; (4) assessment to clarify expectations; (5) providing worthy sources; (6) reduction of uncertainty, surprise, and disappointment; (7) improving efficiency; and (8) keeping up momentum. In the DGC project, due to the unique nature of each translation, PM scaffolding is particularly evident in four types of posts: task announcements on QQ, which help members decide whether they want to take up the tasks; assignment of translators and peer reviewers, task preparation and asset management. When these four types of posts are mapped on a timeline—Figure 6.3 shows that these activities are particularly active and intensive at the beginning but become sparser over time. This pattern aligns with

The DGC project under the microscope 115

Figure 6.3 How four types of scaffoldings provided by PMs change over time.

Source: Image created by the author based on post counts generated from the DGC project.

116 *Project-based Learning in Translation and Interpreting Studies*

Lee-Jahnke's (2009) emphasis on the gradual removal of scaffolding in learning. The decreasing frequency of these posts indicates the participants' growing independence, familiarity with the workflow, and increasing translation competence with DGC tasks.

6.4 Assessment of membership and leadership transitions

6.4.1 *Gaining full membership*

From March to April 2019, the recruits accumulated firsthand experience in translating the DGC materials. This period was crucial in that it not only gave the new members time to assess their suitability for the role but also allowed the old PMs to assess objectively whether the new recruits were suitable for the job.

On April 13, the three PMs sent a group email to all recruits asking them to make two decisions: 1) whether they'd like to stay in the project or quit, and 2) whether any of them were interested in running for the PMs. All new members were expected to reply in a day. In the email, they reminded each one:

> 我们想事先请大家知悉：以后没有整期纪事翻译，不会出现周期性的集中翻译情况，纪事内容会分散到网页翻译之中，所以团队以后面临的是不可预知的网页翻译，时间、频率具有很大的不确定性，其中很大一部分稿件要求当天返回。成为正式成员，代表着肩上的责任更大。我们不仅要求大家准时提供高质量译文，还要求团队所有成员，在自己值班周内，认真负责，随叫随到，任何时候都要积极作出响应。请根据自己的实际情况，谨慎做出选择。

(Formal membership entails a strong sense of responsibility and a willingness to commit your spare time. As the paper issue of the *UN Chronicle* stops, many web content may come on an irregular basis and demand quick turnaround, if you have already had other engagements, please plan your time and make a prudent membership decision.)

Out of 22 new recruits, 20 expressed a clear interest to stay in the project. Six also indicated their intention to run for the PM. Two decided to leave because they had found other internship opportunities and could not guarantee availability.

On April 16, the three PMs sent another group email informing the recruits that 16 of them had been selected as formal members and explaining their evaluation criteria. In the attachment, they provided comprehensive, clear records of each person's performance (see Table 6.8). The rubrics were based on two main components: translation of website content, which accounted for 70% of the evaluation, and proofreading of the *UN Chronicle*, which accounted for 30%. An additional ten points were awarded to those who participated in the terminology work for the translation of the final issue of the *UN Chronicle,* and five points were awarded to those who volunteered to proofread translations done by members of the Class of 2017.

Table 6.8 New recruits training evaluation scores

Name	Web content translation					Web content weighted score 70%	UN Chronicle proofreading score	UN Chronicle weighted score 30%	UN Chronicle Terminology (extra points)	Web content proofreading for 2017 class (extra points)	Total score
	Translation output	Review output	Weighted review output*30%	Total output	PM assessd score						
2232	1794	538.2	2770.2	8.83	61.81	8.5	25.5			87.31
1752	1081	324.3	2076.3	8.5	44.6	10	30	10		84.6
1829	2120	636	2465	8.83	55.00	6.5	19.5	10		84.50
1922	1718	515.4	2437.4	8.67	53.40	9	27			80.40
1582	1924	577.2	2159.2	9.17	50.03	10	30			80.03
1034	1225	367.5	1401.5	8.75	30.99	9.5	28.5	10	10	79.49
1385	1207	362.1	1747.1	8.5	37.53	8	24	10		71.53
1710	2314	694.2	2404.2	8.5	51.64	6.5	19.5			71.14
1610	1100	330	1940	8.5	41.67	7.5	22.5		5	69.17
909	868	260.4	1169.4	8	23.64	10	30	10		63.64
543	1969	590.7	1133.7	8	22.92	9.5	28.5		5	56.42
1031	974	292.2	1323.2	8	26.75	9.5	28.5			55.25
974	795	238.5	1212.5	8	24.51	9	27			51.51
894	958	287.4	1181.4	8	23.88	9	27			50.88
0	403	120.9	120.9	9	2.75	10	30	10	5	47.75
1037	0	0	1037	8.33	21.83	8.5	25.5			47.33
632	353	105.9	737.9	8	14.92	9	27			41.92
795	1031	309.3	1104.3	8	22.32	6	18			40.32
0	0	0	0	0	0	7.5	22.5			22.5

Source: Image created by the author based on information provided by the DGC project.

Here, we began to see how the community leaders exercised their authority in evaluating membership status. The three PMs deliberately introduced variations in expectations for recruits by assigning tasks and activities. They believed that those who participated more fully were likely to develop a deeper understanding of the material and be able to apply it in different contexts. Conversely, those with limited involvement might have a superficial understanding of the material and not be a good fit for the project.

From the perspective of the recruits, those aspiring for membership must actively demonstrate their participation before being accepted into the community. Since their primary mode of learning involved dialogues with the PMs, their sense of community and identity was closely tied to the level of interaction within the practice. Instead of passively waiting for others to facilitate their growth, they were encouraged to take charge of their own learning and show initiative. In the words of Lave and Wenger (1991, 53), "Learning as legitimate peripheral participation means that learning is not merely a condition for membership but is itself an evolving form of membership." The more engaged the new recruits were in the practice, the greater their likelihood of acquiring knowledge, feeling a sense of belonging, and gaining acceptance among senior members. This also aligns with Wenger's (1998) observation that in communities of practice, identity, knowledge acquisition, learning, and social membership are closely intertwined.

Furthermore, Wenger (1998) highlights that community members may exhibit varying levels of participation and move fluidly between these levels as their needs and interests evolve. Engagement can range from being a core member, actively participating in shaping the community's direction, to more peripheral involvement or occasional contributions, and even transactional involvement, providing specific services to the community when required. Core members play a central role in organizing, guiding, nurturing, and operating the community, which is exemplified by the teacher reviser and the three PMs in the DGC project. Active members collaborate closely with core members, contributing to the definition and development of the community. They readily take on tasks and responsibilities. In contrast, occasional members participate infrequently, while transactional members offer specialized services as needed. Not everyone progresses toward the core; some individuals remain on the periphery, and others may choose to disengage from the community. The PMs' assessment of each recruit's membership status reflects this dynamic observation.

6.4.2 Taking the mantle of leadership

The issue of power is another inherent feature of a community. Participation in a CoP is shaped by and shapes the participants' experiences of power (Risku and Dickinson 2009). As team members move to the center of production, some become more identified with the team culture and being more competent in the practice.

Following the announcement of the formal members, the three PMs decided to follow the same merit-based process their predecessors had used on them to select new PMs. A total of three PMs would be selected, rotating weekly as leaders.

This approach not only lightened the coordination load but also fostered stronger connections among the core team members, steering the community toward a collective leadership model.

The entire selection process spanned a month and consisted of four key steps. First, the names of the six candidates who announced their intention to run for PMs in the email were made public. Each of them was asked to write an election plan, which listed their personal reflections on their journey as project members, an assessment of the problems and weaknesses they observed in the practices, and a clear outline of the areas they believed needed improvement and how they planned to lead the team as PMs. These plans were then uploaded to the project's chat group and served as the foundation for their fellow members to cast their votes.

Subsequently, in the following month, whenever new tasks came, these six candidates were expected to sign up quickly and demonstrate their translation competence with DGC content. This experience was also designed to prepare them for their future roles as PMs.

Finally, a closed-door interview took place, with the panel consisting of the three outgoing PMs and the teacher reviser. During these interviews, the candidates each had ten minutes to explain their motivation, followed by a series of impromptu questions from the panel. The objective was to assess their readiness, willingness, and ability to assume leadership roles within the project.

Leadership is one of the most important factors in a community's success. They help the community focus on its domain, maintain relationships, and develop its practice (Wenger, McDermott, and Snyder 2002). Despite a high degree of self-rule and democracy, communities do not manage themselves. "If no one takes charge, they run the risk of dissolving into an unstructured mess or fading away due to lack of interest. PMs play a key role in the structure and continuity of communities, define rules, make important decisions, and resolve conflicts." (Risku and Dickinson 2009, 55). Along with member replacement, leadership transition is also a way to maintain the continuity of the team. The election process, with each candidate proposing ideas for development, brings the community's attention to how it could evolve. It is a chance for the community to enhance team building, find new energy and rejuvenate their ideas and practices.

By this time, we have built a more comprehensive view of the responsibilities expected of a PM. These responsibilities are categorized into those related to translation workflow management and those to the logistical management of the project.

To manage the entire lifecycle of each assignment (initiation, planning, design, execution, monitoring, controlling and closure of each assignment), including:

- Make advance preparations: announce the work shift every three months; make sure four student translators are on duty each week.
- As the dedicated point of contact with the DGC, check Teambition multiple times throughout a day to see if there are any incoming assignments.
- Once an assignment is received, analyze specific requirements; prepare and maintain the documentation of the name of each assignment, the deadline, its work volume, and features.

- Notify the four translators on duty on the QQ platform of the assignment; depending on the actual length, make sure the roles of translator and peer reviewer are taken up.
- Import the document to be translated in Yicat and assign portions to each translator.
- Monitor and control projects status when translation is in progression.
- Coordinate all the project phases and efficiently predict the lifespan of all the stages of the project.
- Assist translators if they experience technical glitches and seek troubleshooting help from the teacher reviser or the outside expert.
- Alert the translators to export the revised translations and start proofreading the translation once the teacher reviser completes the revision.
- Perform final eye or final quality check before sending off the translation in a bilingual Word document to DGC on Teambition.
- For any errors and mistakes caught in the final quality check, provide feedback to the concerned translator and peer reviewer.
- Update the style guide regularly if the mistakes and errors they identified at the final round of quality checks are not covered in the style guide.
- After the week on duty, align the completed translations in Yicat from the past week for the purpose of asset management.

To manage the logistic side of the project, including:

- Control the access to the project (run the entire recruitment campaign, select materials for the translation test, design the revision test, and organize the grading of their test papers).
- Foster the development of community members by training new recruits (organize the orientation and design each training task).
- Selection of formal members (keep detailed assessment record of their performance).
- Organize the selection of new PMs.
- Keep and maintain documentation for each member's performance and work volume.
- Help build the practice—including the knowledge base, lessons learned, best practices, tools, methods, and learning events. Organize regular or ad hoc plenary offline meetings to review the team's performance.

Given the range of responsibilities entailed, it is critical that the right person is picked to fill this position. In the second anonymous questionnaire, the student participants believed that the top five traits that a competent project manager should have include a strong sense of responsibility (100%), detail-minded (100%), time commitment (77.78%), good translation competence (72.22%) and technology competence, good communication skills, and able to enforce rules (33.33%).

While the previous members hadn't established specific criteria for evaluating prospective PM candidates, they did outline this process that required candidates to announce their intentions to run for the PM position, followed by an additional month dedicated to observing their performance. Importantly, the selection of PMs wasn't solely at the discretion of current PMs or the teacher reviser; it involved the participation of every member. This democratic approach aimed to facilitate change and engagement within the group.

Encouraging PM candidates to reflect on their practices and suggest improvements not only promotes their sense of involvement but also establishes a foundation of legitimacy. In a CoP, the concept of legitimacy holds more significance than the mere act of providing instruction. From the perspective of seasoned members, legitimacy hinges on an implicit commitment to assist new members in reaching their full potential within the community. For newcomers, legitimacy implies a willingness to invest effort in enhancing their skills and knowledge to earn formal recognition.

On May 15, 2019, the outgoing PMs announced the scores of the six candidates via email. These scores were derived from a balanced assessment approach: 40% from the teacher reviser, 30% from the old PMs, and the remaining 30% from the votes cast by the current members. The top three scorers were then appointed as the project's new PMs.

6.5 Moving to full participation

6.5.1 Variety and frequency of tasks

The election of the new PMs marked the complete takeover of practice by members of the 2018 class and their full independence. From May 16, 2019, to April 3, 2020, in total, the team, now comprised of 16 members from the 2018 class, handled more than 182 tasks (see Figure 6.4) and provided 154,854 words of translation. The maximum of daily words required to translate was 8,864 words, composed of 11 texts. The smallest task had only 139 words in one text. Tasks came on 92 days, among which, on 33 days, multiple texts were sent, some of the same type and others of different types. The single piece of text with the highest word count to translate was for a thematic web content page with 4,200 words and was divided among four students. Each task demanded a different turnaround time: the smallest commission had to be delivered within the day, and the biggest was given ten days (which was sent on February 7, 2020, and comprised 11 texts).

In terms of post counts generated by each translation (see Figure 6.5), they ranged from a maximum of 244 (in one task of 7,241 wordcounts) to a little of five (which appear twice, one for a task of 914 words for an official bio in web content and the other at 1,005 words for a *UN Chronicle* article). The translation with the smallest word count of 139 words produced nine post counts. This indicates that the word count of a task is only one of a multitude of factors that affect the number of post counts. The biggest factor has to do with the difficulty and their familiarity with the subject matter of a task. The task that produced 244 posts, for example, was on newly requested digital articles of the *UN Chronicle*, which forced the team to spend extra time discussing the arrangement of the workflow. The next biggest post count, at around 140, was on terminologies related to media campaigns and the use of the Twitter hashtag #, which was a new subject matter for the team.

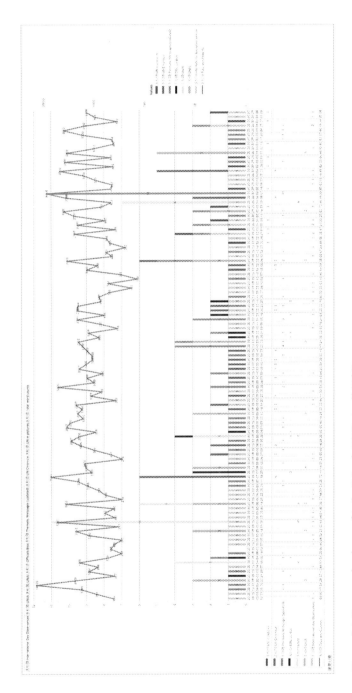

Figure 6.4 Types and volume of tasks (March 2019–April 2020).

Source: Image created by the author based on information provided by the DGC project.

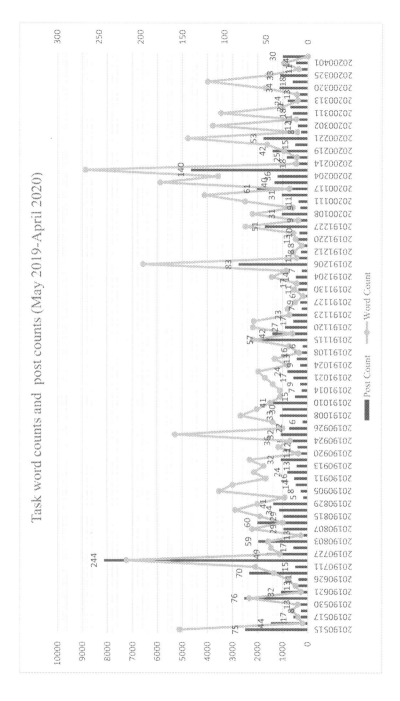

Figure 6.5 Posts per task (March 2019–April 2020).

Source: Image created by the author based on information provided by the DGC project.

Judging by the activities logged by month, from May 2019 to January 2020, discussions took place online every month. Since these tasks were not sent following a schedule but purely based on the needs of the external partner, the discussions also appeared irregular. They took place not only on weekdays but also on holidays and weekends. In some months, such as September, online discussions took place almost every day, while in other months, such as late December and early January, discussions decreased. This was because, in keeping with Western tradition, UN staff were on Christmas and New Year's holidays and, therefore, sent fewer tasks to the team during this time.

While giving us a glimpse of the variety and frequency of the DGC tasks, the graphs also provided evidence that the once fledgling members had grown more capable of taking on complex tasks within this community. In traditional one-off class projects, although the students are given opportunities for real practice, they have no chance to build their familiarity with a particular genre of text through repeated practice. In expertise studies, repetition is one of the five conditions of deliberate practice, which ultimately leads to the attainment of high levels of proficiency. Repetition offers students a valuable opportunity to solidify their existing knowledge and expand their understanding. As Ausubel, Novak, and Hanesian (1978) put it, true learning occurs when fresh information is imbued with meaning by connecting it to the knowledge students already possess. This process of consolidation unfolds through confirmation, correction, clarification, differential practice, and review, all of which take place during repeated exposure to learning materials, accompanied by feedback. By maintaining a continuous cycle of practice and reflection, individuals engaged in an internship project can anticipate a seamless progression. Each instance of practice integrates newly acquired knowledge into the existing reservoir of learned information, enabling participants to develop a clearer understanding of the interconnectedness between concepts, norms, and procedures within the community.

6.5.2 Human–human collaboration

Mutual engagement is a defining feature of a CoP. Through participation in the community, members establish norms and build collaborative relationships. These ties bind them together as a social entity.

The way members engage with each other is first conditioned by how they are grouped and how tasks are assigned. Before the recruits gained their membership, the old PMs asked them to sign up to work on their own initiative to make training fair and competitive. The translators and the peer reviewers were randomly formed, and collaborations and role assignments were constantly changing. Now that the number of participants in the project had been determined and that the members had already had some idea of the amount of work expected, there was a need to develop a more effective work allocation and scheduling system. Many participants at this stage (who were now at the end of their first year of study) had started their internship/work placement at another outside employer and had to balance different engagements. With no clear work allocation schedule, everyone had to check task announcements constantly and might be afraid to make up their personal schedule. This would be a wasteful use of resources and add to the additional work for the PMs to assign work.

Therefore, the three new PMs first checked with each member about their availability. Using the experience learned from the old PMs, they soon published a clearly marked work schedule on the chat group: all members (including the three PMs) were put into a fixed group of four people and were expected to take weekly turns to handle the website content and the UNIA documentaries. In other words, one week every month, each small group must remain responsive to all task announcements on their shift. To give it a bit of flexibility, if emergencies crop up, the assigned translators can swap with people in another group. The three PMs themselves would also take weekly turns to manage the team, in addition to performing their duty as translators. The team had originally assumed that the DGC would stop the paper's publication, and thus, there was no need for a translation of the *UN Chronicle*. However, on July 18, 2019, articles for the digital version of the magazine were sent for translation. This means that rather than translating an entire issue on a quarterly basis, the team must be ready for more frequent and small article translations. At the suggestion of the old PM and in the interest of convenience, another schedule, which put all 16 people into groups of two people per group, was made and duly implemented for this specific task.

The fixed grouping gave members the flexibility to arrange their time and the choice to decide whom they wanted to work with. A small group also gave members a chance to form closer ties. Over time, collaboration began to evolve in a routine and patterned way. The way tasks were divided and assigned became fixed with the creation of the work schedule.

The members assigned to each task engaged with each other in collaborative dialogue for the purpose of providing a joint product. So mutual engagement was reflected by the way they coordinated, cooperated, and collaborated with each other. Their dialogues gave us hints on the degree of their mutual dependence. The quantitative analysis of their interactions shows that the PMs mainly played a mediator and coordinating role in each task (see Figure 6.6). Most of their posts were non-conceptual. Their posts were most active in the beginning stage of the workflow when the PMs asked the four translators on duty to sign up tasks quickly and to make sure the roles of the translator and of the peer reviewer were taken up. Figure 6.6 shows that irrespective of the number of the translators assigned, the number of the posts on task announcements stayed relatively stable (one or two at most), which means that the PMs were efficient at this initial step of work. However, when assigning the translators and peer reviewers, the number of such posts was directly correlated with the number of translators involved, particularly on days when multiple tasks came from DGC. This is understandable because, compared with task announcements, it is more important to have the right resources in place and to make sure the translators receive the tasks and understand their roles and obligations.

The number of posts relating to time management also changed with the number of translators assigned but remained constant at less than five posts per task (see Figure 6.7), suggesting these non-conceptual posts were a routine part of interaction and were meant to push the workflow to the next stage. They were cooperative in nature.

126 *Project-based Learning in Translation and Interpreting Studies*

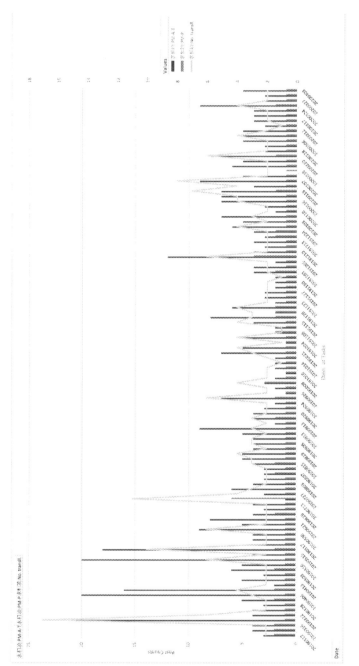

Figure 6.6 Task announcement and preparation posts by PMs (March 2019–April 2020).

Source: Image created by the author based on post counts generated from the DGC project.

The DGC project under the microscope 127

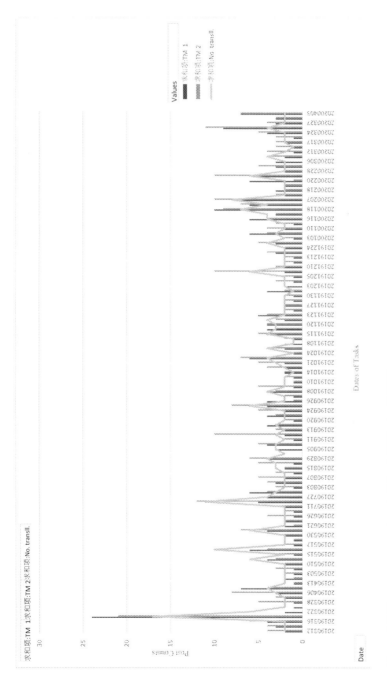

Figure 6.7 Time management posts (March 2019–April 2020).

Source: Image created by the author based on post counts generated from the DGC project.

128 *Project-based Learning in Translation and Interpreting Studies*

What truly encouraged collaborative learning were the dialogues initiated by the teacher during the revision process, the teacher's evaluations upon completion of this revision, and the subsequent dialogues initiated by students with the teacher-reviser. As Dillenbourg (1999) points out, collaboration involves a dynamic interplay where roles can shift, different perspectives are exchanged, and the final product is the result of this intertwining process. During the revision of a text, there are various scenarios that prompted the teacher reviser to ask questions or engage in discussions. Firstly, if the translation appears awkward or unnatural, the teacher-reviser may require the original translator to conduct additional research to pinpoint the source of the problem. Secondly, if there was a clear misunderstanding of a particular sentence or phrase, the teacher reviser would clarify it with the students in the chat group. Thirdly, if the original translator had failed to add a term to the termbase, and there was no prompt from Yicat, the teacher-reviser may raise this issue.

There were also instances where the teacher reviser and the original translator engaged in online discussions to foster mutual knowledge development. Likewise, after receiving the revised translation, the translator may have questions for the teacher reviser, particularly if the feedback contradicted their initial understanding or if they believe the revision was incorrect. For example:

E.g.:

Teacher reviser:	前三十几条你马上看看，我不懂这个内容
PM:	确实是第一次接触，我和**也讨论了挺久[表情]
PM:	我明白您的意思了。这篇主要是讲怎么在推特、脸书、Medium这些社交平台上传播#A4P#的内容，所以有一些涉及到怎么加#标签，怎么@链接到相关主页或账号的情况。
Teacher reviser:	就是整合在一个标签下面
PM:	可以这么理解
PM:	原文表格下包括Facebook posts、Tweets、Instagram posts、Monthly Instagram Stories这些内容
Teacher reviser:	最后一行这个是什么玩意儿
Teacher reviser:	应该不是先发布再@
PM:	可以理解为unpeacekeeping的主页
PM:	应该不是艾特
PM:	这样似乎说得通
Teacher reviser:	实锤了

(*Teacher reviser:*	Check the first thirty or so content right away, I don't understand your translation.
PM:	This is the first time I'm seeing this. I discussed it with ** for quite a while.
PM:	This task mainly talks about how to spread #A4P# content on social media platforms like Twitter, Facebook, and Medium. So, it is about how to add hashtags and how to link to relevant pages or accounts.

The DGC project under the microscope 129

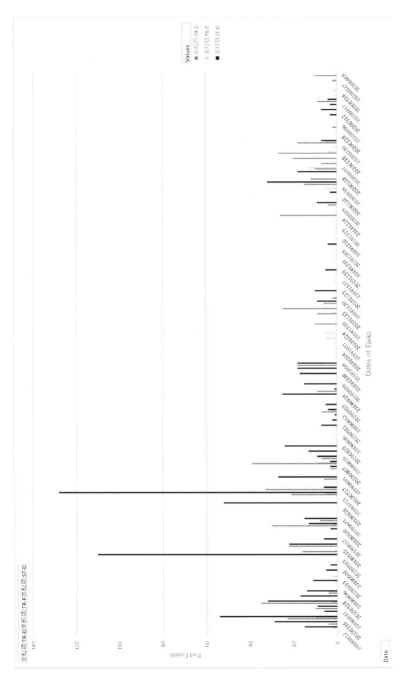

Figure 6.8 Post of teacher reviser initiated-dialogues (dark gray lines), teacher evaluations (light gray lines), and student-initiated dialogues (black lines) (March 2019-April 2020).

Source: Image created by the author based on post counts generated from the DGC project.

Teacher reviser:	It's about integrating everything under one hashtag.
PM:	You could put it that way.
PM:	The original table includes content like Facebook posts, Tweets, Instagram posts, and Monthly Instagram Stories.
Teacher reviser:	What's this thing in the last row?
Teacher reviser:	It shouldn't be about posting first and then tagging.
PM:	Is it about the UN peacekeeping homepage?
PM:	Anyway, "tagging" does not make any sense.
PM:	I think this is plausible.
Teacher reviser:	Yeah. It is.)

Even in cases where the teacher did not pose questions during the revision process, he may provide comments that involve pointing out areas for further improvement or reminding the translators to proofread the text after formatting. These dialogues were beneficial not only because they helped enhance the quality of the product but also because they encouraged participants to articulate and justify their knowledge (Baker 2009).

If we shift the angle, the teacher reviser not only gave the feedback on the product but during his revision, he was actively seeking feedforward from the original translator. In this sense, the translators were no longer put in the middle of the workflow, between the PMs and the reviser, but were more intimately involved in the entire workflow. They not only receive feedback on the product from the reviser but also are given the chance to make their thinking process visible. This makes participants not only more engaged with the translation as a joint activity but also more engaged with the product. Since the two sides might be questioned by each other, both the translator and the teacher must be more careful with their segment of production.

Judging by the frequency and the level of activity of these three types of dialogues in Figure 6.8 (p. 129), the student-initiated dialogues were the most dominant form of interaction. They appeared intensive in the beginning but became less frequent in later stages. If the translators didn't ask questions, one possibility is that problems, if there were any, had already been solved before they reached the teacher reviser; the other possibility is that the teacher reviser only made some minor changes that could be easily understood. If we examine more closely the content of the teacher reviser's evaluation and comments, in the beginning, the evaluation was more about pointing out weaknesses in translation (see the example below), whereas, in later stages, there were more praises and positive confirmations. We thus interpret this change as a sign that in the mid-late stages, student participants' competence has improved in translating the DGC text.

E.g.:

Teacher reviser:	我感觉目前的纪事翻译不够流畅，可读性比较差。大家可以注意一下充分性和可读性的结合。充分性包括两个方面，一个是术语和表达惯例，是词与词组级别的，另一个是信息的完整性，不要随意遗漏信息。可

	读性主要是信息流的组织问题，在不牺牲篇章连贯的前提下，可以提取重点信息，信息之间的逻辑进行重组，该省略的省略，该替换的替换，英语中有些衔接是英语语法要求，不一定要传达到中文里面去的。
Teacher reviser:	要明确主要观点，围绕主要信息构建句子，同时注意上下句的衔接连贯。
Teacher reviser:	总之，我们要说人话。
(Teacher Reviser:	I think our chronicle translations aren't very smooth and could be more readable. Let's balance thoroughness and readability. First, we need to be thorough in two ways: make sure we're using accurate terminology and common expressions, and ensure the information is complete without arbitrarily leaving out details. For readability, focus on the flow of information. Highlight key points, reorganize the logic, cut out unnecessary parts, and make substitutions where needed, but don't lose coherence. And remember, some English transitions don't need direct translation into Chinese.
Teacher Reviser:	We need to make sure the main ideas are clear and build sentences around the key information, while maintaining smooth connections between sentences.
Teacher Reviser:	In short, let's make it sound natural.)

Wenger's description of mutual engagement (1998) emphasizes the participants' capacity to interact with others and respond to each other's actions. Our analysis of the members' interactions in the DGC project indicates that collaborations, in fact, exhibit three characteristic patterns: coordination, cooperation, and collaboration. It is the latter type of interaction that makes ongoing practice a rich learning experience.

6.5.3 *Human–machine collaboration*

In addition to human–human collaboration, human–machine collaboration is another dimension worth examining. Digital tools are now part of a community's habitat (Wenger, White, and Smith 2009). Technology and activities of a community are intertwined because technology has affordances that allow a community to "have asynchronous collaboration" and "the ability to store and manipulate information in a variety of formats" (Hoadley 2012, 295). If we use the same translation technology categorization in Chapter 3, tools that are deeply embedded in the DGC project include the following (see Table 6.9).

As one of the most popular free social networking tools, QQ mainly works to connect the participants across time and space by allowing both synchronous and asynchronous conversation. It is easy to use, can be easily installed on both desktop and mobile devices and can save and transmit large files. It has been used in the project since its very beginning, but each cycle, the participants create their own

132 *Project-based Learning in Translation and Interpreting Studies*

Table 6.9 Technologies used in the DGC project

Translators' computer equipment	Participant's personal computer	HT
ICT tool	QQ chat group	
Text editing and desktop publishing	Word/Shimo	
Language tools and resources	Linguee/UNTERM	CAT/MT
Translation tool	Yicat	
Project management tool		

chat group. Although Yicat was taken up by the 2017 class members, its use was not enforced. It was only when the members of the 2018 class began to independently translate tasks in March 2019 that a complete switch to the tool was made.

These tools combine to create the technological ecosystem for the DGC project: The three PMs use Yicat to do project statistics, track project status and maintain and update the TM and TB saved by the tool. The translators access Yicat using their personal PCs. When they translate, they use Linguee and UNTERM to check on terms and phrases; they consult the internet to check for background information and parallel text. They use Yicat for either computer-assisted translation (CAT) or machine translation of the source text, though the latter is paid if the text exceeds their free quota of usage. The original translator, peer reviewer and teacher reviser work in the same editor on Yicat. Once the revision is completed, the original translator exports the translation and goes back to Word for final desktop editing. Shimo is used only when a commission has a lot of terms that need to be extracted and translated beforehand. Meanwhile, the members stay connected with each other using QQ.

Since Yicat has completely redefined that workflow and is the only translation tool used by the team, we are curious about the participants' user experience with this tool. In late June 2019, we asked the participants in the third anonymous questionnaire to self-assess their degree of acceptance of Yicat on a seven-point Likert scale, with one being totally resistant and seven being completely accepting; the average score was 5.29. We also asked them to self-assess their familiarity with the tool. All of them believed that they knew how to use the tool. One believed he/she was particularly good at the tool; 11 were familiar, and four were moderately familiar. The average familiarity score was 5.36. Considering that when they were first recruited for the project, only six had heard of the tool, and by this time, most members had become competent users of Yicat.

However, the journey wasn't without its challenges when the team had to rely on Yicat for their daily work. Figure 6.9 provides an overview of the number of posts when they encountered technical difficulties. Initially, problems occurred more frequently, but over time, they became less frequent. When we conducted a content analysis of the conversations, we found that most of the help came from one specific person in the chat group, who turned out to be a Yicat employee. A graduate of GIIT's MT program, she now held the role of Yicat's product manager. She had been added to the chat group by the teacher reviser. At first, the participants only consulted her when instructed by the teacher reviser. Over time,

The DGC project under the microscope 133

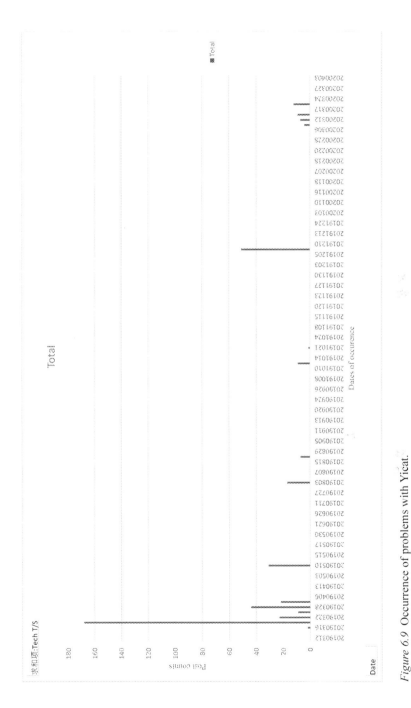

Figure 6.9 Occurrence of problems with Yicat.

Source: Image created by the author based on post counts generated from the DGC project.

however, she became known to the team, and participants began to approach her directly for solutions.

If we break down these technological problems, some were attributed to members' unfamiliarity with the tool, such as neglecting to confirm translations on Yicat. Others were related to the inherent limitations of the free service account, such as restrictions on project members, the inability to lock changes across files, and a cap on the number of terms prompted by the terminology base. Some were caused by sporadic, temporary downtime in the cloud service. There were also challenges stemming from the tool's inadequacies, such as the inability to undo accidental deletions, platform stability issues, and compatibility problems with different browsers. In late March of 2020, the team used the financial support received from the university to upgrade to a business account, gaining access to more comprehensive services.

In summary, having an employee from the tool developer actively participate in the chat group allowed the team to seek prompt support. Simultaneously, the tool developer benefited from real-time feedback provided by our team, enabling them to refine their service. This engagement between the team and the service provider established the foundations of a mutually beneficial partnership.

We also asked the participants to provide a critical assessment of the benefits and drawbacks associated with Yicat. When it comes to the positive aspects of this tool, a substantial 78.59% of respondents believed that Yicat allowed them to collaborate seamlessly with both their peers and the teacher-reviser. 71.43% of participants highlighted the tool's user-friendly interface and its cost-effectiveness. Furthermore, 64.29% mentioned the convenience of being able to develop and manage translation memories and the term base on the go. A notable 35.71% expressed ease in tracking revisions and changes within Yicat. Some participants (21.43%) also noted that Yicat's APIs facilitate effortless machine translation integration. A smaller fraction (14.29%) of respondents pointed out that since Yicat stores language data in a standard format, it can be transferred to other platforms. Lastly, a few participants (7.14%) highlighted their ability to utilize Yicat for translation using the "machine translation (MT) and post-editing (PE)" model.

The team also raised concerns associated with Yicat. One common issue was the time-consuming process of copying and pasting the revised translations into a Word document. 64.29% said that when they translate in the cloud, they inadvertently grant the tool developer access to their data. Another concern was the limitations of the free package, with half of the team (50%) expressing dissatisfaction. The team must pay to access term banks available on Yicat's marketplace or if they want to customize the tool. Moreover, it can be frustrating when the text to be translated is segmented incorrectly, requiring translators to invest extra time in merging or subdividing problematic segments.

Despite the availability of machine translation, 42.87% did not have confidence in the quality of the translations generated by Yicat. Moreover, 35.71% experienced platform breakdowns when multiple translators work on a project. For example, in March 2019, when 17 students were assigned to a large project, confusion arose as translators could not easily identify their designated text segments despite project managers having divided the text beforehand.

Another inconvenience reported by 35.71% was the challenge of building and maintaining TM and TB within the platform. Furthermore, 14.29% of respondents expressed dissatisfaction with the restrictions imposed by the free service, including limitations on the number of members and the fact that translation access was restricted to assigned translators and revisers rather than being open to all project members.

Wenger, White, and Smith (2000) developed a framework to evaluate the suitability of digital tools adopted by a community, which includes criteria related to pricing, adequacy, integration, vendor relationships, and accessibility. In the DGC project, Yicat stands out as a simple and user-friendly tool that supports the collaborative workflow. It provides all the essential features our team currently requires, such as translation memory and terminology management, along with machine translation capabilities. Furthermore, it is freely available and can be accessed from anywhere, even without an internet connection, offering participants remarkable flexibility. What's particularly commendable is the robust support we receive from the service provider, ensuring immediate assistance during challenging moments.

As Cronin (2020, 526) puts it, "technology is not from an ecological perspective simply a lifeless tool or an instrument but an animated part of the human ecosystem, a constituent element of the translator's transversal subjectivity." Indeed, the team's interaction with technology and their discussions about the challenges they encounter online, as well as their search for solutions, provided us with a comprehensive understanding of both the advantages and disadvantages of this tool. These reflections hold value for the members as they help them recalibrate their expectations regarding the capabilities of machines. They also benefit the community by enabling them to adapt practices to maximize the advantages offered by these tools and assist the service provider in making necessary optimizations.

Furthermore, this assessment contributes to the professional development of the participants. Their experiences with Yicat may equip them to quickly utilize features that may arise in the future. Despite not having the opportunity to work face-to-face, their use of the tool and their dialogues on the chat group have fostered a sense of togetherness across time and space.

6.5.4 Collaboration in building shared asset

A CoP is also marked by its shared repertoire built by its members, a shared point of reference and a common discourse arising from the use of these resources (Wenger 1998). In a way, the participants preserve the resources not only by using and sharing this pool of resources but also by constantly contributing to and renewing these resources.

Before we examine how the participants build and maintain their shared pool of resources, it is important to first review the features of the DGC text. According to Cao and Zhao (2006, xxv), the text the UN needs to translate is marked by their "technical nature, diversity of subject areas, a strict turn-over deadline; and continuity." As the largest intergovernmental organization, the UN deals with a wide range of subject matters and disciplinary fields. Many of the issues are sensitive and concern the vital interests of some/all countries. Being an organization with a history of more than 75 years, most of the UN's documents refer to other documents over the years in terms of contents and feature many repetitive elements (Chen 2017). Although the content DGC publishes online is not as technical and sensitive as other UN official documents, the same requirement for accuracy, consistency and continuity also applies. Therefore, translators must be very meticulous and thorough in the background research. The importance of consistency is stressed at recruitment, during training and throughout their entire time in the project.

To achieve consistency of the terms and phrases, the team relies on UNTERM, Linguee, and the UN online content as the most trustworthy resources. If one member has spent considerable time locating a correct term or phrase but only uses it once, it would be a complete waste of time for another member to repeat the same search next time. It would be equally wasteful if the text quality controlled is not capitalized on in future tasks. Hence, there is a compelling need for the team to digitalize and maintain all the validated terms and translation memories for easy recycling.

Previously, when the old members used Word to translate, the validated terms from each task were saved in an Excel form and sent to the teacher reviser and the project manager for review. One member was appointed to move them to a centralized Excel file. But this file was not updated in real time and to use it also required manual research. All the texts that had been translated were saved on the PM's computer. No one had been tasked to track down what the final published version looked like. There were also no procedures in place to make the glossaries and the translations into ready-to-use resources.

The switch to Yicat provided conditions for the centralized management of the TB and TM. Figure 6.10 lists the occurrences of such discussions on the timeline. All the dialogues were initiated by the teacher reviser, either between him and the PMs or between him and the student translators. In the beginning, the dialogues tended to happen before a translation began and were mostly on the approaches the teacher reviser expected the students to take up to develop TB and TM. Later, the discourse shifted to the need to appoint an asset manager and improve the quality of the database. There were also times when the teacher reviser found out during his revision that the original translators had failed to add a new term to the TB and reminded them to do so. Compared with the student participants, who seemed more consumed by the immediate need to complete their assigned task, the teacher focused more on long-term cumulative gains from the management of the translated terms and documents. These dialogues reflected his clear vision of using the industry's best practices to guide the team's translation asset management practice.

With the content analysis of these dialogues, we get a glimpse of the approaches the teacher reviser has in mind for asset management. For a start, if the translator(s) assigned have located the parallel text or previously translated segments online, they should first align them into a bitext. When translation begins, rather than using exact match or full match, the translator can use the fuzzy match to raise the probability of reuse. This is seen in the following dialogue:

The DGC project under the microscope 137

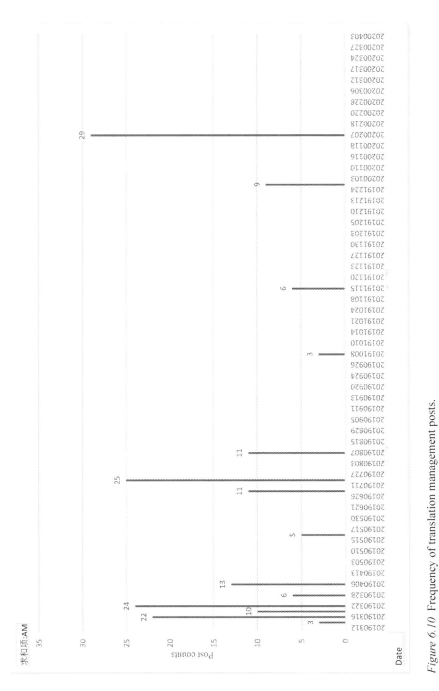

Figure 6.10 Frequency of translation management posts.

Source: Image created by the author based on post counts generated from the DGC project.

E.g.:

Teacher revise:	这个新的任务有语料吗？
PM:	没有
PM:	以前的维持和平系列的网站建设
Teacher reviser:	接活的同学请首先建语料
PM:	这个没什么资料可以参考
Teacher reviser:	用网站网页用好，用linguee也好，需要找到
(Teacher reviser:	Do we have any TM for this new task?
PM:	Nope.
PM:	It looks like the previous peacekeeping website content.
Teacher reviser:	Those taking on this task should first create a TM.
PM:	There aren't many reference materials available.
Teacher reviser:	Make good use of the UN website or Linguee. We need to find something.)

In making the bitext, the teacher reviser would remind students to break a long segment into smaller chunks for a better chance of matching. Conversely, there were also times when he asked the translators to merge segments together if they were too small to have any meaning. For instances:

E.g.:

Teacher reviser:	有些句段很长，拆分开可能更清楚
Teacher reviser:	也更有利于语料利用
One student translator:	好的，我补做一下拆分，下次也会注意～
Teacher reviser:	这次不用了
Teacher reviser:	我是提设想
(Teacher reviser:	Some sentences are quite long. Breaking them up might make them clearer.
Teacher reviser:	It would also make our TM useful.
Student translator:	Okay, I'll break them up in a minute. I would first break text up next time.
Teacher reviser:	No need to do it this time.
Teacher reviser:	I was just thinking this is the right way.)

E.g.:

Teacher reviser:	但务必先合并句段
PM:	老师 合并句段的目的是啥呀
PM:	因为机器翻译只有200条吗 还是说这样不会切分意群
Teacher reviser:	示例图片
Teacher reviser:	像这样句子被割开了，要并在一起

(Teacher reviser:	Make sure to merge the sentences first.
PM:	Teacher, what is the purpose of merging the text?
PM:	Is it because the machine translation only handles 200 entries? Or is it to avoid chunking up the wrong meaning?
Teacher reviser:	Here. Look at this example.
Teacher reviser:	See how these sentences are split? They need to be combined.)

In terms of the ways to maintain TB, the team has already imported the Excel glossaries into Yicat, but they still need to vet new terms. The teacher reviser, therefore, asked the translators to add each new term on the go and not to send a separate Excel file containing the new terms again.

E.g.:

Teacher reviser:	起码要建好术语库，导入yicat翻译，不用单独给我发术语表，我直接在平台上看。
PM:	好。
PM:	老师，您的意思是，初译同学拿到文件后，先通读全文、提取术语，然后把新术语加到以前的术语表里面，再导入平台翻译吗？
Teacher reviser:	差不多，新术语不用加到以前到术语表里，可以新建术语库，导入后在项目设置那边选定增加就好。
(Teacher reviser:	We need to build a TB and import it into Yicat for translation. Do not send me the term list separately; I'll check it directly on Yicat.
PM:	Okay.
PM:	Do you mean that the initial translators should first read through the document, extract terms, then add the new terms to the existing TB, and finally import it for translation?
Teacher reviser:	That's about right. We don't need to add new terms to the old TB. You can create a new term base, import it, and then add it from the settings menu.)

Furthermore, the teacher reviser asked the team to add not only the terms from the UNTERM but also the frequently used expressions and phrases from Linguee into the TB. By migrating carefully selected resources from the UNTERM and Linguee, he expected the team to build a more project-specific database.

E.g.:

Teacher reviser:	有些术语翻译过后要提出来，更新术语库
PM:	好的 片语要不要也提出来？
Teacher reviser:	尽量提出来
Teacher reviser:	是资产，也是自己学习
PM:	好的明白
Teacher reviser:	其实主要是从unterm搬到我们的术语库，还有从Linguee找到的片语都没有更新到术语库里，这个也要补进去。

(Teacher reviser:	Some terms need to be highlighted after translation and added to the TB.
PM:	Got it. Should we also highlight phrases?
Teacher reviser:	Yes, try to include them.
Teacher reviser:	They are assets and help with our learning.
PM:	Understood.
Teacher reviser:	Basically, we need to move terms from UNTERM to our term base and add phrases from Linguee. The phrases in the TB are not kept up to date. This needs to be done as well.)

There's more to a term entry. For example, the same abbreviation may stand for terms with widely different meanings. Therefore, the teacher reviser felt a strong need to create standardized metadata for each term entry by including the source, usage details, and the grammatical properties of that term. He also asked the translators to add comments in Yicat so that in case they feel they need to alert fellow translators down the chain. When each time a term is introduced into Yicat, it results in the creation of a new entry. Over time, multiple entries for the same term may accumulate, each with slight variations. For instance, the Chinese equivalent of the term "2030 Agenda for Sustainable Development" can sometimes include a special punctuation mark and sometimes not. Additionally, the term may be used in its abbreviated form as "the 2030 Agenda" with the definite article "the" or without any article. If these terms are left unattended, they can lead to inconsistencies in translations, potentially resulting in different definitions or the inclusion of signs and marks that require extra time for revision.

As a result, the teacher reviser found it urgent not only to increase the size but also to increase the quality of the TB. He asked the three PMs on multiple occasions to appoint a dedicated asset manager who can work as the quality control manager to merge different TBs, clean the TB from duplicate entries, and check if the added terms are prompted by Yicat next time the appear in a source text and how many options are provided. These ideas are reflected in the following posts of the teacher reviser.

E.g.:

Teacher reviser:	现在得安排人手整理术语库，合并术语库，然后去重
Teacher reviser :	建议在18级的同学里设一位专门盯术语的，特别关注提取和导入的术语在平台上是否能跳出来
Teacher reviser:	你们有没有设置资产管理专员？术语管理和语料管理谁在做？
(Teacher reviser:	We need to assign a dedicated person to organize the term base, merge the term lists, and remove duplicates.
Teacher reviser:	I suggest appointing a specific person to manage terms, particularly ensuring that extracted and imported terms are correctly displayed on the platform.

Teacher reviser: Do you have an asset manager? Who is managing our TB and TM?

In response to the teacher's request, the three PMs took weekly turns to work as the asset managers. They would review the new terms submitted from each commission, identify errors, track down each published version, and update the changes made by DGC in the TB/TM.

    E.g.:

Teacher reviser: 我发现术语管理工作还是做得不够，希望一边翻译一边提取，随时更新到术语库里，yicat上有这个功能。
PM: 有时候查证的术语可能不完全正确，还是需要先把一下关再更新到术语库，不然还是提交Excel表，最后PM来更新？
Teacher reviser: 涉及到两个人协同工作，可以先统一，也就是先实时更新，然后根据最后定稿再修订。
PM: 好的可以，后期我们再根据网站上挂出来的修改。

(*Teacher reviser:*   The terminology management isn't thorough enough. We should continuously extract and update terms in the term base during translation. Yicat can help with this.
PM: Sometimes, even if we've verified terms, they're not entirely correct. Should we review them first before updating the term base, or should we still submit an Excel sheet to update after each task?
Teacher reviser: This requires collaboration. It is best to update in real-time first, then revise based on the final version.
PM: Got it. We'll make changes based on the updates posted on the website.)

If a task was on unfamiliar subject matter, the teacher reviser would alert the PMs and original translators to extract terms in advance rather than in the task. If a translator forgot to highlight newly added terms and expressions in the interface, the teacher reviser would quickly point out the problem during the revision. For example:

    E.g.:

Teacher reviser: 相互看看，可能还有许多需要协调
Teacher reviser: 方便的话，大家组织一下术语提取
Teacher reviser: 几个PM一起看看。这次协调工作要做好

(*Teacher reviser:*   Take a look at each other's work; there are many things that need coordination.
Teacher reviser: Ask the team to extract the terms first.
Teacher reviser: You three PMs then review the terms together. Coordination is crucial.)

142 *Project-based Learning in Translation and Interpreting Studies*

If the teacher noticed that the translators failed to extract key terms, he would also point this out in the chat group.

Teacher reviser:	很多关键词和高频词都没有提成术语
Teacher reviser:	隐患很大啊
(Teacher reviser:	You didn't add key terms and high-frequency words to the TB, did you?
Teacher reviser:	This is a big risk.)

In addition to maintaining the terminology database and translation memory, the team must also ensure that the style guide is kept up to date. A well-maintained style guide serves as both a standard reference tool (Washbourne 2012) and a training resource. When users open the style guide, they will notice sections highlighted in blue as "new additions" and sections highlighted in yellow as "items requiring special attention." It is the PM's ongoing responsibility to include common translation and formatting errors made by team members, as well as new insights gained, all supported by screenshots and solutions in the guide. When we began our observations in 2018, the book was 28 pages long, with 12,954 words. By 2021, it had grown to 33 pages with 13,657 words.

To sum up, the continuity of practice increases the "shareability of data" for the team. By using the translation technology, each previously translated term and segment becomes relevant to future practice and becomes training data for the machines. In a sense, this creates a bond between the participants and the translation technology, between participants in the same cycle and across cycles. It also builds trust in the data and trust in the quality of each production. In the words of the teacher reviser:

> 所以这一届要为下一届着想，每一届到要为下一届着想，尽量减少工作量，我们的利用机器就是，其实我们现在是在给机器做培训，机器如果能够识别的是速度快，它的效率自然就会提高，否则机器就没用。

(As current participants engage in translation, it's important for them to understand that their translations can benefit subsequent participants in the next cycle, reducing their workload. As we gather more data, the likelihood of their translations being utilized increases, ultimately leading to a more precise and effective tool. Moreover, our meticulous management of linguistic assets contributes to the training of Yicat. When the tool can swiftly and accurately identify each term and segment, our overall efficiency will see a significant boost.)

In this context, it becomes evident that there exists a third dimension of collaboration within the DGC project. It goes beyond the mere act of working together with technology to create a shared product. Collaboration also takes shape when multiple translators come together to build a common repository of resources. According to Lave and Wenger (1991), a shared repertoire serves to solidify a community's history of past engagement, enabling its members to participate more effectively in future activities. Translation asset management represents just one facet of this overarching principle, yet it is an integral component of a thriving community. By developing and maintaining the term base and translation memories, participants gain a stronger sense of ownership over the artifacts they create. These resources continue to influence subsequent practices, ensuring that each member bears a responsibility to contribute to the growth of this shared pool of resources.

6.5.5 Changes in motivation and learning accrued

Motivation is crucial for engagement and performance. Moreover, it is important for the participants to not only be motivated in the beginning but to stay motivated over time. In June 2019, seven months into their participation, we assessed how their motivations had changed compared with at the beginning of your training. The results suggested that only 7.14% significantly became more motivated; 35.71% grew marginally motivated; 42.86% remained at the same level of motivation; 14.29% reported a marginal decrease in their motivation. No one reported a significant decrease in motivation. Overall, they appeared to be quite engaged with the practice.

As to the reasons that continued to draw them into the DGC project, the top five reasons included improving translation competence (78.57%), improving revision competence (64.29%), chances for being selected for internships at the UN (64.29%); improving project management competence (64.29%); having different experience from the formal curriculum (64.29%); opportunities for scholarship and other forms of compensation (42.86%); opportunities to interact with teachers and classmates through the project (42.86%). Compared to the previous two sets of responses, the order of ranking for different types of motivations seemed to remain the same, except that by now, the students knew that participation would bring some sort of compensation[5] and the opportunity to apply for Chinese government scholarships to intern at the UN, so some explicitly acknowledged this as an extrinsic source of motivation.

Following the retirement of the three PMs in May, it appeared that once student participants passed their mid-point training assessment, their membership status became unchangeable, and no one else could revoke their membership except themselves. To dispel this perception, the three newly elected PMs swiftly devised a performance assessment system to encourage members to remain focused and motivated. They also published the assessment results publicly on the chat group.

Under this new scheme, within each translation, if the reviewers could not identify any errors or proofreading mistakes during the final round of quality control, they would award translators a full score of ten points. Conversely, for each style or consistency mistake, they would deduct 0.5 points. Starting in June 2019, the results of these reviews were published online bi-monthly. There were no penalties or rewards associated with these reviews; the sole purpose was to encourage everyone to be more vigilant and remind members that even though they believed they had given their utmost effort to each task, there was still a chance that some errors might have slipped past their attention.

While the scoring process didn't adhere to any strict translation quality assessment models, these public reviews had a significant impact on the team. They served as benchmarks and created a sense of peer pressure, causing each member to measure their performance against their peers.

When the next performance review results were released in early September, there was a notable improvement in the average score. Many team members scored nine or higher. Convinced that the reviews had served their purpose, the three PMs discontinued the effort.

It should be noted that it is not only peer pressure, but also peer influence that can push students for better performance. Bandura's (1977) social learning theory holds that when the participants view positive behaviors, they may imitate and change behaviors as well. When asked if they are made more careful after seeing how careful and committed the teacher/reviser and their fellow collaborators are, unsurprisingly, all members agree or strongly agree with the statement. Many believe the teacher reviser has set up a role model. He has never once refused to revise student work due to personal reasons, and he always returns the revised translation on time. Over time, by working together on an ongoing basis, the traditional teacher-student relationship has taken on a spirit of camaraderie of equal partners. There is great deference from the student participants to the authority of the teacher reviser, not because of his senior position but because of his own dedication, efficiency, and performance record. Previous sampled studies tend to depict the teacher participant as a facilitator to help the students produce a better product, but seldomly as a role model that instills into the students the importance and values of being professional.

As we delve deeper into the DGC project and its potential impact, we find that applying a traditional competence model to assess PjBL's effectiveness may counter its core objectives. This is primarily due to several reasons.

Firstly, the idea of translation competence is a subject of ongoing debate and can be defined in various ways. Furthermore, competence models themselves can vary, with some being role-based and continuously evolving in response to technological advancements. It is unrealistic to expect a single model to encompass all the diverse elements necessary for a successful group project. Secondly, translation competence models typically focus on individual skills, whereas PjBL emphasizes learning within a community context. It's important to recognize that competence is not solely "a property of individuals and the representations in their heads," as emphasized by Hoadley (2012, 288). Thirdly, learning is a dynamic and cumulative process. Expecting a community's knowledge to be built solely through a one-time practicum is overly simplistic. Instead, according to Brown, Collins, and Duguid (1989), knowledge is shaped, acquired, developed, shared, and validated through continuous social interactions. Fourthly, learning is a holistic experience. It is influenced by students' emotions, motivations, and mental activities. This was evident in our anonymous questionnaires, where participants unanimously agreed that the emotional tone of feedback significantly impacts its reception. Learning is also enriched by sensory and kinesthetic experiences and incorporates both tacit and explicit knowledge (Wenger, McDermott, and Smith 2009). Over time, the routines and trust established within a learning community contribute to shaping its identity and sustaining motivation among its members to actively participate.

Hence, aligning with the social perspective on learning, we prefer to utilize the overarching concept of "learning" to describe the advantages that members have gained. It's important to note that we may not possess a precise means of quantifying the extent of these improvements. However, by employing the benchmarks established at the outset and the end of their internship, we have discerned a wide spectrum of benefits. These encompass cognitive enhancements, emotional growth, strengthened interpersonal skills, a heightened appreciation for team values and quality standards, improved translation proficiency and knowledge, as well as the development of valuable soft skills relevant to employability.

To illustrate these points, we select a few snippets from participants' reflections collected during plenary meetings or recorded interviews. The most direct validation of students' progress in translation competence stems from evaluations conducted by the teacher reviser.

> 这两届下来，尤其是这一届现在正在工作的这一届，我觉得都很愉快。就是说我在给他们入审校的时候，我就不会觉得说我要扛着整个一个团队在走，我就是一个流程里面的一个普通的一个环节，有时候是在用欣赏的眼光来读他们的译文，这是很大的一个进步。

> (I enjoy working with the latest two cycle of students, particular the current one. When I revise their work, I don't feel I'm the one exclusively responsible for quality. I am just taking care of one stage on a production line. Sometimes, I find their draft translations very readable. They have been making big progress.)

The following is how one PM describes her typical day and the changes that have taken place in her life since taking up the position.

> 作为PM我每天醒来的第1件事情就是查看消息，确认是否有稿件待译，然后每天确认当天的一稿，顺利交付之后才能安心的睡一下。很多时候就已经是过了凌晨12点了。我们会主动研究CAT的翻译辅助软件，去帮助我们管理术语，去把语料库给积累起来，然后开学后我们也会专门召开项目总结会，反思我们项目的经验跟不足，就是说有了这个团队之后，我们希望把我们做的东西去积累起来，然后不断地指引我们后面更该怎么做的更好。然后我现在那个百度网盘里，我就是会有一个项目的文件夹，我会去看一些资料，然后也有各种培训的PPT，就回想起来真的是激情澎湃，热血沸腾。

> (As a PM, the first thing I wake up every day is to check if there is any incoming commission. Even after a task is assigned, I would check the chat group every few minutes to see if everything runs smoothly. I do my best to make sure every translation is thoroughly proofread before sending it off. I cannot remember

the number of days when I go to bed after midnight. The biggest change since becoming the PM is that we start to study how to use technology to build the resources. We start to hold review meetings to reflect on the weaknesses in the practices. We have a very simple goal: we want to make the workflow procedures more efficient. I have an online storage folder that saves all our translations and documents. Whenever I look at them, I feel very proud of being part of the team.)

Other team members listed the benefits they have taken away from the DGC project. Here are a few examples:

联合国这一套东西和我们平常的作业还是有不同的区别的，它有自己的术语体系、规则体系，所以能够接触到这方面的内容，我觉得是一个很好的锻炼机会，刚开始大家难免会犯错，包括我现在也还会犯很多错，但是大家都总会在错误中一步步成长起来的。

(Translating the DGC content forms its own system. It is so different from the homework assigned in our formal curriculum. We have never been made so acutely aware of the importance of consistency in terminology and in style. It is beneficial to be able to work in this new area. In the beginning, everyone made mistakes. I still make mistakes, but we learn from these mistakes and learn to never make the same mistakes again.)

首先你肯定会学到一个专业的态度，就是比如说对待文本的时候会一种严谨的态度，光光SG就已经有几十页了，就可以研究很久了。一开始你可能就要研究好几天，才能把这些SG里的东西完全的融入到自己的工作流程当中，这样才不会出错，就即便我们做到现在，可能有时候也是会出错的，所以我们也有互校的环节，相互纠错。大家讨论的时候其实还非常有劲的，大家会一起扣网站什么的，非常有趣，在这里能结识到很好的朋友，然后共同成长。

(In my experience working on the DGC project, I've learned what it takes to be a true professional. One notable aspect of this is the precision required when handling texts. We have our own comprehensive style guide, spanning dozens of pages. I vividly recall the days I spent poring over it when I first received it, diligently trying to grasp every single rule. However, it wasn't until I had the opportunity to put these rules into practice that their true essence became clear to me. I still make mistakes from time to time. Fortunately, I have the privilege of working closely with a peer reviewer on each project, who helps me navigate and rectify these errors. Occasionally, my partner and I find ourselves engaged in impassioned debates, unable to convince each other of our respective viewpoints. In such cases, we often return to the style guide and the original text to find common ground. Through these experiences, I've forged numerous friendships, all of us grateful for the growth we've achieved together.)

在DGC团队成长了特别多，最大的变化愿意钻研，愿意为了一个小点去抠，不管从事什么工作。它会塑造你的职业道德。让你特别重视deadline， 以后跟客户合作，跟上下级沟通，长期的守时会让别人觉得你是一个靠谱的人，在很多环境中能够成长的更好。在DGC项目中，我又要实习，又要上课，写作业，还要做稿子，很多事情压在一起，很多人会觉得自己的心理压力太大了，承压能力很弱。然后在这种情况下身兼数职的时候也可以知道自己的极限在哪里。这是一个长期历练的过程。

(The DGC project has brought about significant changes in my approach to work and time management. One of the most notable transformations is my increased attention to detail and my willingness to explore a multitude of online resources to resolve even the smallest issues. I believe that this newfound meticulousness is highly valued in the professional world. Another important shift is my growing respect for deadlines. I have come to realize that consistently meeting deadlines is crucial for building a reputation as a reliable individual. As a member of this project, I've been compelled to juggle various responsibilities, including project tasks, coursework, and homework. Balancing these demands has helped me identify my limits and gradually extend them. While it's been a gradual process, I've become more adept at managing my time effectively.)

很重要的一点就是加入团队就有一种共同责任感。别人都做你怎么不做，这个事情压倒我头上我怎么能不完成？如果我不做，下面给我互校的同学时间就卡不上。然后会因为我影响项目进度。我就有了责任感，不能因为一个人拖团队后腿。有时候自己确实也会想偷懒，想睡懒觉或是，不想做，想出去玩，很正常，但是这时候就会有"别人做我怎么能不做呢？"那种心态。就把自己揪过来了。

(For me, the most important change is that I start to value accountability. When I see my fellow members sign up a commission, I feel bad if I don't sign up. And if I don't finish my share of work on time, I know other people would have to wait for me. The progress of the translation will be held up because of me. Sometimes, I do want to give it a slack; I also want to sleep in or go out for fun, but when I start to think that my teammates would have to wait because of me, I become more engaged.)

As the only reviser on the team, the teacher reviser clearly felt the weight of his responsibility.

一开始我说我们要时刻保持敬畏之心，我们在翻译的时候应该战战兢兢，如履薄冰。没想到我这句话会成为当口头禅，一直传承下来。非常感谢同学的一种不懈的追求，然后和我一起经历各种艰辛，当然也是一种荣耀。我们一直有一种，说大一点的话，就是使命感，就是说我们很珍惜和UN合作，我们任何人包括我都不希望说这条路砸在我们自己手里面，我希望能够把这个路呢给下一届的同学们、学弟学妹们能够延续下去，能够开拓更多的这种机会。所以我们每天在做的时候都会战战兢兢、如履薄冰，不想让这个事情砸在自己手里，成为历史的罪人。

(I still vividly recall the inception of this project, where I consistently emphasized the importance of thoroughness to both myself and our students. It was as if we were treading on delicate eggshells. Little did I know that this metaphor would become a guiding principle, passed down through subsequent cycles. I'd like to express my heartfelt gratitude to all the students who have embarked on this journey with me. Being part of the DGC project has given us a sense of purpose, as we highly value the training opportunities offered by the UN. None of us wish to see the end of this collaboration. I sincerely hope that this internship project will not only endure but also attract more students in the future. This is precisely why we must maintain precision and consistency in our translations, as we cannot afford a single mistake that might erode the trust bestowed upon us.)

These alternative perspectives provide evidence that learning is taking place in the seemingly mundane and repetitive routines of the practice. Like many small strands, each instance of learning combines to bring out transformative changes in each participant and help them feel more competent, more connected, and more empowered.

6.6 Taking in new blood

New members provide an opportunity for a community to evolve and grow. In less than a year, the members of the 2018 class had taken full ownership of the DGC project. As November 2019 approached, it was time to welcome a new group of first-year students to the team.

The three PMs began developing their recruitment plan well in advance. Similar to the previous year, in October 2019, they announced openings through WeChat groups to all MT and MI students. A total of 60 students from both tracks expressed their interest by submitting their resumes.

On November 1, 2019, the first round of translation examinations was distributed via email to all applicants. This time, the chosen article was again sourced from the *UN Chronicle* digital magazine, which had been recently translated by two current members. Applicants were given four days to complete the translation and submit it to the specified email address. Subsequently, on November 6, 2019, the second round of revision examinations was sent out via email. This test consisted of six short paragraphs intentionally containing various errors, designed by the three PMs to assess applicants' understanding of textual conventions and attention to detail. Applicants were required to submit their modified versions using Microsoft Word's comment function by November 13. Ultimately, a total of 54 students successfully completed both rounds of examinations.

On November 14, the members of the 2018 class organized a plenary meeting to prepare for the annual recruitment process. As usual, the translation papers would be evaluated by the teacher-reviser using a five-level letter grading system. All 16 current student members participated in the grading of the revision tests. The three PMs assigned four test papers to each member, along with a fully marked reference text, giving them one week to complete the grading process.

During the following week, many members turned to the PMs online to address their questions when they discovered that the provided reference did not cover all the correct answers comprehensively. Engaging in lively discussions in the chat group, the current members gradually developed a shared understanding of the grading criteria. Surprisingly, they even identified a couple of errors in the reference answers and urged the PMs to create an updated version. Since this was the first recruitment led by the three PMs, they were newcomers to this aspect of activities. In a community, no single individual bears the sole responsibility for knowing it all (Lave and Wenger 1991). The fact that members requested clarification on ambiguous answers from the PMs illustrated that knowledge was distributed among the team, with each contributing their knowledge and skills to the collective endeavor. Learning evolves through inheritance and cumulative modification. When grading was completed, the PMs again reviewed all revision tests to ensure fairness and tallied the final scores.

It is evident that homogeneity characterizes the recruitment process in both cycles. A year before, the three PMs from the 2018 class were test-takers evaluated by the 2017 class PMs. Now, they sent out test notification emails following the exact model they had received a year earlier and applied the same principles to design the recruitment test. This demonstrated their recognition of the practical value of the artifacts left behind by their predecessors. Continuity involves passing on the stories, artifacts, and practices from one generation to the next, creating enduring connections between newer and older members and the artifacts themselves.

However, they also introduced incremental changes. For instance, when combining the two scores to calculate the final scores, the three PMs realized that using the same weighting as the previous year would result in minimal differentiation between applicants. Consequently, in consultation with the teacher reviser, they decided to distribute the weighting equally between the translation exam and the revision exam. They eventually welcomed 23 new recruits, two more than in their own cycle.

Another noteworthy change was the announcement of test results to applicants. They introduced a completely new component and provided an explanation for why they deducted points from applicants who had failed to follow the test instructions. This included those who had incorrectly named their test papers, submitted their work late, or used the track-change function instead of the comment function. While such errors might seem inconsequential on other occasions, they bore consequences as they reflected on the entire team, as the real client judged them collectively. Consequently, the three PMs decided to deduct five points from the final scores as a lesson highlighting the importance of adhering to instructions. In the email notifying applicants of their results, they presented the breakdown of the final score transparently and clearly, marking an improvement compared to the test results announced by the 2017 class PMs.

The changes, however small, are evidence that current members are keeping their eyes open to potential deficiencies and are seeking to optimize the practices. As a result, the new members would come away with a more positive impression of the project. It also shows that legitimate peripheral participation is far more than just a process of learning on the part of newcomers. Old members also learn to identify new features from the young members and learn how to better acclimate young members to the established values and practices.

6.7 Grooming new members

The next step is to introduce the new recruits to the community. In conjunction with the upcoming visit of DGC partners in celebration of the two side's sixth year of collaboration, the program administrator organized a special one-day orientation event for newer recruits. In the morning, DGC representatives gathered with the current members and some seasoned members from previous cycles for a discussion. The experienced members shared their insights and reminisced about their time working on the project with the new recruits.

In the afternoon, the entire group met face-to-face with the newer recruits. Following a similar format to the previous year, the three PMs from the 2018 class and the teacher reviser guided the new members of the 2019 class through the workflow, tools, and procedures used in the practice.

This event provided a unique opportunity for members from both the 2018 and 2019 classes to connect with each other and the broader community. One of the project's founders, a student from the 2015 class, shared the story of how she and her classmates came together to handle DGC tasks and the initial steps they took, such as creating a style guide, to ensure consistency. She even mentioned how this experience helped her secure a job in media communication. The DGC partners also discussed how the partnership with GIIT came into existence and the transformations they've witnessed in the team over time.

As the sole reviser in the project for the past six years, the teacher reviser reflected on how the work instilled in him a sense of commitment and reverence for the project. Three members from the 2017 class briefly shared their experiences of completing three-month internships at the UN European Headquarters in Geneva and Vienna during the summer of 2018, highlighting how their work on DGC materials contributed to their success in the internship application process.

The three current PMs then provided the DGC partners with an overview of the new workflow that the team adopted since transitioning to a cloud-based tool. This allowed everyone to stay updated on the latest developments within the team and their approach to work.

The event culminated in the presentation of a congratulatory letter written by the then Undersecretary-General of the DGC, Ms. Melissa Fleming, which read:

> This year also marks the sixth anniversary of the cooperation between the United Nations Department of Global Communications and Shanghai International

Studies University. On behalf of the Organization, I express my deep gratitude for your immeasurable contributions to our work.

SISU has been an important and steady partner in helping to produce rich, multilingual content that reaches a global audience. Your contributions have made possible Chinese-language versions of important UN products, including the UN Chronicle magazine, the *UN In Action* feature television programme, various web pages for www.un.org, news about international days and the two Chinese editions of *Basic Facts of the United Nations*.

The complexity and range of the subjects you have covered is a testament to the professional quality of your translation and behind-the-scenes effort you have put into this work over many years. In addition, we appreciate the many interns you have provided to the United Nations. We look forward to strengthening this fruitful collaboration in the future.

On this milestone anniversary, please accept my sincere best wishes for your continued success.

According to Wenger, McDermott, and Snyder (2002, 56), meaningful participation in a CoP is "a complex process that combines doing, talking, thinking, feeling, and belonging. It involves the whole person, including bodies, minds, emotions, and social relations." Seen in this way, training new recruits is not only about providing them with practical information, but also a chance to show them the culture of the community. Clearly, these narrations have sketched out the history of the project from different points of view. Their accounts have sparked the imagination of the possibilities new recruits might have once they become formal members. The reflections on the meaning of the practice and on the identity of being a member feed back into the cultural heritage of the community. "Heritage," in this sense, is not only about the artifacts and documents that are visible but also consists of immaterial elements, such as traditions, culture, and values. It represents a shared history and identity and helps the members develop mutual respect.

Following the orientation, the first training exercise was sent through email on January 11, 2020, which asked the new recruits to review the translations made by the 2018 class members and to write a reflective report. The second training exercise was sent in late February, asking them to translate a *UN in Action* documentary. Unlike a year before, the current members adopted a mentorship scheme and asked every older member to provide one-on-one feedback to the recruits of the 2019 class. Meanwhile, the formal members continued to engage in the routine practice for the DGC.[6]

Notes

1 The print edition of the *UN Chronicle* was discontinued following the publication of a special 2018 double issue. The magazine was moved to an all-digital format on 1 January 2019.
2 This is the platform used by DGC to send/receive translations to/from the team.

3 The print edition of the *UN Chronicle* was discontinued following the publication of this special 2018 double issue. The magazine was moved to an all-digital format on 1 January 2019.
4 All the posts we pulled directly from the chat group as evidence are followed by their translations in brackets in this chapter.
5 Although the DGC project is not financially supported by the UN, GIIT has been able to obtain a grant from the university to compensate the participant's time and commitment to the project.
6 Due to the breakout of COVID-19 pandemic in late January of 2020 and the subsequent lock-down of campus, we had no way to connect with the new recruits of the 2019 class face to face and therefore, were forced to skip this part of research. But at the same time, we continued to observe online how the members of the 2018 class continued to translate the routine tasks sent by the DGC all the way to early April of 2020.

References

Ausubel, D. P., J. D. Novak, and H. Hanesian. 1978. *Educational Psychology: A Cognitive View*, 2nd ed. New York: Holt, Rinehart & Winston.
Baker, M. 2009. "Argumentative Interactions and the Social Construction of Knowledge." In *Argumentation and Education: Theoretical Foundations and Practices*, edited by N. Muller Mirza and A. Perret-Clermont, 127–144. Dordrecht and Heidelberg: Springer.
Bandura, A. 1977. *Social Learning Theory*. Saddle River: Prentice Hall.
Brown, J. S., A. Collins, and P. Duguid. 1989. "Situated Cognition and the Culture of Learning." *Educational Researcher* 18 (1): 32–42. doi: 10.3102/0013189X018001032.
Cao, A., and X. Zhao. 2006. *Translation of United Nations Documents. [联合国文件翻译.]*. Beijing: China Translation Corporation.
Chen, Z. 2017. "Unlocking the Everyday Work of United Nations Translators: An Exclusive Interview with Chen Zhongliang, Chief of the Chinese Translation Service at the UN Headquarters on the International Translation Day." https://news.un.org/zh/audio/2017/09/309942.
Cronin, M. 2020. "Translation, Technology and Climate Change." In *The Routledge Handbook of Translation and Technology,* edited by M. O'Hagan, 516–530. London and New York: Routledge.
Dillenbourg, P. 1999. "What Do You Mean by Collaborative Learning?" In *Collaborative-Learning: Cognitive and Computational Approaches*, edited by P. Dillenbourg, 1–19. Oxford: Elsevier.
Dunne, E. S. 2011. "Project as a Learning Environment: Scaffolding Team Learning in Translation Projects." In *Translation and Localization Project Management. The Art of the Possible*, edited by K. J. Dunne and E. S. Dunne, 265–288. Amsterdam and Philadelphia: John Benjamins.
Hoadley, C. 2012. "What Is a Community of Practice and How Can We Support It?" In *Theoretical Foundations of Learning Environments*. 2nd ed., edited by D. H. Jonassen and S. M. Land, 287–300. London: Taylor & Francis.
Lafeber, A. 2012. "Translation Skills and Knowledge-Preliminary Findings of a Survey of Translators and Revisers Working at Inter-Governmental Organizations." *Meta* 57 (1): 108–131. doi: 10.7202/1012744ar.
Lave, J., and E. Wenger. 1991. *Situated Learning: Legitimate Peripheral Participation*. Cambridge: Cambridge UP.

Lee-Jahnke, H. 2009. "Doppelter Praxisbezug und Kompetenzvermittlung als Problem der Qualitätssicherung Translatorischer Studiengänge." In *CIUTI FORUM 2008. Enhancing Translation Quality Ways, Means, Methods*, edited by M. Forstner et al., 133–195. Frankfurt am Main: Peter Lang.

Risku, H., and A. Dickinson. 2009. "Translators as Networkers: The Role of Virtual Communities." *HERMES – Journal of Language and Communication in Business* 42: 49–70. doi: 10.7146/hjlcb.v22i42.96846.

Sawyer, D. 2004. *Fundamental Aspects of Interpreter Education: Curriculum and Assessment*. Amsterdam and Philadelphia: John Benjamins.

Shang, X., M. Russo, and C. Chabasse. 2023. "Introduction to the Special Issue Revisiting Aptitude Testing for Interpreting." *The Interpreter and Translator Trainer* 17 (1): 1–6. doi:10.1080/1750399X.2023.2170042.

Vallerand, R. J. 1997. "Toward a Hierarchical Model of Intrinsic and Extrinsic Motivation." *Advances in Experimental Social Psychology* 29: 271–360. doi: 10.1016/S0065-2601(08)60019-2.

Vygotsky, L. S. 1978. *Mind in Society: The Development of Higher Psychological Processes*. Massachusetts: Harvard University Press.

Washbourne, K. 2012. "Translation Style Guides in Translator Training: Considerations for Task Design." *The Journal of Specialised Translation* 17, 2–17.

Wenger, E. 1998. *Communities of Practice. Learning, Meaning, and Identity*. Cambridge: Cambridge UP.

Wenger, E., R. McDermott, and W. M. Snyder. 2002. *A Guide to Managing Knowledge: Cultivating Communities of Practice*. Cambridge: Harvard Business School Press.

Wenger, E., N. White, and J. D. Smith. 2009. *Digital Habitats: Stewarding Technology for Communities*. Portland: CPSquare.

Wenger-Trayner, E., and B. Wenger-Trayner. 2015. "Introduction to Communities of Practice: A Brief Overview of the Concept and Its Uses." https://wenger-trayner.com/introduction-to-communities-of-practice/.

7 Analysis, comparison and discussion of the DGC project

7.1 Research features of the DGC project

7.1.1 Research design

An internship project differs from a one-off class project in that it offers members the opportunity for consistent practice. Consequently, it may necessitate a distinct research approach. Class projects are frequently investigated through action research or case studies. Action research is driven to address a specific educational problem, conducted by individuals intimately involved in the context, and the findings are directly applied to their practice (Efron and Ravid 2013). However, this approach isn't suitable for our situation. In line with the principles of social learning theory, we hold the belief that learning in an internship project is not about completing a single task but an ongoing, evolving process. This learning is not solely derived from productive activities but also from tasks that may not be directly related to translation. As a result, instead of selecting a single task as a sample and describing its progression, we have opted to employ an ethnographic perspective to chronicle the sequence of events within the community.

7.1.2 Research foci

A key feature characterizing most studies on PjBL is that they aim to correlate the effects of PjBL with the participants' improvement of translation competence. Indeed, many of them have reported positive results, providing unequivocal evidence of the value of PjBL in complementing traditional classroom instruction.

Nevertheless, there are two problems with this approach. One is that they tend to use a single translation competence model for students to tick after a learning event[1], but due to individual differences in role specification and levels of engagement, participants may gain a wide range of benefits, some of which may not be amenable to assessment. We cannot develop a perspective on the effects of PjBL that is deterministic and restrictive. The other problem is that most projects are one-off learning events. As expertise studies inform us, people need constant practice and repetition to consolidate their learning. Kolb (1984) suggests that in an experiential learning cycle, knowledge is continuously created and recreated. A single

DOI: 10.4324/9781003542469-7

experience alone does not necessarily lead to learning that can be sustained and transferred to unfamiliar circumstances. Practitioners need to consciously examine knowledge gained from one task and apply it to new contexts to achieve deep learning.

Initially, we have indeed tried to ask the student participants to self-assess their competence improvement using the European Master's in Translation (EMT) wheel of competence (EMT Expert Group 2009) at three points in their participation. But there was no apparent improvement in the three sets of data. We assumed this had to do with the long interval between each questionnaire. It was midway past their learning journey, after the participants had accumulated some experience with the DGC text that we began to frequently hear positive gains from interviews and from their group meetings. Contrary to what we initially expected, the biggest benefits they reported were not some abstracted translation competences, but generic competence and tacit knowledge of workflow. For instance, through teamwork, they started to value each other's contribution more. They were made more aware of the importance of juggling different priorities and working to meet deadlines. There was a renewed appreciation of advance planning and time management. There were also improvements in their self-perceived efficacy and wider knowledge base. In terms of the translation competence *per se*, they began to set more store by information and communications technology (ICT) and information literacy, the importance of translation asset management and the ability to adapt to the workflow.

This led us to believe that it was impossible to assess the full extent of the participants' competence acquisition by using a single explicit translation competence model. Our findings validate the co-emergent competence model (Kiraly 2016). Where we part ways, however, is that Kiraly does not make a distinction between the subcategories of authentic PjBL and, therefore, focuses only on class projects. We believe, in addition to class projects, internship projects represent another way of authentic, collaborative learning. If we shift our perspective to use legitimate peripheral participation as the theoretical lens, there is a clear learning trajectory taking place. The participants learn by establishing a clear routine that helps them produce quality work over different cycles. In a way, the findings convince us that competence is not fostered by a single task. It requires regular practice for participants to be fully competent in a domain.

7.1.3 Data elicitation and analysis methods

Previous research on PjBL often uses a combination of the teacher's personal reflections, questionnaires, reflective journals, interviews, and product-based examples to make a claim, which are all qualitative offline methods. Being introspective and retrospective, the data generated run the risk of being incomplete (Hansen 2005) and may even be constrained or manipulated due to assessment concerns (Boud 2001). There is an inherent need to triangulate them with more online methods.

With the growth of the Internet, digital media and translation tools have opened new ways in the provision of translation services. They also provide powerful ways to connect people across distributed work environments. That is why we can't easily dismiss the activities captured by the ICT and translation tools. In learning sciences, encouraging learners to engage in collaborative dialogue and examining the dialogic artifacts for the presence of such new knowledge is an established way to examine learning in online environments (Paulus 2005). But this method has not been applied widely in translation pedagogy[2]. Written verbal data reflect participants' reflections, justifications, emotions, and experiences (Hansen 2005). Tracking how various interactions shift over time can reveal changes in individual and collective learning.

7.2 Changes identified in the DGC project

Schön (1983) promotes an epistemology of practice grounded in the concept of reflection-in-action. A community should not remain static. As new members inherit practices from their predecessors, they often introduce changes in response to evolving demands within the practice. This dynamism not only enhances motivation and engagement among community members but also underscores their ability to contribute to growth. In retrospect, we have been able to identify several changes in this cycle. They include:

- In the past, opportunities for participation were only available to the students enrolled in the translation stream, but from this cycle, the first-year interpreting students were allowed to participate as well. This reflects a clear recognition at the Graduate Institute of Interpretation and Translation (GIIT) that the students need to be prepared for a wide range of career options. It aligns with the idea of equal access to opportunities, promoting fairness and inclusivity in education.
- When the participants were under training, they saw how the old members used Word to translate, but when they took on tasks themselves, they were asked to use a cloud-based translation tool to translate. Consequently, they revamped the workflow and were able to experience more real-time human–human and human–machine collaboration.
- With the adoption of the new tool, the team started to pay more attention to translation asset management. Previously, except an integrated term base saved in an Excel file, all the content translated were distributed in different places. Now the team started to build their own domain-specific TB and TM in the tool, with the three project managers (PMs) doubling up as translation asset managers.
- It is not only the team, but the external partner that is also changing with the times. In early 2019, DGC stopped the paper-based quarterly publication of the *UN Chronicle* and launched an exclusively web-based digital magazine. As a result, new articles that needed to be translated were sent on a more varied basis. Previously, it would take the team a month to complete the translation of a whole issue. Now a shift schedule has been put in place for this specific type of work, allowing quicker turnaround and higher flexibility.

Analysis, comparison and discussion of the DGC project 157

- When it was time to select the new recruits from the 2019 class, the project managers devised a more differentiated grading scheme to take in the most qualified candidates.
- When the participants of the 2018 class were under training, although each was paired with an older member, it was hard to assess the scaffoldings provided. Now, as they began training the newer members themselves, they provided more targeted one-on-one feedback.
- The team started with a free basic version of the cloud-based tool, but as they became more adept with the tool and as more new members joined the community, they felt an acute need to update the service and successfully obtained funding to do so.

These continuous improvements illustrate that participants are consciously examining their practices and striving to enhance their efficiency. It's important to recognize that communities are in a constant state of reinvention, as asserted by Wenger (1998). This process of continuous improvement can be seen as a collaborative effort between both old and new members. Teams that embrace change and consistently seek to refine their practices are better positioned to stay ahead of the curve, mitigate quality risks, reduce costs, and meet the demands of clients.

7.3 "Best" practices in the DGC project

Although each project is unique, they all need to have the right people, tools, processes, and resources in place to achieve the "best" practice.

7.3.1 Participants

Quality in translation starts from finding the right people (Jääskeläinen 2016). This is mainly reflected in the ways new students are selected and trained in the DGC project. The recruits are qualified in the sense that they appear to possess specific skills that are valued by the team. But what is more special is that they must prove their qualifications through training, which lasts half a year, until they gain formal membership. Training establishes a clear policy on the procedures to follow and gives the new members access to all the tools, resources, and information. It is supervised by the older members rather than by a teacher, which fosters team cohesion. Training continuously engages recruits and enables them to engage back.

Of all the student participants, project managers are the most important mediators. The responsibilities they assume are many and various. In all previous studies we have reviewed, the PMs are either appointed by the teacher, elected by the student participants, or assumed by the teacher themselves. In the DGC project, the recruits have observed for months the performance of the old PMs to build knowledge of what the job is about. When the time comes to picking the new PMs, running for the position is voluntary, and selection criteria are competitive and merit-based. The PM candidates regard the old PMs as their role models, but on the other hand, they are asked to reflect on their management deficiencies. Such a practice assists them in reviewing and refining the ways to manage a team once they are elected.

The teacher reviser is the most crucial cog in helping the team achieve quality. In the industry, there is fear that a revisor may introduce new errors to the translation because he or she may not have invested the same amount of time as the translator in research (Martin 2012). In the DGC project, the teacher reviser is the only one involved in the project since its very beginning. Therefore, he has developed an uncanny take on the external partner's preferences, more knowledge of the subject matter, and a broader perspective on the continuity of tasks. He systematically improves each translation, starting from checking the translator's understanding of the source text to spotting mistranslations and omissions to making sure the target text flows idiomatically and maintains consistency across sections handled by various students. Moreover, he gives the students opportunities to revert his revisions through online discussion. His commitment and expertise in the tasks are a key factor underpinning the success of the DGC project.

7.3.2 Collaborative workflows and quality control

Compared with the previous sampled projects that proceed in a linear manner, the DGC project adopts a collaborative workflow model. There are seven steps of quality control, with each step designed to address pitfalls of the previous one[3] (see Table 7.1).

The workflow starts with the translator(s) machine translating the source text or translating the source text using the TB and TM to produce a rough draft. Doing so helps them save time on repetitive element and increases the consistency with legacy translations. It can also help them avoid obvious mistakes, such as omission, misspelling, and grammar errors.

The second step entails the translators using his/her own translation competence and the quality assurance (QA) functions provided by the tool to improve a translation's accuracy and smoothness. However, the hidden danger is that the translators may be unwittingly influenced by the draft, or they may develop blind faith and skip research on the United Nations Terminology Database (UNTERM) and Linguee for correct terms and expressions.

Table 7.1 Layers of quality control in the DGC project

Step 1: Translating text assisted by machine translation/translation memory
Step 2: Post-editing and self-checking
Step 3: Peer revision
Step 4: Teacher revision
Step 5: Student translator validating teacher reviser's modifications
Step 6: Student translator exporting and formatting the target text
Step 7: PM proofreading each translation

At peer revision, the initial translator and his or her partner switch to revise each other's work. This is an opportunity for them to fill in gaps in each other's knowledge and skills. However, there are some potential pitfalls. For instance, they might get caught up in rewording sentences they find awkward or poorly phrased, even though such changes might not significantly impact the overall quality. Additionally, if one of them doesn't identify any issues, it is possible that the other may miss them as well. As argued by Martin (2012), when both translators are inexperienced and of mediocre skill, critical errors may persist, and peer revision essentially acts as a mere "second set of eyes" without contributing to the overall quality.

As a result, the thrust of quality control is put on the shoulders of the teacher reviser. Since all the edits and changes are recorded by Yicat, the teacher reviser can tell which term comes from the integrated term base and which is newly added. The changes and comments the translators made during peer revision also give him clues of the problems they have experienced. He poses questions to the original translator on the chat group whenever he feels the need for more information, and whoever is being asked is expected to respond to the query quickly. This back-and-forth flow of information is vital to overcome knowledge asymmetry and improve quality.

After the teacher reviser completes his revision, the initial translators read the revised translation from beginning to end to see what changes have been implemented. They can ask the teacher reviser to explain if they don't understand a particular change. The subsequent negotiations and discussions helped both sides connect the dots.

Once all the queries are clarified, the original translators export and format the translation and send it to the PM, who proofreads the bilingual text and posts additional questions to the teacher reviser and the original translator for clarification.

At first glance, this workflow does not look very much different from those adopted in previous research, but we see more feedforward and feedback flowing in the process. With the teacher revising the students' translations and students validating the teacher's revisions, the team learn by exchanging alternate points of view, being more exact in quality control and assuming mutual accountability for the final product.

7.3.3 Technology

Based on our cross-case analysis, tools used in sampled projects tend to be communication, documentation, and desktop editing tools. Translation tools are only used in three studies, all of which are server-based proprietary tools, and are all decided by the teacher(s). We do not see how the tools shape, and more importantly, being shaped by the members' experiences of use.

In the DGC project, the team took up Yicat early in this cycle. The best part of the tool is that it allows the original translator(s), the peer reviewer(s) and the teacher reviser to work in the same browser-based editor and to have their resources updated in real-time. Once the original translator confirms his/her translations, every subsequent change is saved and marked out by the tool, which helps the people down the chain make decisions quickly.

The team has been using QQ as the communication tool all along. Being the most popular free chat tool in China, it can be easily installed on the participants' desktop and mobile devices. It saves all the posts with a searchable history, which gives everyone equal access to information. It can even be used as an online storage device. When posts are visible to all, the team would know who is praised by the teacher reviser and whose translation has produced mistakes. In this way, the use of QQ fosters the individual sense of accountability.

Technology is always evolving. The use of these two pieces of technology has helped the team overcome the geographical barrier and avoid financial and infrastructure impediments that often afflict in-house translation projects mentioned by Li and He (2011).

7.3.4 Resources

It would be incomplete to examine the workflow and technology without mentioning the scaffolds used to help the team produce consistent and accurate translations.

First, the team uses two open-source corpus-based databases—Linguee and UNTERM—to identify correct terms and expressions. Situating the most fitted term from copious similar examples takes time. To maximize value from each research and make the resulting TB more DGC-domain specific, the translators now directly add each new term and their metadata to the cloud-based tool.

The same goes for the text translated each time. One big problem with translating with Word is that each translation remains in the hands of whoever has produced it, which means its value is lost to other members who are not involved in that task. Now all the translations are digitalized in the cloud-based tool; they are accessible to all, easily scalable and up to date.

Lastly, the style guide. The now 33-page document specifies the norms governing every imaginable aspect of translation. New recruits must read it during training. Formal members consult it again and again until they can apply the principles automatically in formatting and proofreading. The style guide is growing with the project and encapsulates the members' shared repertoire and representations of the knowledge.

7.3.5 External partner

The client, the UN Department of Global Communications is not merely the end user of all translations. It is involved in the project in several ways. This is first reflected in the feedback it provides to the team. DGC has its own inhouse reviewers to go through every translation before putting it online. They will send back the opinion if they feel the quality has dropped. This pushes the team to maintain and improve quality. Secondly, DGC issues a certificate to everyone who

Analysis, comparison and discussion of the DGC project 161

successfully completes the internship. The Under-Secretary of the DGC has sent several official letters praising the participants' excellence in work. Other officials of the department have also come to visit the team on a regular basis. They would sit down with the members to learn what procedures are put in place to achieve the quality that meets their expectations. In return, they would share with the team the procedures they use in-house to edit and publish each translation, which helps everyone understand the larger picture and the ethos represented by the UN. As the chief of the DGC's Chinese translation unit points out, his division has been working with several universities in China to produce translated website content. The most challenging part of such cooperation is to make sure translations are of consistently high quality, but they are gratified that the DGC project implemented at GIIT, SISU has achieved this goal and is the most successful among all similar schemes. As he puts it,

> 严格专业的团队选拔和培训机制是翻译质量的保证，以老带新教师督导是团队长期稳定发展的秘诀。上外高翻基于项目的实战训练教学模式和联合国全球传播部的项目需求完全吻合，这样呢就保证了双方默契的配合，既实现了联合国全球传播部翻译中文资料的诉求，也保证了学生在翻译实行过程当中专业与综合能力的提升，真正做到了互利互惠、合作共赢。

(The quality of translation derives from the team's strict selection and training mechanism, and the supervision by older members and the teacher reviser. The training model set up by GIIT gives us assurance and confidence in the partnership. This collaboration has not only helped us reach more audience but has also given the participants a way to improve their professional and generic competence. This is a truly mutually beneficial partnership.)

7.3.6 *Strong support network*

A community cannot thrive without the support of its wider network of stakeholders. The team is first supported by the professionals employed by the cloud-based tool provider. A couple of them were once project participants themselves. This allows the team to contact tech support in crisis situations and have the problems solved soon.

The program provider has provided an institutional context that is conducive to reflective practice. They would frequently roll out news reports on its official WeChat account about the work carried out by the team. They would invite back the graduates and older members to share their internship and career stories with the current members, which creates a sense of continuity of the project and identification and pride among the members. They have been working to improve the working conditions of the team and have obtained a grant from the university to update Yicat service. They have also provided strong references if members wish to apply for intern scholarships from the UN.

The synergy formed with the technology stakeholder and with the program provider thus provides a source of vitality for the community to develop its enterprise.

7.4 Deficiencies of the DGC project

While the factors mentioned above have contributed to the overall strength of the DGC project, we have also identified several limitations.

The primary issue concerns the team's approach to task delegation. Currently, the team employs a shift schedule to ensure a constant availability of translators for incoming tasks. However, a drawback of this system is that PMs rarely assign tasks directly to translators; instead, they allow translators to choose the tasks they wish to work on. This approach may work well for small and familiar tasks, but it becomes a significant weakness when dealing with larger and less familiar tasks.

For instance, consider a task involving the translation of a 4,000-word document on the topic of producing social media content for UN peace operations, a subject area that was new to the team. During the revision process, the teacher reviser noticed marked stylistic differences among the four translators assigned to the task. In fact, one translator, Jim (a pseudonym), produced a translation that was crisp and comfortable but significantly differed from the others. The reviser's comment succinctly captured the issue: "**的翻译很简单，读起来很舒服，可是跟大多数人不一样，这是个问题，要是** 一个人翻就好了。" (Jim's translation is excellent, but it stands out too much from the others. This poses a problem. I wish the entire piece had been translated by him)

In short, when the team faces the challenge of completing a complex task within a tight timeframe, the PMs need to be more flexible in how they assign work to ensure stylistic consistency across multiple translators.

Secondly, by switching to the cloud-based tool, the team aims to achieve centralized management of translation assets, which means the terms generated from each task must be added to the TB. There are times when some translators have forgotten to do so. In a similar vein, the team now needs to invest time to manage the accrued resources by 1) vetting every newly added term, 2) standardizing the metadata, 3) removing inconsistencies or different forms of the same term, and 4) tracking down the final edits from the published version and reflecting these changes in the TM. The teacher reviser has been calling on the PMs to appoint a dedicated asset manager. Eventually, the three PMs decided to share this work, mainly because they were not sure what exactly was entailed in the job, and thus, no one stepped forward. The consistency of the three PMs and lack of supervision of their asset management practice might be a problem.

The third area concerns the management styles of the PMs. The teacher reviser admits that different PMs carry different styles. Some PMs like to be "the nice guy," but they also need to confront a wrong action, for instance, when a member picks up the tasks only when prompted or when fellow members do not attend group offline meetings. They must themselves identify with the practice and work closely with the teacher reviser to promote the "best" practices. When choosing a project manager, the team often leans toward individuals who actively engage with the established practices. However, it is essential to recognize that effective translation skills are one aspect, while the ability to lead and manage the team represents a different facet of the equation.

Fourthly, we have detected differences in the participants' learning styles and personalities. For instance, when a revised translation is returned to the original translators for validation, some engage with the teacher reviser immediately by asking all sorts of questions, but there are also those who appear disengaged and unassertive. In one of the interviews, one PM noted that sometimes, when probed by the teacher reviser on their understanding of a particular sentence or phrase, some students would simply ask the teacher: "翻成这样可以吗?"(can I change it to …?) without defending their own position or simply following the teacher's advice. It is important to create a culture that encourages and empowers the participants to ask questions and to stick to their ground when they are challenged by a more competent member.

Currently, there is only one teacher reviser to handle all the revision work in the project. This is only sustainable to the extent that the daily work does not exceed his maximum limit. There was a short period of time when the teacher reviser came down with a sudden illness; although he still managed to carry out all the revision work, the team soon heard from the DGC that the quality began to dip. To run the project in a sustainable way calls for the participation of more revisers to share the workload. But this opens the floodgate of other questions. For example, how to shorten the learning curve of the new teacher reviser(s)? How to make sure other revisers perform to the standard of quality?[4]

Finally, in a class project, the supervising teacher has an assortment of assessment methods at his/her disposal. In comparison, since the DGC project is carried on the sidelines of the curriculum and is self-governed by the students, there is no incentive to enforce effective assessment methods. As a result, once the new members are given full membership, some remain very proactive, but there are also those who end up not pulling their weight and prioritizing it less. This is seen in the divergence of words translated by different members[5] (see Table 7.2). The teacher reviser once floated the idea that even if the recruits were given full membership, they might still be removed from the group. But this idea has never gotten off the ground. The team adopts a system to calculate the words each of them has handled, but there are no effective methods to assess the quality of their translation. The only quality appraisal ever implemented was based on a rough calculation of their stylistic errors rather than translation errors, and it lasted less than four months. Simply put, the participants are only assessed by the volume rather than by the accuracy or efficiency of work. One remedy to the problem is to ask the teacher reviser to give a score based on the global assessment of each translation, but doing so would take extra time and effort and may not be popular with the student participants.

Table 7.2 Participant output (March, 2019–April, 2020)

No.	Name	Web content translation (including UNIA)	UN Chronicle translation	Total Output*
1		25635， 52546 (PM)	5417， 18106 (PM)	31052， 70652 (PM)
2		16316	4619	20935
3		17238， 54338 (PM)	6259， 9638 (PM)	23497， 63976 (PM)
4		27538	4665	32203
5		16427	4648	21075
6		25830， 53305 (PM)	3803， 25294 (PM)	29633， 78599 (PM)
7		12113	3026	15139
8		28999	5186	34185
9		14839	6611	21450
10		16573	4842	21415
11		10561	7233	17794
12		12533	7261	19794
13		25242	5442	30684
14		29894	3663	33557
15		15970	6510	22480
16		20953	6965	27918

Source: Provided by DGC project, with participant names deleted for anonymity.

Notes:
*Total output = Translation output (Web content + UN Chronicle) + Project management output ×10%.

Notes

1 The most recent example of this trend is seen in Zhang and Wang (2020). We are of the opinion that efforts of this nature may run counter to Kiraly's proposition that learning is an emergent phenomenon.
2 For the limited number of research using online data collected in natural settings, see Kußmaul (1995), Tirkkonen-Condit and Jääskeläinen (2000), Alves (2003), Pavlović (2009) and Pym (2009).
3 These steps are presented in a linear way for the sake of convenience. In reality, with the use of a cloud-based translation tool, steps 1–5 can be carried out in real time.
4 According to Brunette, Gagnon, and Hine (2005), dividing the revision work among several revisers to meet deadlines may bring risks to interrater and intra-rater reliability. Therefore, having a new reviser on board might contribute to inconsistency.
5 For example, the active members translate nearly three times as many words in web content as the least active members. There are likely two explanations for this discrepancy: some members may wait for others in the group to sign up for tasks, or they may tend to choose only the easier and smaller tasks.

References

Alves, F., editor. 2003. *Triangulating Translation: Perspectives in Process oriented Research.* Amsterdam and Philadelphia: John Benjamins.
Boud, D. 2001. "Using Journal Writing to Enhance Reflective Practice." In *Promoting Journal Writing in Adult Education. New Directions in Adult and Continuing Education,* edited by L. M. English and M. A. Gillen, 9–18. Hoboken: John Wiley & Sons.

Brunette, L., C. Gagnon, and J. Hine. 2005. "The Grevis Project: Revise or Court Calamity." *Across Languages and Cultures* 6 (1): 29–45. doi: 10.1556/Acr.6.2005.1.3.
Efron, S. E., and R. Ravid. 2013. *Action Research in Education: A Practical Guide*. London and New York: The Guilford Press.
EMT Expert Group. 2009. *Competences for Professional Translators, Experts in Multilingual and Multimedia Communication*. European Commission. http://ec.europa.eu/dgs/translation/programmes/emt/key_documents/emt_competences_translators_en.pdf.
Hansen, G. 2005. "Experience and Emotion in Empirical Translation Research with Think-Aloud and Retrospection." *Meta* 50 (2): 511–521. doi:10.7202/010997ar.
Jääskeläinen, R. 2016. "Quality and Translation Process Research." In *Reembedding Translation Process Research*, edited by R. Muñoz Martín, 89–106. Amsterdam and Philadelphia: John Benjamins.
Kiraly, D. 2016. "Beyond the Static Competence Impasse in Translator Education." In *Translation and Meaning. New Series,* edited by B. Lewandowska-Tomaszczyk, et al., Vol. 1. 129–142. Frankfurt am Main: Peter Lang.
Kolb, D. A. 1984. *Experiential Learning: Experience as the Source of Learning and Development*. Saddle River: Prentice Hall.
Kußmaul, P. 1995. *Training the Translator*. Amsterdam: John Benjamins.
Li, R. L., and Y. He. 2011. "Researching Translation Project-Based Learning Models from the Perspective of Learning Science. [学习科学视角下的项目翻译学习模式研究.]" *Foreign Language Education* 32 (1): 4–98.
Martin, C. 2012. "The Dark Side of Translation Revision." *Translation Journal* 16 (1). https://translationjournal.net/journal/59editing.htm.
Paulus, T. M. 2005. "Collaborative and Cooperative Approaches to Online Group Work: The Impact of Task Type." *Distance Education* 26 (1): 111–125. doi: 10.1080/01587910500081343.
Pavlović, N. 2009. "More Ways to Explore the Translating Mind: Collaborative Translation Protocols." In *Behind the Mind: Methods, Models and Results in Translation Process Research*, edited by S. Göpferich, A. L. Jakobsen, and I. M. Mees, 81–106. Copenhagen: Samfundslitteratur.
Pym, A. 2009. "Using Process Studies in Translator Training. Self-Discovery through Lousy Experiments." In *Methodology, Technology and Innovation in Translation Process Research*, edited by S. Göpferich, F. Alves, and I. Mees, 35–156. Copenhagen: Samfundslitteratur.
Schön, D. A. 1983. *The Reflective Practitioner*. New York: Basic Books.
Tirkkonen-Condit, S., and R. Jääskeläinen, editors. 2000. *Tapping and Mapping the Processes of Translation and Interpreting: Outlooks on Empirical Research*. Amsterdam and Philadelphia: John Benjamins.
Wenger, E. 1998. *Communities of Practice. Learning, Meaning, and Identity*. Cambridge: Cambridge UP.
Zhang, Z., and Y. Wang. 2020. "Project-based Translation Teaching and Translation Competence Development: Theory and Practice. [MTI 项目化翻译教学与翻译能力培养：理论与实践]." *Foreign Language World* 2: 65–72.

8 Conclusions and pedagogical implications

8.1 General synthesis

The research begins by setting the scene with a brief overview of the rise of competence-based training within T&I education. The quintessential feature of the CBT is that it is student-centered, competence-based, and process-oriented. Although there is no single widely agreed definition of translation and interpreting competence, CBT overall uses the top-down multi-componential view to inform the curriculum design (Massey 2017). However, when the teaching content is linked with component(s) of translation competence and role-based competence, there might be a lack of integration and coherence in different modules (Kelly 2007), underscoring the need for authentic, collaborative training at the advanced stage to achieve interconnectedness in learning and increase student adaptability and overall effectiveness.

This is followed by a summary of understanding of the translation process and an overview of industry standards and workflow models. While most models are sequential in nature, the emergence of cloud-based translation tools has created possibilities for real-time collaboration for a distributed team. By comparing the workflow of a school translation project with these industry-informed perspectives, we can identify gaps and areas for improvement.

PjBL is also rooted in the interdisciplinary developments in learning sciences, cognitive science, and expertise studies. With the rise of social constructivism, PjBL can bridge the gap between school and the profession and further promote learning as active participation and enculturation. The new "4EA" cognition paradigm (e.g. Muñoz Martín 2016) specifies that knowing is not a fixed totality but a contextual phenomenon that emerges as people interact with each other, with technologies and with evolving artifacts. In expertise studies, learners need to watch models of expertise-in-use to improve their skills (Collins, Brown, and Holum 1991). Expertise is not absolute nor concentrated in a single individual. Of the five conditions of deliberate practice that leads to expertise (Ericsson 2010; Shreve 2020), informative feedback, opportunities for repetition and the correction of errors, and motivation and support, can be purposely provided in PjBL.

Empirical studies on authentic translation projects are dominated by anecdotal accounts. By cross-analyzing 11 sampled studies, we find a lack of conceptual

Conclusions and pedagogical implications 167

differentiation of the concept. We first try to establish a distinction between traditional class projects and the new emerging internship projects. Class projects are sourced from a teacher as a one-off practicum. Students who sign up for the class automatically become participants. Internship projects, on the other hand, are organized by a program provider in collaboration with an external partner. Student and teacher participation in such projects is optional. If the external partner has regular needs for translation, the project may be sustained. Compared with the wealth of publications that describe how a single class project contributes to student translation competence, we perceive a lack of investigation on the latter type of PjBL.

Consequently, we try to fill the gap through a case study called the DGC project. With "Community of Practice" as a general theoretical toolkit (Lave and Wenger 1991), we adopt an ethnographic lens to track the journey of the student cohorts recruited at the project's fifth year. Our data comes from eclectic sources. In particular, we analyzed the participants' real-time collaborative dialogues, task by task, day by day, to highlight their human–human collaboration, human–machine collaboration and collaboration in building a shared asset for the community. The study shows that along the way, the participants took increasing pride in their identity. Individually, all of them have reported improvement in multidimensional competence in translating the DGC's content, tacit knowledge of the workflow, enriched appreciation of technology, ability of ad-hoc learning and better research skills, indepth understanding of the UN and the UN system, a broad knowledge base, and a close identification with the norms and values of the community. Collectively, they have contributed to the practice by adopting a new browser-based CAT tool, a new workflow technique, and have achieved some centralized management of translation resources. In the end, they have successfully maintained the continuity and viability of the project.

8.2 Response to the research question

If the cross-case review gave us a surface impression of the difference between class projects and internship projects, the observation of the DGC project has only made their differences more salient on the fundamental quality level.

In one-off projects, all the participants are involved in the production. The priority is to make sure the holistic work to be delivered is accurate, consistent within itself, and meets the deadline. To this end, the team must build an integrated term base and a style guide and follow fixed work procedures, but they generally don't concern themselves with the stakeholders, resources, and procurement management. Despite the reflections and assessments held at the completion of the project, the team does not have the chance to improve upon the practices in follow-up projects. All the resources and knowledge gained are for one-time use only. Once the product is delivered, the participants disband.

In contrast, in an ongoing internship project, the team must maintain the same level of quality from task to task (Bass 2006). This is a difficult goal to achieve because, first, the DGC has its own strict translation consistency requirements, to begin with; second, each task sent to the DGC is translated by different students; and third, the team reproduces itself cyclically. As the teacher reviser of the team put it, their biggest challenge is to make sure that "all translations read as if they were done by the same person all the time."

Therefore, a standard workflow and a common set of resources are essential, but they are not enough. To achieve consistent quality over successive groups of participants, the people taken in must have some initial qualification. This is why the older members used the real tasks they had translated as the examination material and developed the criteria in direct alignment with the team's quality metrics to measure an applicant's fitness.

They must put in place an onboarding and training system to make everyone identify with the philosophy and norms of the team. This is why, instead of putting the recruits on the job immediately, for the first three months, the PMs let the new members watch on the periphery how the old members interacted with each other. Gradually, the new members were allowed to help at the two ends of a real task so as to be acquainted with the types of work, the resources and tools, the vocabulary used in online discussion, and the organizing principles of the community.

A community is "held together by member's passion, commitment, and identification with the group and its expertise" (Wenger, McDermott, and Synder 2002, 42). This is why the project managers never force a task on a member but ask them to pick up work of their own volition. A community needs to retain committed members. This is why, after several months of training, the PMs gave each recruit the choice to leave or stay and awarded full membership to those truly committed. A community must have leaders who can diligently record and monitor each task. This is why it took an extra month and extra procedures to select the candidates interested in the position. The team believes that deeper engagement will generate enthusiasm and stimulate interest, which in turn will help the team develop a sense of identity and cohesion.

To ensure quality, there must be a common and constantly updated set of resources that include a style guide, term base, and translation memories. That is why the new members were given access to these resources from day one. This is why all the members can access the artifacts and documents saved in the tools, in order to learn at their own convenience. To prevent "garbage in, garbage out" from happening and to keep the resources up to date, there must be a dedicated person to organize translation assets accrued each time. This is why the teacher reviser has made repeated calls to select an asset manager and why some preliminary efforts have been made to this end.

A community must have a consistent and more experienced person who, like a stalwart, has a holistic view of the tasks and the practice, who can define the metrics of good translation and who can give student participants guidance on the industry's best practices and push students to make continuous improvement. We see these traits in the teacher reviser of the DGC project.

When the team adopts a new piece of technology, there must be robust support in place for those experiencing difficulties. To ensure the continuity of the project, the external client must have a sustainable need for translation service, understand the practice, make interventions when needed, and appreciate the value created by the team. There must be coordination and financial support from the program administrator in case of a need. In short, there must be an ecosystem at work to make sure the community runs productively.

All the above ingredients are indispensable for a community to achieve its strength and continuity. We have seen with our own eyes how each of them falls into place in the DGC project. But the more pertinent question is: what do the student participants learn from their experience in the community?

Studies on class projects invariably use some explicit translator competence model to gauge their effects and benefits. Our view is that we cannot use a single translation competence model, or any revision, project management, post-editing, or terminology competence model, for that matter. Because for one, the boundaries and content of the competence models are malleable to change and subject to individual interpretation, for another, any improvement depends on a person's level of engagement with the practice. On this point, we particularly agree with Kiraly's (2016) assertion that learning is an "autopoietic process."

Learning in the DGC project is authentic because, in terms of the degree of authenticity to market practice, the project has prepared students in more ways than a one-off task. On top of the direct translation experience and different role-based competences, the participants get to experience so many simple truths in life. For example, if they wish to be accepted by the project, they must make careful and thorough preparations to maximize their chance of being selected. If they want to stay in the project, they need to pay attention to all the announcements and activities taking place. They need to show an agency to decide how to learn, and how much time to spend on it and when to modify plans and strategies. They need to grab the chance to act when an opportunity presents itself. The participants learn by juggling competing responsibilities. They feel peer pressure from others, but they may also be held as role models because of their commitment and performance. They are made more conscious of their role as part of a bigger whole.

Learning in the DGC project is collaborative and iterative. It is enacted when the members coordinate with, monitor and critique each other to produce a joint product. It is enacted when they learn to use a new tool, evaluate its strengths and weaknesses, and contribute to building a common resource pool and a common set of values and discourse. It is enacted when the young members network with the old members and the DGC partner to know more about the background story of their translation. It is enacted when the technological supplier tells the members why a problem would occur and what measures can be taken to solve it. As the team works on various tasks, they have a better understanding of roles and responsibilities, which enhance overall team efficiency and effectiveness. When new challenges crop up, the team works together to address the difficulties. Each strand of individual and collective learning is closely knitted to help the team grow. Trust and cohesion are built through these shared experiences, fostering a positive team dynamic and a knowledge-sharing culture. This culture encourages team members to proactively share information, insights, and best practices. Perhaps the most succinct way to characterize such learning comes from Wenger himself (1998, 7):

For individuals, learning is an issue of engaging in and contributing to the practices of their communities. For communities, leaning is an issue of refining their practice and ensuring new generations of members.

8.3 Originality of the research

We believe that this research holds significance on multiple fronts. Firstly, it underscores the complementary roles played by individual cases and meta-analysis when examining a phenomenon. Individual cases provide a deep dive into specific details, contextual factors, and unique aspects, while meta-analysis helps uncover underlying patterns and themes. Given the scarcity of efforts to conduct cross-case comparisons of studies on authentic translation projects, we take a step back and adopt a holistic perspective. Using a bipartite framework, we conducted a comprehensive assessment of the sample projects' research and practice features. Our findings reveal that all samples follow a linear workflow model, predominantly employ desktop proprietary translation tools, and extensively explore human–human collaboration within the workflow and quality control aspects, but they only briefly touch upon human–machine collaboration and resource management. Most samples rely on offline data to assess PjBL's impact on individual student achievement, operationalized through various translation competence models.

As we delve deeper into these projects, we uncover that PjBL is not a monolithic entity but encompasses various subtypes. While many are one-off class projects, China's T&I education is witnessing the emergence of program-level internship projects. We proceed to introduce this new categorization for authentic translation projects. Furthermore, we argue that it is more appropriate to characterize ongoing internship projects rather than one-off projects as CoPs. We explore the operation of one such project within a single cycle. Along this journey, we identify numerous sensible practices in recruitment, training, assessment, leadership selection, technology utilization, workflow management, quality control, and knowledge and asset management. We also identify changes and the factors driving these changes and capture shifts in participants' motivations and identities. The DGC project has illuminated our understanding of the degree of authenticity and different dimensions of collaborative learning. It proves that the formal curriculum is not the primary locus of PjBL. By organizing an internship project in partnership with external partners, academia can foster a small ecosystem and benefit from the synergy brought forth. The greatest strength of the study, therefore, is its relevance to these new developments in project-based T&I pedagogy.

Regarding research questions, while previous studies have primarily focused on the benefits of PjBL for individual learning, we posit that to comprehend the dynamics of teamwork, problem-solving, decision-making, and creativity within ongoing internship projects, a broader perspective is necessary. We need to scrutinize how knowledge, ideas, and information are shared, processed, and collectively constructed within the group. This approach allows us to explore how group norms, leadership, and communication patterns influence the learning process and outcomes. It also opens the door to the emergence of novel solutions that individuals may not have conceived on their own, thereby enhancing the value of learning in social settings. Furthermore, it deepens our understanding of how individuals contribute to and gain from collective learning experiences.

In terms of research methodology, we employ a combination of methods to enhance the validity and reliability of our findings. Notably, we use collaborative verbal analysis to examine participants' online dialogues as a source of real-time activity data. We collect all posts, categorize them by task, initiator and content, and create a timeline to visualize the evolution of these activities. We also zoom in to scrutinize specific interaction details. This data-driven method represents a departure from previous empirical studies on PjBL, which primarily rely on "soft" data such as researcher observations and participant self-reflection. Analyzing verbal protocols allows us to capture dynamic changes objectively, maintaining ecological validity and replicability.

8.4 Limits of the research

There are a few limitations inherent in this research that we must acknowledge. The cross-case analysis in Chapter 3 should have included more recent projects, particularly those utilizing machine translation and artificial intelligence. Yet, despite diligent efforts, we encountered challenges in identifying cases that offer sufficient detail for comparative analysis. Several factors contributed to this difficulty. Trainers are often constrained by a prescribed curriculum, necessitating trade-offs between incorporating real-world tasks and covering other essential content. Real-world tasks may demand resources such as budget, time, personnel, and tools that educational institutions may not readily provide. Their complexity may require substantial time and effort to adapt for classroom use, and simultaneous involvement in translation tasks can hinder teachers' ability to act as researchers and document the process comprehensively. Then, the confidentiality constraints surrounding translation work may limit the disclosure of certain details in publications. Consequently, many educational programs resort to simulated projects for training purposes. We hope to address this lack of representation in future studies.

In investigating the DGC project, the biggest drawback of ethnographic design concerns the choice of the case, which tends to be based on convenience due to time constraints and limited resources (Saldanha and O'Brien 2014). Admittedly, convenience does play a large part in our study. Not every T&I program can partner up with the United Nations in offering students internship opportunities. The DGC project happens to be among the very few limited success stories we know and can access. But given the rise of such internship projects in China, we believe the case might herald a trend and deserves to be studied for the significance of the issues raised.

Nevertheless, we find it difficult to do full justice to the complexity of the DGC project. We came to understand the team's productive activities mostly through their online collaborative dialogues. Guba and Lincoln (1994) posit that it is best for a researcher to have prolonged immersion to establish trustworthiness. We have only observed one cycle of the project. If the observation had more iterative elements, we would have built a more solid understanding of the evolution of the practices.

In analyzing the collaborative dialogues taken from the team's chat group, we note that they mostly took place between the project manager and the translators, between the project manager and the teacher reviser and between the translators and the teacher reviser. This gives us reason to believe that some translators have chosen to talk bilaterally in private. It certainly would be more exhaustive if we could observe their bilateral interactions.

The coding and counting of each type of dialogue turned out to be an extremely labor-intensive and time-consuming process. We relied on double coding and built-in functions of Microsoft Excel for counting. It would be more accurate if a third independent person were involved for the study to reach intercoder reliability. Additionally, ethnographic case studies require tact and respect in negotiating continued access with all participants. As much as we wanted to interview every member of the project, we could only rely on a few key informants for information. We have tried to mitigate this weakness by triangulating with other sources of evidence, but it should be noted they represent not all but a subsection of all participants.

8.5 New paths of investigation

According to Wenger, McDermott, and Synder (2002, 68–69), like a human being, a CoP also goes through some natural stages of development:

> They typically start as loose networks that hold the potential of becoming more connected and thus a more important part of the organization. As members build connections, they coalesce into a community. Once formed, the community often grows in both membership and the depth of knowledge members share. When mature, communities often take active stewardship of the knowledge and practices they share and consciously develop them. One community would stall when its passionate leader changed roles.

Our findings indicate that the DGC project has reached a mature and thriving stage. However, when we compare this progress to the typical growth trajectory of a community, the period we've described represents just one phase of its stewardship. It would be intriguing to investigate how the project will continue to evolve in the future. For instance, as our observation ended in early 2020, coinciding with the onset of the COVID-19 pandemic, we noticed a significant shift in the project's operations toward a fully online format. This transformation posed challenges in terms of supervision, communication, and networking. However, it also compelled the team to be more resilient, resourceful, and adaptable. The coping strategies they developed in response to such disruptive events may prove to be invaluable assets in their ongoing professional growth and future careers.

Secondly, while our research has primarily focused on the learning effects experienced by student participants, we have overlooked examining the perspectives of the teacher reviser, the program administrator, and the client who has been involved in the project since its inception. An important challenge in organizing translation internship projects lies in supporting teachers as they juggle their project commitments alongside their teaching responsibilities. Trainer competence has gained increasing attention in recent years, as translation is fundamentally a skill-based activity (Englund Dimitrova 2002; Kelly 2008; Massey, Kiraly, and Ehrensberger-Dow 2019). Given the rapid changes in the translation market, Bowker (2015) argues that one obstacle for teachers in integrating technology into their classes is their own limited training and practical experience with these technologies. We can reasonably assume that exposure to internships would motivate teacher participants to stay current with the latest developments. Moreover, the program administrator and the client likely have valuable insights into both the strengths and shortcomings of the project's practices. Their observations could serve as constructive feedback to implement changes that better align with their respective needs and expectations.

The third area of investigation we wish to embark on focuses on the connection between the DGC project and its impact on the curriculum. Our current study is unable to definitively determine the extent to which the improvements in students' learning can be attributed solely to the project. This is because students are exposed to formal instruction and various practicum opportunities alongside the project. However, it is essential to acknowledge that the internship project can serve as a litmus test, reflecting the learning outcomes students have achieved or failed to achieve within their formal curriculum. Persistent mistakes made by students should serve as warning signals to teacher participants, prompting them to optimize their classroom instruction. The gaps in students' skill sets that are exposed should provide valuable feedback to curriculum designers, enabling them to create more integrated courses that better align with societal and student needs. Given the fast-evolving nature of the translation profession, T&I program providers should also remain responsive to market demands and foster best practices.

Fourthly, within the DGC project, there is inherent value in the transition to a cloud-based translation tool and centralized management of translation assets. As student participants aggregate data from translated DGC content, the teacher reviser has been advocating for a complete shift to the "MT/TM/TB/PE" model. We are just beginning to grasp how this change accelerates the translation process and enhances the quality of the product. It could be particularly intriguing to quantitatively explore the productivity gains resulting from this tool and new procedure, as well as the reflections of teachers and students that impact further utilization of this technology. With the emergence of new deep learning models in natural language processing, such as ChatGPT, our curiosity is piqued about whether the team will embrace advanced technologies and what exciting transformations will be introduced to their work.

In summary, the DGC project exemplifies the potential of providing students with continuous, authentic, and collaborative project-based learning experiences alongside the formal curriculum. In higher education, institutions often grapple with numerous obstacles when it comes to offering internship opportunities for their students. They must continually monitor and evaluate internship placements to ensure that they remain in alignment with their educational objectives. The strengths observed in the DGC practices highlight how GIIT has navigated these challenges, offering valuable experiences that contribute to the professional development of its students. However, it is important to note that this project should not be seen as the sole viable model. Instead, by sharing the research findings and practices, we hope to inspire fellow educators to innovate and adapt approaches to suit their unique contexts. We are left pondering whether internship projects could potentially become a prevalent model for situated learning in T&I education. In this context, we strongly resonate with Kiraly's (2012, 93) call for "a reassessment of existing and emerging pedagogical approaches with a view toward improving their coherence, consistency, and cogency."

References

Bass, S. 2006. "Quality in the Real World." In *Perspectives on Localization*, edited by K. J. Dunne, 69–94. Amsterdam and Philadelphia: John Benjamins.

Bowker, L. 2015. "Computer-aided Translation: Translator Training." In *Routledge Encyclopedia of Translation Technology*, edited by S. Chan, 88–104. London and New York: Routledge.

Collins, A., J. S. Brown, and A. Holum. 1991. "Cognitive Apprenticeship: Making Thinking Visible." *American Educator* 15 (3): 6–11.

Englund Dimitrova, B. 2002. "Training and Educating the Trainers: A Key Issue in Translators' Training." In *Teaching Translation and Interpreting 4: Building Bridges*, edited by E. Hung, 73–82. Amsterdam and Philadelphia: John Benjamins.

Ericsson, K. A. 2010. "Expertise in Interpreting: An Expert-performance Perspective." In *Translation and Cognition*, edited by G. M. Shreve and E. Angelone, 231–262. Amsterdam and Philadelphia: John Benjamins.

Guba, E. G., and Y. S. Lincoln. 1994. "Competing Paradigms in Qualitative Research." In *Handbook of Qualitative Research*, edited by Norman K. Denzin and Yvonna S. Lincoln, 105–117. Thousand Oaks: SAGE.

Kelly, D. 2007. "Translator Competence Contextualized Translator Training in the Framework of Higher Education Reform: In Search of Alignment in Curricular Design." In *Across Boundaries: International Perspectives on Translation*, edited by Dorothy Kenny and Kyonjoo Ryou, 128–142. Newcastle upon Tyne: Cambridge Scholars Publishing.

Kelly, D. 2008. "Training the Trainers: Towards a Description of Translator Trainer Competence and Training Needs Analysis." *TTR* 21 (1): 99–125. doi: 10.7202/029688ar.

Kiraly, D. 2012. "Growing A Project-Based Translation Pedagogy: A Fractal Perspective." *Meta* 57 (1): 82–95. doi:10.7202/1012742ar.

Kiraly, D. 2016. "Beyond the Static Competence Impasse in Translator Education." In *Translation and Meaning. New Series*, edited by B. Lewandowska-Tomaszczyk, et al., Vol. 1., 129–142. Frankfurt am Main: Peter Lang.

Lave, J., and E. Wenger. 1991. *Situated Learning: Legitimate Peripheral Participation*. Cambridge: Cambridge UP.

Massey, G. 2017. "Translation Competence Development and Process-Oriented Pedagogy." In *Handbook of Translation and Cognition*, edited by J. W. Schwieter and A. Ferreira, 496–518. Hoboken: John Wiley & Sons.

Massey, G., D. Kiraly, and M. Ehrensberger-Dow. 2019. "Training the Translator Trainers: An Introduction." *The Interpreter and Translator Trainer* 13 (3): 211–215. doi: 10.1080/1750399X.2019.1647821.
Muñoz Martín, R. 2016. "Reembedding Translation Process Research: An Introduction." In *Reembedding Translation Process Research*, edited by R. Muñoz Martín, 1–20. Amsterdam and Philadelphia: John Benjamins.
Saldanha, G., and S. O'Brien. 2014. *Research Methodologies in Translation Studies*. London and New York: Routledge.
Shreve, G. M. 2020. "Professional Translator Development from an Expertise Perspective." In *The Bloomsbury Companion to Language Industry Studies*, edited by E. Anglone et al., 153–177. Bloomsbury: Bloomsbury Academic.
Wenger, E. 1998. *Communities of Practice. Learning, Meaning, and Identity*. Cambridge: Cambridge UP.
Wenger, E., R. McDermott, and W. M. Snyder. 2002. *A Guide to Managing Knowledge: Cultivating Communities of Practice*. Cambridge: Harvard Business School Press.

Index

access 70, 76, 91, 99, 120, 132, 134–5, 156–7, 168, 171–2
action research 39, 52, 154
adaptive expertise 26
analytic induction 2
anchored instruction 18
application programming interface (API) 22, 112, 134
artifact 24, 65, 80, 108
assessment 40, 41, 44, 46–8, 50, 53, 76, 101, 106, 121, 135, 143, 155, 163
asset management 47, 114, 162, 170, 173
authentic projects 1–2, 38, 49, 54

bachelor of translation 49
best practice(s) 4, 50, 120, 136, 157, 163, 168, 169, 173

case study 4, 37, 77, 78, 167
chat group 4, 42, 44, 78, 80, 84, 89, 101, 103–4, 109–10, 119, 125, 128, 132, 134, 142–3, 145, 149, 159, 172
class projects 2, 5, 19, 43, 52, 56, 67–9, 124, 154–5, 167, 169, 170
cloud-based tool 4, 22, 44, 57, 77, 101, 104, 112, 156, 157, 160, 161, 166, 173
co-emergent competence model 19, 52, 155
cognitive science 5, 9, 13, 23–4, 166
collaborative model 22, 57
communication management 66
community of inquiry 3
Community of Practice (CoP) 2–3, 5–6, 24, 70–1, 76, 109, 118, 121, 124, 135, 151, 167, 170, 172
competence-based training (CBT) 10, 11, 166
computer-assisted translation (CAT) 15, 21–2, 42, 45, 58, 113, 132, 145, 167

consistency 76, 103, 108, 136, 146, 148, 158, 167, 174
continuity 60, 76, 119, 135–6, 142, 149, 158, 161, 167–9
cost management 44, 54, 66
cross-case analysis 5, 37, 51, 159, 171
crowdsourcing 23
curriculum 10, 18, 49, 55, 69, 166, 171, 173

deadline 43–4, 47–8, 54, 59, 76, 91–2, 110, 113, 119, 135, 147, 167
deliberate practice 11, 26, 124, 166
Department of Global Communications (DGC) 3–6, 75–8, 83, 88–9, 91, 94, 97–104, 109–51, 154–60, 171–4
desktop-editing 132, 159
digital legacy 67, 102
direct corrective feedback 44, 49, 50
direct observation 80–1
distributed team 4, 77, 156, 166
documentation analysis 5, 80
domain 60, 76, 96, 98, 119, 155–6, 160
double coding 88, 172

emic perspective 52
employability 1, 10, 145
ethnographic study 5, 77, 171
etic perspective 52
European Master's in Translation (EMT) Competence Framework 13, 51, 52, 155
exit 4, 70, 76, 78
expertise 3, 11, 14, 17, 25–6, 101, 104, 158, 166, 168
expertise studies 5, 23, 25, 124, 154, 166
expert scaffolding 44, 58
extrinsic motivation 97

feedback 4, 11, 14, 16, 18, 20, 22, 40, 42, 44, 49–51, 53, 58–9, 68, 93, 100, 103, 105, 108, 114, 120, 124, 128, 130, 144, 157, 160, 166, 173
feedforward 130, 159
formal curriculum 4, 97, 98, 108, 143, 173
"4EA" cognition 25, 166
free/open-source software 57
functional theory 9

generic competence 10, 13, 44
Graduate Institute of Interpretation and Translation (GIIT) 3, 43, 75, 76, 91, 97, 108, 132, 150, 156, 161, 174

heritage 3, 71, 76, 94, 151
hidden curriculum 98–9
human–human collaboration 25, 40, 66, 67, 124, 156, 167, 170
human–machine collaboration 40, 66, 67, 131, 156, 167

identity 3, 71, 88, 91, 96, 118, 145, 151, 167
incremental workflow 22
industry standards 20, 21, 76, 166
information and communication technology (ICT) 38, 77, 155
integrated translation management system 17
international governmental organizations (IGOs) 94
internship 2, 67, 70, 101, 124, 143
internship projects 3, 5, 52, 55, 67, 69, 71, 124, 154, 167, 170
interpreter competence 14
interpreting competence 14–15, 166
interview 24, 48–9, 53, 76, 80–2, 88–9, 93–5, 101, 103, 113, 119, 145, 155, 163, 172
intrinsic motivation 97
iterative workflow 22

Kiraly, D. 1–3, 9, 11–14, 19, 37–42, 46–7, 50, 52–9, 65, 70, 155, 173–4
knowledge community 3

language service provider (LSP) 1
language service provision 10
Lave, J. 2–3, 24, 70, 99, 104–5, 109, 118, 142, 149, 167
leadership 4, 17, 71, 116, 119, 170
learning 23, 59, 118, 143, 145, 169

learning community 3, 145
learning science 13, 23, 37
Lee-Jahnke, H. 1, 3, 10–11, 18, 23
legacy translation 87
legitimate peripheral participation 24, 49, 70, 76, 109, 118, 150, 155
licensed software 57
linear workflow 57, 158, 170
Linguee 100, 102, 114, 132, 136, 138–40, 158, 160
linguistic theories 9

machine translation (MT) 12, 16–17, 21, 114, 134, 173
Massey, G. 38–9, 52–9, 166, 173
Master of Arts (MA) 50
Master of Interpreting (MI) 93, 94, 98, 144
Master of Translation and Interpreting (MTI) 38
Master of Translation (MT) 44, 76, 91, 94, 98, 132, 148
meta-analysis 37, 39, 170
metadata 57, 140, 160, 162
motivation 26, 50, 96, 97, 109, 143, 145, 166
multi-componential models 13, 52
mutual engagement 2, 76, 125, 131

natural language processing (NLP) 42, 173
News and Media Division (NMD) 75, 76

offline data 53, 78, 170
one-off project 2–3, 38, 50, 76, 167, 170
online data 78
open curriculum 99
open-ended questionnaires 53

PACTE 12, 16, 52
parallel text 41, 97, 132, 136
participant observer 4, 78
peer assessment 52
peer revision 16, 45, 159
peer scaffolding 44
PMBOK® Guide 17, 66
post-editing competence 13, 16
post-editing (PE) 16, 21, 134
pre-editing 16, 21
process 19, 20, 38, 40, 45, 47–9, 166
procurement management 167
professionalism 11
project-based learning (PjBL) 1–6, 9, 18–19, 23–6, 37–9, 41–2, 44–5, 52, 54, 56, 60, 67, 96, 108, 144, 154–5, 166–7, 170–1

project management competence 17
Project Management Institute 2, 54, 66
project manager (PM) 1, 17, 42–5, 51, 56, 78, 80–7, 91, 100, 103, 110–20, 125, 128, 130, 138–41, 145, 157–9, 163
project timeline 2, 49
proofreading 16, 20, 42, 47, 100, 103–5, 108, 116, 120, 143, 160
proprietary tool 170
published translation 54, 69, 102

quality assurance (QA) 16, 22, 44–5, 51, 158
quality control 4, 17, 47, 75, 87, 140, 143, 158–9, 170
quality management 66
questionnaire 39, 41, 43, 46, 48, 51–3, 81–2, 89, 94–6, 101, 103, 105, 109, 113–14, 120, 132, 155

recruitment 4, 43, 50, 52, 76, 78, 91, 94, 120, 148, 170
reference material 39, 42–3, 45, 49, 57–8, 138
reflection-in-action 156
reflective reports 43, 52–3, 102–3
repetition 11, 26, 60, 124, 154, 166
reproduction 3, 71, 76
resource management 4, 66, 167
reviser 1, 16, 41, 43, 45, 56, 69
revision competence 16, 95, 143, 169
risk management 66
role-based competences 15, 17, 144, 166, 169
routine expertise 26
routine practice 110, 114, 151

scaffoldings 4, 18, 40, 41, 47, 49, 58, 59, 114, 157
scope management 66
SDL Trados 43, 58, 113
self-assessment 52
self-checking 16, 58
self-scaffolding 44, 47, 114
sequential workflow 19
Shanghai International Studies University (SISU) 3, 43, 75, 161
shared repertoire 76, 135, 142, 160
simulated projects 1, 38
situated learning 1, 3, 23–4, 49–50, 57, 69, 71, 174
skopos 9, 49, 65, 146
social constructivism 49, 50, 166

social learning 3, 5, 24–5, 144, 154
soft skills 15, 145
software as a service (SaaS) 22
source text 9, 16, 25, 42, 45, 49, 57–8, 102, 108, 132, 140, 158
specific competence 10
stakeholder management 66, 167
style guide 42, 59, 102, 112, 120, 142, 146, 160, 168
subject matter expert (SME) 16, 42
subscription models 57

target text 9, 16, 21, 51, 158
task-based approach 18, 47
TAUS 2, 20, 57
terminologist 1, 11, 15, 41, 47, 51, 56, 78, 106, 108
terminology base (TB) 22, 45, 110, 132, 135–6, 139–42, 156, 158, 160, 162, 173
terminology competence 15, 17, 169
terminology management 15, 16, 42–4, 46, 47, 56, 135
T&I education 1–3, 5, 9–12, 14–15, 18–19, 67, 70–1, 166, 170, 174
time management 66, 125, 147
T&I pedagogy 6, 9, 170
trainer competence 173
transcreation 38
translation asset 22, 87, 101, 136, 143, 168
translation competence 10–14, 16–18, 38, 43–4, 52, 70, 94–5, 112, 116, 119–20, 143–5, 154–5, 158, 166–7, 169–70
translation-editing-proofreading (TEP) 19–20, 40–1, 43, 47
translation memory (TM) 21–2, 43, 50, 102, 110, 112–14, 132, 135–6, 138, 141, 156, 158, 162, 168, 173
translation service provider (TSP) 17, 20
Translation Studies Bibliography 37
translation technology 5, 21, 45–6, 48, 50, 57, 97, 131, 142
translator competence 11, 14, 19, 169
trust 3, 69, 71, 100, 142, 145, 148, 169
turnaround time 4, 47, 54–5, 100, 121

UN Chronicle 99, 100, 103, 104, 108, 109, 116, 121, 125, 151, 156
UN In Action (UNIA) 99, 102, 125, 151
United Nations Multilingual Terminology Database (UNTERM) 92, 100, 102–3, 114, 132, 136, 139–40, 158, 160
United Nations (UN) 3, 75, 76, 135, 167

UN Memorandum of Understanding (MoU)
    Institution 75

verbal analysis 5, 81, 171
verbal data 80, 82–3, 87–8, 156

Wenger, E. 2–3, 24, 70–1, 91, 99, 102, 104,
    105, 109, 118–19, 131, 135, 142, 145,
    149, 151, 157, 167–9, 172
wheel of competence 13, 51, 52, 155

workflow 3–5, 18–22, 25, 41–5, 47–8, 57,
    59, 66–7, 76, 83, 93, 97, 100–1, 105,
    109–10, 116, 119, 121, 125, 130, 132,
    135, 146, 150, 155–6, 158–60, 166–8, 170
work placement 1, 49, 67, 110, 124

Yicat 93, 101–2, 105, 110, 112–14, 120,
    128, 132–5, 139–42, 159, 161

zone of proximal development 114

Printed in the United States
by Baker & Taylor Publisher Services